MARIE HENRI BEYLE, known through his writings as Stendhal, was born in Grenoble in 1783 and educated there at the École Centrale. A cousin offered him a post in the Ministry of War and from 1800 onwards he followed Napoleon's campaigns in Italy, Germany, Russia and Austria. In between wars he spent his time in Paris drawing-rooms and theatres.

After the fall of Napoleon he retired to Italy, adopted his pseudonym, and started to write books on Italian painting, Haydn and Mozart, and travels in Italy. In 1821 he left Italy because of the political situation and, returning to Paris, he finished his book *De L'Amour*. This was followed by *Racine et Shakespeare*, a defence of romantic literature. *Le Rouge et le Noir* was his second novel, and he also produced or began three others, including *La Chartreuse de Parme*, none of which was received with any great understanding during his lifetime.

Beyle was appointed Consul at Civitavecchia after the 1830 revolution, but his health deteriorated and six years later he was back in Paris and beginning a life of Napoleon. In 1841 he was once again recalled for reasons of illness, and in the following year he suffered a fatal stroke. Various autobiographical works, his *Journal*, his *Souvenirs d'Égotisme* and his *Vie de Henry Brulard* were published later.

STENDHAL

LOVE

TRANSLATED BY GILBERT AND SUZANNE SALE
AND WITH AN INTRODUCTION BY
JEAN STEWART AND B.C.J.G. KNIGHT

PENGUIN BOOKS

Penguin Books Ltd, Harmondsworth, Middlesex, England
Penguin Books, 40 West 23rd Street, New York, New York 10010, U.S.A.
Penguin Books Australia Ltd, Ringwood, Victoria, Australia
Penguin Books Canada Ltd, 2801 John Street, Markham, Ontario, Canada L3R 1B4
Penguin Books (N.Z.) Ltd, 182–190 Wairau Road, Auckland 10, New Zealand

This translation first published by The Merlin Press 1957
Published in Penguin Books 1975
Reprinted 1977, 1980, 1982, 1984

Made and printed in Great Britain
by Richard Clay (The Chaucer Press) Ltd,
Bungay, Suffolk
Set in Monotype Bembo

CONTENTS

APPENDIX

INTRODUCTION

Biographical Background

1783–99. Marie-Henri Beyle (Stendhal) born 23 January 1783 in Grenoble, son of Chérubin Beyle and his wife Henriette, *née* Gagnon, who died in childbed November 1790. Lived in Grenoble, went to Central School, passed examinations for entry to the École Polytechnique in Paris where he went on 10 November 1799. He did not attend the Polytechnique and lived at first alone and later in the house of his cousin Pierre Daru, who took Stendhal into his offices in the Ministry of War.

1800. Went with the army of Napoleon over the St Bernard Pass into Italy and moved from garrison to garrison in Lombardy and various towns in Northern Italy as aide-de-camp to General Michoud. At end of 1801 obtained leave and returned to France. Began his *Journal*.

1802–5. Various occupations and love affairs; interested in the theatre and tried to write a play; much reading, including in particular the *Ideology* of Destutt de Tracy.

1806–14. Returned to Paris from Marseille and renewed contact with his cousins Pierre and Martial Daru, important military persons.

Went with Napoleonic armies to Germany, Austria, Hungary.

1810–11. Held official posts: *auditeur* to the Council of State, inspector of furniture and buildings of the Crown. Travelled in Italy (Florence, Rome, Naples) and first had the idea of writing an *Histoire de la Peinture en Italie*.

1812. Went with the headquarters staff of Napoleon's army into Russia, entered Moscow, saw it in flames; was sent back to organize provisioning for the retreat from Moscow at Smolensk, Mohilev, Vitebsk.

1813. New post as commissariat officer at Sagan in Silesia. Obtained leave and went to Milan.

1814. At Grenoble appointed assistant to Count de Saint-Vallier, commissioner extraordinary of the 7th military region, to organize resistance to the Allied invasion. Allies entered Paris and Napoleon exiled to Elba. The end of Stendhal's fortunes under Napoleon.

Wrote *Vies de Haydn, Mozart, et Metastase*. Went to Milan, where he spent most of the next seven years.

1815. Stendhal remained in Italy, not returning to France during the Hundred Days when Napoleon came back from Elba; Waterloo, and final exile of Napoleon to St Helena.

1816. Stendhal in Milanese society, attended La Scala in box of Lodovico de Breme, met Byron and other liberals.

1817. *Histoire de la Peinture en Italie* and *Rome, Naples, et Florence* published in Paris.

1818. 4 March, beginning of the 'great musical theme', which was his painful love for Mathilde Viscontini Dembowski, whom he called Métilde.

1819. Milan, Volterra, Grenoble; deeply in love with Métilde. 29 December, had the 'brilliant idea' of writing a book which would express all that Métilde had made him feel. This became *De l'Amour*. The political situation in Milan grew more and more difficult for the liberals.

1820. Journeyed to Northern Italy. In Milan, occupied with his book concerning his feelings for Métilde, who treated him more and more coolly. Arrests of prominent liberals. Rumours began to spread in liberal circles that Stendhal was an agent of the French Government. First draft of *De l'Amour* sent to France.

1821. The Austrian Government suspected Stendhal of being connected with the *Carbonari* movement. 13 June, Stendhal finally left Milan on urgent advice from friends and because he recognized the hopelessness of his love for Métilde, who was even colder towards him.

1821–30. Lived in Paris, frequented literary circles, wrote for English reviews, and published books.

    1822. *De l'Amour* published.

    1823. *Vie de Rossini* and *Racine et Shakespeare I* published.

    1824. Journalism in French and English papers and reviews.

    1825. *Racine et Shakespeare II*; *D'un nouveau complot contre les industriels*.

    1826. Second, much changed edition of *Rome, Naples, et Florence*. Wrote *Armance*.

    1827. *Armance* published.

    1828. January went to Milan and was immediately expelled.

    1829. Published *Promenades dans Rome*. Various short stories:

'Vanina Vanini', 'Le coffre et le revenant' appeared in *Revue de Paris*, 'Mme de Vanghel' (then unpublished).

1830–31. Wrote story 'Le Philtre' and his great novel *Le Rouge et le Noir* which was published in November 1830.

1831. After the revolution of July 1830, which overthrew Charles X and established Louis-Philippe and the Charter in France, he eventually obtained the post of French Consul at Trieste; but the Austrian Government would not accept him and he had to leave.

1831. He was then sent as French Consul at Civitavecchia, the port near Rome, and he frequently went to Rome.

1832. 20 June–4 July wrote *Souvenirs d'Égotisme* about his life from June 1821 to November 1830.

1833. September–December on leave in Paris; returned to Civitavecchia via Lyon and Marseille, meeting George Sand and Alfred de Musset en route for Venice.

1834. Began novel *Lucien Leuwen* inspired by an idea of his friend Mme Jules Gaulthier, but left unfinished.

1835. In November began his autobiographical *La Vie de Henri Brulard*, covering his earliest years to 1801.

1836–9. On prolonged leave in Paris. Various short stories. Travels in the centre of France; *Mémoires d'un touriste* published June 1838. More journeys in south-west and south-east France, Switzerland, Rhineland, Holland, Belgium. Published stories 'La Duchesse de Palliano', 'L'Abbesse de Castro'. September 1838 had first idea of *La Chartreuse de Parme*, which masterpiece he wrote in fifty-two days, 4 November–26 December 1838; published April 1839.

1839–42. Returned to the consulate at Civitavecchia August 1839. Began a new novel *Lamiel* (unfinished); wrote story 'Don Pardo'.

 March 1841 had an apoplectic stroke; given leave and returned to Paris. Died suddenly from a stroke 23 March 1842 – as he had wished.

Background to De l'Amour

The above chronological sketch of the life of Stendhal gives a background to *De l'Amour*. To quote Henri Martineau:

Stendhal always considered this his principal work because in it he had expressed his most cherished ideas, his most intimate beliefs, all that science of happiness to which he attached so much importance, above all because he had enclosed in it his most painful secrets about love. Perhaps he even preferred the book less for its theories than for the memories with which he had filled it. His personal experience has a preponderant part in it, and the sense of the book would escape us if we were unaware of certain circumstances of his life and of his love for Mathilde Dembowski. (H. Martineau, *L'œuvre de Stendhal*, p. 203)

With the fall of Napoleon in 1815 and the break-up of the Napoleonic empire, the province of Lombardy in North Italy was annexed to Austria and ruled as a police state. During Stendhal's residence in Milan from 1815 onwards there was a smouldering anti-Austrian patriotic movement among the circles of Italian intellectuals in which Stendhal moved. Manifestations of Italian nationalism, attempts at emancipation, and the spread of liberal ideas were rigorously suppressed. There were conspiracies, the formation of secret societies (for example the *Carbonari*) aiming to throw off the Austrian yoke; and the situation was similar in the adjacent state of Piedmont. Leaders of these patriotic movements were arrested and sentenced to long terms of imprisonment in the Spielberg citadel at Brno in Moravia, which became a state prison for political prisoners. For example, Count Federico Confalonieri, the outstanding Italian patriot, Silvio Pellico, Pietro Maroncelli, and many others were arrested in 1820, and Alexandre Andryane, cell-mate of Confalonieri, in 1823. They were sent to the Spielberg for long incarcerations under severe conditions. The wives, relatives, and friends of the Spielberg prisoners and many others participated in attempts to succour the prisoners and to maintain and develop the revolutionary movements. Among these cultured, ardent, and daring women were the intimate friends Teresa Confalonieri, wife of Count Federico Confalonieri, Mme Frecavalli, and Mathilde Dembowski – Stendhal's Métilde.

Métilde

Since Stendhal's obsession with one woman is the core of his book, she must be introduced without further delay. Stendhal was no novice in love when in 1818 he met Mathilde Viscontini Dembowski, whom he called Métilde. His first real affair had been with a young actress, Mélanie Guilbert, with whom, at the age of twenty-two, he had lived for some months; there had been another actress, Angelina Beryter, in Paris, as well as several more ephemeral or unsuccessful involvements; then had come his tempestuous relationship with the exciting Angela Pietragrua, whom he had shyly admired on his first visit to Milan in 1800 and who became his teasing mistress when he returned to that city in 1811.

But Mathilde Viscontini Dembowski was in a totally different category. She was a Milanese, twenty-eight years old when Stendhal first met her in Milan. She had been married at seventeen to a Polish officer, a naturalized Italian, from whom she was separated; she had two schoolboy sons. She was an ardent patriot and was deeply involved in the nationalist revolutionary organization of the *Carbonari*.

In Andryane's *Memoirs of a State Prisoner in the Spielberg*, Andryane's sister is reported to have heard from Mme Frecavalli – an intimate friend of Teresa Confalonieri and Mathilde – the following account of Mathilde Dembowski:

She [Métilde] died at the age of thirty-five – died in my arms, still beautiful, when everything should have preserved her for her two sons whom she idolized ... But she also loved the glory of her country and the men who aspired to make it illustrious; she suffered too long, from our subjection and the loss of her friends, for her constitution not to be shattered; the energy of her soul consumed her, not finding any other nourishment ... And yet, what goodness, what angelic sweetness in that noble heart!

... When she was arrested in December 1822, at night in the street just as she was entering her house and they dared to keep her a prisoner there by putting a gendarme at the door of her bedroom, a general feeling of indignation arose against the magistrates and in support of the accused.

Brought next day before the Inquisitorial Commission, she had to undergo interrogation for ten hours. It was then that Salvotti, wanting to insult her dignified answers, asked her ironically whether she thought she was in the midst of *Carbonari* where she was presiding.

'No', she replied, 'in the Venetian Inquisition.' Then, protesting against the violence they were doing to a woman's weakness, she declared that she would answer no more questions, and the enraged Salvotti was obliged to set her at liberty. Continually harassed by the police, her devotion to our unhappy exiles and those condemned to the Spielberg never flagged. She never ceased to be like this and was justly called the Niobe of her friends. (A. Andryane, *Mémoires d'un Prisonnier d'État au Spielberg*, III, 1837–8, Chapter 9)

Teresa Confalonieri, to whom Andryane's book was dedicated, described Métilde as 'that angelic woman in whom were united all the perfections of an adorable sensibility with the energy that makes one capable of the most sublime actions' (A. Andryane, *Mémoires*, III, Chapter 9).

Métilde had the enigmatic beauty which Stendhal called Lombardian and which he recognized in Luini's *Salome* in the Uffizi Gallery in Florence (which he thought was by Leonardo da Vinci). She died on 1 May 1825, four years after Stendhal had left Milan. Later Stendhal, who had the habit of writing notes in the margins of books, wrote in one of his own copies of *De l'Amour*:

'1 mai 1825 – Death of the author' [in English].

Such was the woman – a true Stendhalian heroine – with whom Stendhal fell in love in 1818, recognizing the fact on 4 March as the beginning of a 'great musical theme'.

She never yielded to Stendhal's persistent siege; she neither loved him nor understood him; and the more exigent he became, the more Métilde cooled and kept him at a distance. In her relations with Stendhal she was hypersensitive, quick to take offence and touchy about her reputation. She may well also have had political suspicions about him. For, as a Frenchman living in Milan, Stendhal was in an equivocal position: the Austrian police considered him suspect, for his acquaintances were patriotic Italian liberals (it is ironical that 'De Bell, litterato francese abitante de Milano' figures on the same police list of suspects as Métilde herself); and in those circles, always endangered by spies and secret agents, personal enemies could start rumours against him as a French government agent. This situation may account for Métilde's ever-increasing coolness towards him.

As the Austrian police increased its operations against the patriotic liberals and the *Carbonari*, Stendhal became more and more concerned about his personal position in Milan. On 20 July 1820 he wrote to his close friend, Mareste, in Paris:

My dear friend, the greatest misfortune that could possibly happen has just happened to me. Certain jealous people, for who does not have them? have circulated the rumour that I am here as an agent of the French Government.

This rumour has been going round for six months. I noticed that several people were trying not to greet me. I didn't care at all, until good Plana wrote me the letter which you will receive, and which I don't mind about. However, this was a terrible blow! For indeed, what was this Frenchman doing here? The cheerful good-natured Milanese will never understand my philosophic life and that I can live here on 5,000 francs better than in Paris on 12,000 . . . I am too upset to speak about anything else. I assure you that I am not exaggerating. For three months I have not been admitted to a certain circle because an impartial person said, 'if he comes, several people (admittedly people who hate me) will leave'. I learnt this only two hours ago. This is the most shattering blow I have ever had in my life.

There is a desperate letter to Mareste dated 30 December 1820. This is written in Stendhal's English:

Dear Sir,
Write no more to me directly, by terror periculous. Write every fornight to M. Agostoni neg^te in Chiasso, every fornight. You can write as you will, but the names in English by excess of prudence. You can also write to Domenico V[ismara]. We are now what the French were in 1815 in the little reactionary towns of France. I pray you write every fornight. Give me your dear news with all the possible lib[erty]. Yours

Smith and Co.

And from a letter to Mareste dated 1 April 1821:

I believe, my dear friend, that I have at last took the most painful decision in all my life, that of coming back to Bruxelle's hotel [italics indicate Stendhal's English]

He saw Métilde for the last time on 7 June and left Milan for Paris on 13 June 1821. Throughout the rest of his life he continually thought of Métilde, making marginal and other cryptic notes referring to her until he died.

The Book De l'Amour

Take the two volumes of *De l'Amour*; certainly the most bizarre that M. de Stendhal has written. If at the tenth page, you do not throw it down in vexation, you will be surprised on reaching the end how much it has stirred your imagination.

Thus wrote a perceptive contemporary of Stendhal's, Duvergier de Hauranne, in the *Globe* of 24 October 1829.*

Undoubtedly *De l'Amour* is on first acquaintance a disconcerting book; it seems a hotch-potch of analysis and anecdote, argument, apophthegm, and poetry. Some critics have deplored its lack of order,

* H. Martineau, *L'Œuvre de Stendhal*, Paris: Albin Michel, 1951, p. 200.

even of that instinctive organic order that underlies some of Stendhal's least 'composed' books. Most of his contemporaries were completely baffled; the publisher, Mongie, complained bitterly about the unsold copies: 'They must be sacred, for nobody will touch them.' The book's failure can be explained in part by the fact that not even Stendhal's friends were aware of the key to it: his love for Mathilde Dembowski, about which he spoke to no one, but which obsessed him unhappily for years. He wrote this strange and profoundly perceptive book partly to explain his feelings to her, partly in an attempt to exorcise, by dissecting, a hopeless passion. It thus displays the two conflicting sides of his nature – the deeply sensitive and the coolly analytical. These aspects are indeed present in everything he wrote, but in the great novels they are fused miraculously, whereas in *De l'Amour* they are in somewhat uneasy juxtaposition. The effort he made to control his feeling self was too great; these experiences were too close, too traumatic for lucidity to prevail. Emotion was hardly 'recollected in tranquillity'; even when he was correcting the proofs of *De l'Amour* he wept: 'I nearly went crazy,' he said in *Souvenirs d'Égotisme*.

He made a heroic attempt to analyse with detachment the aspects and phases of the passion that was a major influence in his life. To this end he recalled a model which had inspired him in earlier days: the *Éléments d'Idéologie* of Destutt de Tracy, that heir to the 'sensualist' tradition of Helvétius and Condillac, friend and colleague of the psychologist Cabanis, and remembered nowadays chiefly through Stendhal's admiration of him. Stendhal had discovered de Tracy's work at the age of twenty-one and had been fascinated by the clarity and order of the philosopher's attempt to analyse the problems of consciousness. It had seemed to the young Stendhal to be at the opposite pole from the 'hypocrisy' of prevailing attitudes and above all of the pious obscurantism of his early educators. In a footnote to Chapter 3 of *De l'Amour* he acknowledges his debt: 'I have called this essay a book of ideology . . . I beg the forgiveness of the philosophers for having chosen the word ideology . . . If ideology be a detailed description of ideas and of all the parts into which these ideas can be analysed, this book is a detailed and painstaking description of all the feelings which make up the passion called love . . .' De Tracy, who had defined love as 'friendship embellished by pleasure', failed to appreciate either the book or its author, describing *De l'Amour* as 'absurd' and the author as 'a skittish horse'. Fortunately for its readers *De l'Amour* does not in any way adhere to its ambitious and would-be systematic programme. Personal feelings and experience continually get the upper hand over ideology. The brief Chapter 9 reflects the conflict: 'I am trying extremely hard to be *dry*. My heart thinks it has so much to say, but I try to keep it quiet. I am continually beset by the fear that I may have expressed only a sigh when I thought I was stating a truth.'

In fact the book starts drily enough, distinguishing (Stendhal always liked to state things mathematically) between four kinds of love and then between seven stages of falling in love. True, he comments that 'there are perhaps as many different ways of feeling as there are of seeing . . .' But he then proceeds to concentrate on a single kind of love: *amour-passion*, intense, romantic, generally unrequited and perhaps impossible to requite; it alone is deemed worthy of the name. Plain sex, *amour-physique*, which in life he did not despise, is briefly dismissed (no doubt to the disappointment of any naïve reader hoping for erotic details in a book bearing this title). *Amour-goût*, eighteenth-century style, and the *amour de vanité* prevalent in the France of his day, which too often masqueraded as the real thing, are analysed only by contrast with *amour-passion*.

The few poignant letters still extant from Stendhal to Métilde bear witness to the intensity and hopelessness of his passion for her. Always paralysed by excess of feeling, he reacted in ways that offended her all too readily: tongue-tied or garrulous in her company, tactless in his approach or inadequately explicit in his declarations. 'We completely fail to understand one another,' he wrote to her in June 1819. 'How many of my simplest actions must have displeased you! Heaven knows what they mean in Italian.' There was, for instance, the tragi-comic episode, mortifying for both parties, when he followed her to Volterra, where she had gone to visit her sons at school. He was disguised in an overcoat and dark-green glasses, but in a rash moment removed these and was recognized. Embarrassed, he pretended not to know her; but they met again next day – by accident, he swore – in a meadow which happened to be her favourite walk. She was furious, and endless recriminations and apologies ensued; the whole story is told in a pathetic letter of self-justification written on his return to Florence, 11 June 1819. Throughout the course of this one-sided affair, Métilde kept denouncing Beyle's lack of 'delicacy', rationing his visits to one a fortnight (though never wholly forbidding him access), and describing him as 'difficile à désespérer' (hard to reduce to despair) long after he had ceased to hope – although he still clung to the illusion that she might be repulsing him from pride, or fear, or feminine modesty, like some of his own later heroines (Bathilde de Chasteller in *Lucien Leuwen*, for instance). In November 1819 he dreamed of explaining himself in a *Roman de Métilde* written for her eyes alone. A few weeks later (he gave 29 December 1819 as the 'day of genius') he formulated this project in the opening chapters of *De l'Amour*. By the spring of 1820 he had completed his first draft and sketched the Werther/Don Juan antithesis, following this up with the 'Journal de Salviati' and the chapter on marriage. He dispatched his manuscript to France, but it was lost; he only recovered it in November 1821, when he completed the book with the miscellaneous final chapters, borrowing freely from several sources (many of which he indicated in his notes) for the dissertation on love in various countries and the chivalric code of Provence. He added various fragments and *pensées*, all of which served as ballast and as a disguise for the too personal element at the heart of the book.

The genesis of *De l'Amour* thus explains how, under the guise of a generalized 'physiology of love' (as it is described in the third Preface), we find the account of a very special sort of love, the unhappy, diffident, hopeless passion of one man, Henri Beyle, for one woman, Mathilde Dembowski. Yet such is Stendhal's depth and keenness of perception, that the special case reveals a general truth. Métilde's name is never mentioned in the book, although her actions and attitudes and her own words are often cited. She is Léonore, Alviza (Fragment 90; he himself wrote Métilde in the margin of his copy of *De l'Amour*), Madame —; her lover appears as Salviati, Lisio Visconti, Delfante, or 'a young man of my acquaintance'. Only Métilde would recognize the references.

Perhaps the most famous feature of the book is the analysis of the power of the imagination in love – its ability to transfigure the image of the loved one – described in terms of the natural phenomenon of 'crystallization'. This is first set forth in Chapter 2, 'Concerning the Birth of Love', and developed at greater length in a fragment added later, 'The Salzburg Bough'. The metaphor, which is striking, original, and apt, is explained thus:

Leave a lover with his thoughts for twenty-four hours, and this is what will happen:

At the salt mines of Salzburg, they throw a leafless wintry bough into one of the abandoned workings. Two or three months later they pull it out covered with a shining deposit of crystals. The smallest twig, no bigger than a tom-tit's claw, is studded with a galaxy of scintillating diamonds. The original branch is no longer recognizable.

What I have called crystallization is a mental process which draws from everything that happens new proofs of the perfection of the loved one.

This psychological phenomenon is a familiar literary theme – for example Shakespeare's lines:

> The lunatic, the lover and the poet
> Are of imagination all compact . . .

But surely no one before Stendhal, and since Stendhal no one until Proust, has subjected it to such penetrating analysis without loss of feeling, admitting the illusion while still under its spell.

And this is true of Stendhal's whole searching study of the various stages and subtle nuances in the obsession. The paralysing effect of that shyness he knew only too well: 'shyness is a proof of love' (Chapter 5); the agonies of apprehension and self-consciousness (Chapter 14): 'The only way to show courage would be to love her less'; the difficulties of communication (Chapter 24); the importance and at the same time the impossibility of being *natural*, of expressing one's true feelings at the right moment (Chapter 32): '. . . If you are truly in love and your lover says things which make you happy, you will lose the power of speech'; and the way introspection kills candour; the successive phases of hope and jealousy, ecstasy and doubt; the disproportionate delight or despair caused by trifles: '*tout est signe en amour*' (Chapter 39); and above all by the first intimations of intimacy: 'the greatest happiness love can offer is the first pressure of hands between you and your beloved.' When he notes the heart's irrationality: 'we can never understand the whys and wherefores of our feelings' (Chapter 6), 'from the moment he falls in love even the wisest man no longer sees anything *as it really is*' (Chapter 12) (suggesting in a footnote a physiological cause for this 'incipient madness'); when he describes the curious 'blankness' in which the lover's heart is sometimes becalmed (Chapter 15) (what Proust later called *les intermittences du cœur*); when he dwells on the power of music to evoke or translate feelings of love (Chapters 16 and 43) – music which, by giving precise form to elusive emotions, by expressing the inexpressible, satisfied both sides of his nature,* we realize that these insights are based on personal experience, deeply felt and acutely noted, without self-pity, bitterness, or romantic irony.

But it is, perhaps, above all, in his awareness of the power of associations, of the involuntary memory, that Stendhal shows his singular originality (and once again anticipates the Proustian analysis). A distant glimpse of a white satin hat that resembled his beloved's made 'Salviati's' heart miss a beat and he had to lean against a wall for support (Chapter 35); a lover who cannot consciously recollect anything about his rapturous meeting with one who later proved unfaithful is 'visibly shaken' by the sight of an acacia which recalls the bush on which, on that occasion, her dress caught (Chapter 32); a woman falls into the lake while absorbed in watching a drifting laurel leaf, because it brought back words spoken by her lover as he stripped the leaves from a laurel branch and dropped them into the water. Landscape has this evocative power: to 'Salviati' the skyline of rocks at Poligny suggested the anger of 'Léonore' (Chapter 32); the picture of a distant town where one's mistress was once seen for a moment 'throws you into a deeper and sweeter reverie than even her actual presence could evoke'.

Stendhal's explanation is that in the loved one's presence one is too deeply disturbed to notice surroundings; one is aware only of one's sensations (*l'âme . . . est la sensation même*); and later these are powerfully renewed by some extrinsic object which 'recalls her more vividly by some new relevance' (Chapter 14). To which he adds the brief but suggestive footnote: 'Scents'.

Interspersed with the chapters based on Stendhal's own experience of passion there are some in which he attempts to guess at women's feelings; seeking, no doubt, to understand Métilde – her pride, her feminine modesty, her courage, her sensitivity, and perhaps (just as in early days he had hoped, through self-assessment, to attain self-mastery) to discover thereby how to win her. He never won Métilde; but his study of feminine psychology was later embodied, profitably, in the heroines of his great novels.

Several chapters in the second part of the book deal with love

* See J. P. Richard, *Littérature et Sensation*, Paris: Editions du Seuil, 1954.

in different countries and social milieux. Like Stendhal's travel books, they are a mixture of shrewd observation and idiosyncratic prejudice; much is borrowed from various sources, but shot through with original comment. Here again, his picture of vanity-obsessed French society and pleasure-loving, passionate Italy seem like preliminary sketches for *Lucien Leuwen* and *La Chartreuse de Parme*.

Then, with Chapter 54, Stendhal suddenly appears in a less familiar light, as an eloquent champion of the emancipation and education of women. This will not surprise those who know his spirited, high-minded heroines; nor, above all, those who have read his early letters to his sister Pauline, assiduously urging her to study literature, philosophy, and mathematics, and to strive to become a truly cultured, rational, and free person. He recognizes that men have been responsible for keeping women ignorant and narrow-minded, making them prudes and hypocrites – whereby both sexes suffer; he has nothing but contempt for the arguments commonly put forth against women's education, and demolishes these in scathing terms. Girls should have the same cultural opportunities as boys; they should not be allowed to grow up in ignorance of the facts of life and of society. Marriage without love is unnatural: 'there is but one way to ensure greater faithfulness among women to the bond of marriage, and that is to allow freedom for girls and divorce for married couples' (Chapter 56). He even sketches a programme of reform based on – and indeed falling short of – that of his master, the 'ideologue' Destutt de Tracy. But in fact he was far more interested in personal relations than in social reform. And in Fragment 115 he notes, on Métilde's own authority, that 'the only unions which are legitimate for ever are those ruled by a genuine passion'.

As Simone de Beauvoir has said*:

Stendhal is at the same time deeply romantic and decidedly a feminist ... It is not only in the name of freedom in general, it is in the name of individual happiness that Stendhal demands the emancipation of women.

And happiness is a key-word with Stendhal. He sought i t unremittingly: not mere pleasure or the satisfaction of desires, but a rapture accessible only to natures of rare quality – the '*âmes sensibles*', 'the happy few'; the delight that comes from intense feeling, lucid aware-

* Simone de Beauvoir, *Le Deuxième Sexe*, Vol. 1, Paris: Gallimard, 1949, p. 377.

ness, passion and energy; the happiness of reverie, of response to beauty, of the free imagination – and such happiness he found in loving, even without return.

The Text

The text from which this translation is made is that established by Henri Martineau and published by Fernand Hazan *Les classiques du monde* (Paris, 1948). M. Martineau followed the 1822 edition and added those parts of the book (Stendhal's three Prefaces, the chapter 'Concerning Fiascos', the Appendices) which were first incorporated with the original work in the posthumous edition (Michel Levy) of 1853. The last Appendix – an example of love among the wealthy class in France – is the work of Stendhal's friend Victor Jacquemont. English words used by Stendhal are printed in SMALL CAPITALS.

J. S. and B.C.J.G.K.

Suggestions for Further Reading

ADAMS, R. N., *Stendhal: Notes on a Novelist*, Merlin Press, 1959.

GREEN, F. C., *Stendhal*, Cambridge University Press, 1939.

HEMMINGS, F. W. J., *Stendhal: Aspects of his Novels*, Oxford University Press, 1964.

LEVIN, HARRY, *The Gates of Horn*, Oxford University Press, Section 3, 1963.

DEL LITTO, V., *La Vie de Stendhal*, Paris: Albin Michel, 1965.

MARTINEAU, H., *L'œuvre de Stendhal*, Paris: Albin Michel, 1951. *Le Cœur de Stendhal* (2 vols), Paris: Albin Michel, 1952. *Petit dictionnaire Stendhalien*, Paris: Le Divan, 1948. (For biographical details of those persons mentioned in *The Life of Henry Brulard*.)

STENDHAL, *To the Happy Few: Selected Letters of Stendhal*, translated by Norman Cameron, London: John Lehmann, 1952; New York: Evergreen editions, 1955. *The Private Diaries of Stendhal*, edited and translated by Robert Sage, Gollancz, 1955. *The Charterhouse of Parma*, translated with an introduction by Margaret R. B. Shaw, Penguin, 1967. *Scarlet and Black*, translated with an introduction by Margaret R. B. Shaw, Penguin, 1969. *The Life of Henry Brulard*, translated with an introduction by Jean Stewart and B. C. J. G. Knight, Penguin, 1973.

TILLET, MARGARET, *Stendhal: The Background to the Novels*, Oxford University Press, 1971.

PREFACE TO THE FIRST EDITION

IT is of little use for an author to beg the public's indulgence, for the very act of publication gives the lie to this pretence at modesty. He had better submit himself squarely to the justice, patience, and impartiality of his readers. It is chiefly to the last of these qualities that the author of the present work now makes appeal. He has heard much talk in France of writings, opinions, and feelings which are *typically French*, and has reason to fear that his presentation of facts as they really are, and his respect only for feelings and opinions which are *universally typical*, should have played into the hands of that passion for exclusiveness which has of late apparently been classed among the virtues, though its nature is highly equivocal. What, indeed, would become of history, ethics, even science and letters, if they had to be typically German, typically Russian or Italian, typically Spanish or English, the moment you crossed the Rhine, the mountains, or the Channel? What are we to make of geographical justice or truth? When we meet such expressions as *typically Spanish devotion*, or *typically English virtues*, used in earnest in the speeches of foreign patriots, it is high time to grow suspicious of the sentiments which inspire exactly similar statements elsewhere. In Constantinople, and in all barbaric countries, this blind and exclusive partiality for one's own land is a fury which demands blood. Among cultured peoples it is a pained, unhappy, anxious vanity, that turns at bay on the very slightest provocation.

– Extract from the preface to *Voyage en Suisse*, by M. Simond

FIRST ATTEMPT AT A PREFACE

THIS book has met with no success; it has been found unintelligible, and not without cause. In this new edition, therefore, the author has tried above all to express his ideas clearly. He has related how they occurred to him, and has written a preface and an introduction, all for the sake of clarity. Yet despite all this care, for every hundred readers who have enjoyed *Corinne*, not more than four will understand this book.

Although it deals with love, this little book is not a novel, and above all it is not entertaining like a novel. It is simply an exact and scientific description of a brand of madness very rare in France. The conventions, whose sway widens daily, more from a fear of ridicule than from moral purity, have turned the word which serves me for title into something unmentionable, something that even conveys lewdness. I could not avoid using the word, and trust that the scientific austerity of my style puts me beyond reproach on that score.

I know one or two legation secretaries who, on their return, will be able to do me this favour. Until then, I can only suggest that those who dispute the facts I shall relate should kindly pay me no attention whatsoever.

I may be charged with egotism for the form I have adopted. But a traveller is allowed to say: '*I* embarked at New York for South America. *I* went up to Santa Fé de Bogota. Midges and mosquitoes bothered *me* on the journey, and for three days *I* could not open *my* right eye.'

The traveller is not accused of being too fond of the first person singular; all these *I*'s and *me*'s are forgiven him because to use them is the clearest and most interesting way of relating what he has seen.

It is to be clear and graphic, if he can, that the author of this journey into the little-known regions of the human heart says: 'I went with Mme Gherardi to the salt mines of Hallein . . .' 'Princess Crescenzi said to me in Rome . . .' 'One day in Berlin I saw handsome Captain L. . . .' All these little things have really happened to the author, who has spent fifteen years in Germany and Italy. But being more inquisitive than susceptible, he has never met with even the mildest adventure, nor experienced any personal emotion worth recording. If he should be thought proud enough to believe otherwise, let him say that an even greater pride would have stopped him publishing his heart and selling it to the public for six francs, like the folk who bring out their memoirs during their lifetime.

In 1822 the author corrected the proofs of this moral journey, as it were, through Italy and Germany. He had described things the very day he observed them, and his manuscript contained a detailed account of all the phases of that disease of the soul called *love*. He treated this manuscript with the blind respect that a fourteenth-century scholar would have brought to a newly discovered work of Lactantius or Quintus Curtius. When he came across some obscure passage, and to be quite frank this often happened, he always assumed that the fault lay with his later self. He admits that he carried his respect for the manuscript as far as to publish several passages that he no longer understood. This would be crazy for anyone seeking public acclaim, but when he saw Paris again after his travels, the author considered it would be impossible to achieve success without stooping to pander to the press. Now if one is going to cringe, one might as well keep it for the prime minister. Since what goes by the name of success was out of the question, the author pleased himself and has published his thoughts exactly as they occurred to him. In this he follows the example of the Greek philosophers of old, whose practical wisdom is his delight and admiration.

It takes years to penetrate intimately into Italian society. Perhaps I shall have been the last traveller in those regions. Since the advent of the *Carbonari* and the Austrian invasion, foreigners will never again be welcomed in those drawing-rooms so full of light-hearted joy. The monuments, streets, and public squares of a town will still be accessible, but not the society; the foreigner will always be suspect, regarded by the inhabitants as a potential spy. Or they will fear he may laugh at the battle of Antrodoco, and at the mean shifts necessary to evade persecution by the ten or so ministers and favourites who surround the prince. I really loved the people there, and I was able to see the truth. Sometimes I would not speak a word of French for almost a year, and had it not been for the disturbances and the activities of the *Carbonari* I should never have returned to France, for I value good fellowship above all things.

Though I have made every effort to be clear and lucid I cannot work miracles; I cannot give hearing to the deaf, nor sight to the blind. So people with money and coarse pursuits, who have made a hundred thousand francs in the year before they open this book, had better close it again quickly, particularly if they are bankers, manufacturers, or respectable industrialists; in a word, men with highly positive ideas. The book will be less unintelligible to anyone who has won a fortune on the Stock Exchange or in a lottery. Wealth won in such a way is perfectly compatible with a habit of daydreaming for hours at a time, or of enjoying the emotions stirred by one of Prud'hon's pictures, by a passage of Mozart, or by a certain glance from a woman who is often in your thoughts. People who pay two thousand workmen at the end of every week do not *waste their time* like this; their minds are always bent on useful and positive things. The dreamer I am speaking about is the man they would hate if they had the leisure to do so; the man they would most willingly choose as the subject of their funny stories. The industrial millionaire has a confused feeling that such a man would value a thought higher than a banknote.

I take equal exception to the studious young man who, in the year during which the industrialist earned his hundred thousand francs, acquired a knowledge of modern Greek of which he is so proud that he is already aspiring to Arabic. If you have never been unhappy for some imaginary reason *other than vanity*, and which you would be ashamed to hear disclosed in a drawing-room, then kindly leave this book unopened.

I am bound to displease the women who, in those same drawing-rooms, force attention by their perpetual affectedness. I have occasionally caught some of them in an unguarded moment of sincerity, and they were so surprised that they did not know whether a recent sentiment they had expressed was natural or affected. How could such women judge a description of true feelings? This book has indeed been their pet aversion; they have described its author as unspeakable.

Do you suddenly blush when you think of certain things you did when you were young? Have you been foolish because you were tender, and do you reproach yourself, not because you look ridiculous in the eyes of all the room, but rather in the eyes of one particular person there? At twenty-six, did you fall head over heels in love with a woman who loved another? Or again – but the case is so rare that I hardly dare quote it for fear of falling into unintelligibility again, as

I did in the first edition – did you perchance, as you entered the drawing-room that contained the woman you believed you loved, think of nothing but to read in her eyes what she thought of you at that moment, so that you had no thought of conveying your love for her through your own glances? These are the antecedents I require in my readers. It is the description of many of these delicate and rare feelings that has seemed obscure to men with positive ideas. What could I do to be lucid in their eyes? Perhaps announce a fifty-centime rise in price, or an alteration to the customs tariffs of Colombia.[1]

The book that follows explains simply, rationally, and, as it were, mathematically, the various feelings which succeed each other to become, in their entirety, the passion called love.

Imagine a fairly complicated geometrical figure drawn in chalk upon a large blackboard. Well, I am going to explain this figure, but a necessary condition is that it should already be there on the board; I cannot draw it myself. It is this inability that makes it so difficult to write a book about love which is not a novel. The reader requires more than mere intelligence to follow a philosophical examination of this sentiment with interest; it is absolutely imperative that he should have seen love. Now where can one *see* a passion?

Here is a source of obscurity about which I can do nothing.

Love is like the heavenly phenomenon known as the Milky Way, a shining mass made of millions of little stars, many of them nebulae. Four or five hundred of the small successive feelings – so difficult to recognize – that go to make up love have been noted in books, but only the more obvious ones are there. Among the many errors is that of mistaking the lesser lights for the greater. The best of these books, such as *La Nouvelle Héloïse*, the novels of Madame Cottin, the *Letters* of Mademoiselle Lespinasse, and *Manon Lescaut*, have been written in France, a country where the plant called love is chronically afraid of ridicule, stifled by the demands of the *national* passion – vanity – and hardly ever grows to its full stature.

What sort of knowledge of love can be gained from novels? When you have seen it described in a hundred best-sellers but have never

1. 'Cut out this bit,' they tell me, 'it's perfectly true, but beware the business-men; they will cry "aristocrat!"' I was not afraid of the Procurator-General in 1817, so why should I fear millionaires in 1826? The ships sold to the Pasha of Egypt have opened my eyes to *their* little game, and I only fear what I respect.

felt it, is it worth coming to this book to find an explanation of its madness? Like an echo I reply: 'It's madness!'

Poor disillusioned young woman, would you like once again to live through what engrossed you so much a few years ago, something you dared not mention to a soul, and which nearly cost you your honour? It is for you I have re-written this book and tried to make it clearer. When you have read it, never speak of it without a slight sneer, and thrust it into your lemon-wood bookcase behind the other books; I should even leave a few pages uncut, if I were you.

More than a few pages will be left uncut by the imperfect being who imagines himself a philosopher because he has always been a stranger to the mad emotion that can make a week's happiness depend on one glance. Others, as they get older, exert their vanity to the utmost in order to forget that they could once be so humble as to court a woman and so expose themselves to the humiliation of being refused; they will hate this book. Among the many intelligent people who have condemned this book for various reasons – but always in anger – the only ones who struck me as ridiculous were the men whose double vanity could claim always to have been above love's weaknesses, and yet to be gifted with such penetration that they could judge *a priori* the accuracy of a philosophical treatise which is simply a detailed description of these same weaknesses.

People of grave disposition, who enjoy a reputation for unromantic wisdom, are much more likely to understand a novel, however passionate, than a philosophical work in which the author coldly describes the various phases of the disease of the soul called *love*. They are moved in some way by a novel, but when it comes to a philosophical treatise these wiseacres are like blind men asking someone to read them a description of the pictures in the Museum, and saying to the author: 'You must admit that your work is terribly obscure.' And what if these blind men are intelligent, long acknowledged as such, and convinced of their own clear-sightedness? The author gets a rough passage. This is exactly what happened to the writer over the first edition. Several copies of it were actually burnt by extremely intelligent people infuriated by vanity. I say nothing of the insults, none the less flattering for their fury: the author was coarse; he was immoral; he pandered to the public taste; he was a dangerous man, and so on. In countries exhausted by the monarchic system, these epithets are the assured reward for those who choose to write about ethics and fail to dedicate their work to the Dubarry of the day. Literature would be blessed enough if it were not a question of fashion, and if those for whom it is written were the only ones who paid any attention to it. In the days of the Cid, Corneille was just 'my good man' to M. le Marquis de Danjeau.[1] Nowadays everybody thinks himself qualified to read M. de Lamartine; all the better for his publisher, but how hard, how terribly hard on the great poet himself. Nowadays genius has to put itself out for people it should not even have to demean itself by thinking about.

The active, hardworking, eminently respectable and positive life of a Privy Councillor, a textile manufacturer, or a clever banker reaps its reward in wealth but not in tender sensations. Little by little the hearts of these gentlemen ossify; things positive and useful possess them utterly, and they lose the capacity for that sentiment which, above all, requires leisure and makes a man quite incapable of any rational and consecutive undertakings.

The whole purpose of this preface is to proclaim that the book which follows it will be understood only by those who have had leisure enough to commit acts of folly. Many people will think themselves offended; I hope they will read no further.

1. See *Mémoires de Dangeau*, Genlis edition, p. 120.

SECOND ATTEMPT AT A PREFACE

I AM writing for a mere hundred readers, unfortunate, likeable, charming, unhypocritical, unself-righteous people whom I wish to please; I know no more than one or two. I have no respect at all for those who lie in order to attract notice as writers. Fine ladies of this sort have to go and read their cook's account-book and the fashionable sermonizer of the moment, whether it be Massillon or Madame Necker, before they can converse with the dispassionate women who are the dispensers of 'notice'. And, mark you, the only way of reaching this exalted position in France is to become the high priest of some nonsensical doctrine. I would ask anyone who wants to read this book: 'Have six months of your life ever been made miserable by love?'

If you have never experienced an unhappiness beyond worry over a lawsuit, failure to be elected a Deputy at the last election, or not being witty enough when you were taking the waters at Aix last season, then I shall continue my indiscreet questioning and ask you whether within the last twelvemonth you have read one of those outspoken books which force the reader to think; J.-J. Rousseau's *Emile*, for example, or the six volumes of Montaigne? Because if you have never suffered from that weakness of the strong and are not in the unnatural habit of thinking while you read, this book will rouse your anger against its author, for it will make you suspect that there is a certain kind of happiness you do not know, though Mademoiselle de Lespinasse knew it.

FINAL PREFACE

I BEG the reader's indulgence for the curious form of this *Physiology of Love*.

It is now twenty-eight years since the upheavals which followed the fall of Napoleon robbed me of my profession and plunged me, fresh from the horrors of the retreat from Russia, into the life of a friendly town where I fully expected to spend the rest of my days; a prospect which delighted me. In happy Lombardy, in Milan and Venice, the important, in fact the only, business of life is pleasure. No one there takes any notice of what the neighbours do, nor cares very much for what happens to anyone else. If you do perceive your neighbour's existence, it doesn't occur to you to hate him. If you exclude the pastime of envy from a French provincial town, what remains? The absence, the sheer impossibility, of malicious envy is the surest part of the happiness that attracts all the provincials to Paris.

Following upon the masked balls during the Carnival of 1820, which were more brilliant than usual, Milan society witnessed five or six completely crazy events. Although in that part of the world they are used to things which would appear quite unbelievable in France, they talked about these events for a whole month. In this country the fear of ridicule would preclude such strange actions, and indeed it requires all my audacity even to speak of them.

One evening we were speculating deeply on the causes and effects of these extravagances. We were at Mme Pietra Grua's – she is a charming woman who, strangely enough, was not involved in any of these escapades. It occurred to me that perhaps a year later I should have only a vague recollection of the peculiar facts and the causes we were assigning them. I seized a concert programme, on which I scribbled a few words in pencil. We intended to play *faro*, and thirty of us were sitting round a green table; but the conversation was so lively that the game was forgotten. Late in the evening Colonel Scotti turned up – one of the pleasantest men in the Italian army – and we asked him what details he could contribute about the bizarre events we had been discussing. He told us certain things that he had learnt by chance, which put quite a different complexion upon the whole affair.

I reached for my concert programme and added the new circumstances.

This collection of details about love has been continued in the same way, in pencil on scraps of paper picked up in the drawing-rooms where I used to hear the anecdotes. I soon began to look for a common law by which to determine the varying degrees of love. Two months later, fear of being taken for a *carbonaro* drove me to return to Paris, intending to stay only a few months; but I have never been back to Milan, where I had lived for seven years.

In Paris I was bored to death, and it occurred to me to turn again to that lovable country whence fear had driven me. I collected my scraps of paper together and made a present of the lot to a publisher. There was soon a snag, however, for the printer declared that he was quite unable to work from pencilled notes. I perceived that this sort of draft was quite beneath his dignity. The young printer's devil who brought back my notes looked quite ashamed of the discourtesy with which he had been saddled; he knew how to write, so I dictated my pencil notes to him.

I also realized that for discretion's sake I would have to change all the names, and above all shorten the anecdotes. Though they read but little in Milan, the book would have seemed abominably spiteful had it fallen into their hands.

So the book that I brought out was unfortunate. I shall be so bold as to admit that in those days I dared to despise elegance of style, and I could see the young apprentice busily avoiding flat endings to my sentences, and sequences of words which sounded odd. For his part, at every turn, he quite happily altered the details of facts difficult to express. Even Voltaire flinches from things which are difficult to say.

The only value of the *Essay on Love* lay in the number of little nuances of feeling which I begged the reader to verify from his own recollections, if he were fortunate enough to have any. Worse still, I was then, as always, a tyro in literary matters; the publisher to whom I had presented the manuscript had it printed on poor paper, and the layout was ridiculous. He told me after a month, when I enquired how the book was getting on, 'You might call it sacred, for nobody will touch it!'

It had not even occurred to me to solicit newspaper reviews; it would have seemed ignominious to do so. Yet no work was ever in more dire need of an introduction calling for the reader's patience.

Lest it should appear unintelligible from the very first, I had to persuade the public to accept the new word *crystallization*, which was intended vividly to convey the whole congeries of strange follies about the beloved which come to be regarded as true and beyond question.

At that time, steeped as I was in devotion to every slightest detail I had culled from my beloved Italy, I carefully avoided any concessions, any amenity of style that might have made the *Essay on Love* seem a little less peculiarly outlandish in the eyes of men of letters.

Besides, I did not flatter the public at all. It was at the time when we were all bruised by our recent disasters, and literature seemed to have no other object than to soothe our wounded vanity. Everything victorious rhymed with glorious, and never a sword unsheathed but was laurel-wreathed. The tedious literature of this period never seems to bother with the exact details of the subjects about which it claims to be dealing; it merely seeks opportunities to pay compliments to a people enslaved by fashion, whom a great man called the great nation, forgetting that it was only great by virtue of his leadership.

The result of my ignorance of the conditions necessary for the most modest success was that between 1822 and 1833 my book only found seventeen readers; in its twenty years of existence I doubt if it has been understood by more than a hundred or so curious-minded folk. One or two have had the patience to observe the successive phases of the disease of love in those around them who have been afflicted with it; because, to understand this passion which our fear of ridicule has been concealing so carefully for the last thirty years, you must speak of it as a disease. Indeed this is sometimes the first step towards its cure.

It is, in fact, only after half a century of revolutions which have monopolized our attention one by one; only after five complete changes in the form and trend of our governments, that revolution has begun to affect our way of life. Love, or the most common substitute that uses its name, was all-powerful in France under Louis XV; the ladies of the court chose the colonels, and that was the finest position in the kingdom. Now, fifty years later, the court no longer exists, and the most respected women in the ruling middle-class or the disgruntled aristocracy could not influence so much as the grant of a tobacconist's licence in the tiniest village.

We must face the fact that women are no longer in fashion; in our salons, brilliant as they are, young men of twenty affect never to speak to them, much preferring to gather round some coarse driveller with a provincial accent who talks of *capacities*, while they try to get a word in edgeways. Wealthy young men make a point of appearing frivolous, to give the impression that they are carrying on the gay life of bygone days, but they really prefer to talk about horses or to play for high stakes in gambling-circles where women are not admitted. A lethal chilliness seems to characterize the relationships of young men with the women of twenty-five who have been thrown back into society by the tedium of marriage. Perhaps this may lead some wise souls to welcome my scrupulously exact description of the successive stages in the disease known as love.

The frightening change which has plunged us into our present boredom, and which makes us quite unable to understand the society of 1778, such as we find it in Diderot's letters to his mistress Mademoiselle Voland or in the memoirs of Mme d'Epinay, may lead us to enquire which of our successive Governments destroyed our faculty for amusing ourselves and increased our resemblance to the gloomiest people on earth. We do not even know how to copy their *Parliament* and the integrity of their parties – the only tolerable thing they ever invented. On the other hand, the stupidest of all their gloomy conceptions, the spirit of dignity, has come among us to replace French gaiety, which is hardly to be found anywhere now except in the five hundred suburban ballrooms round Paris, or in the *Midi* south of Bordeaux.

But which of our successive Governments did commit the frightful atrocity of *anglicizing* us? Should we lay the blame on the energetic Government of 1793 which stopped foreigners from camping on Montmartre? A Government which, in a few years, we shall regard as heroic, and which was a fitting prelude to the one that, under Napoleon, was to carry our name into all the capitals of Europe.

We may pass over the well-intentioned stupidity of the Directoire as illustrated by the talents of Carnot and the immortal Italian campaign of 1796-7.

The corruption at court under Barras still recalled the gaiety of the *ancien régime*, and the graces of Madame Bonaparte were evidence that at that time we still had no taste for the sourness and arrogance of the English.

Despite the envious spirit of the Faubourg Saint-Germain, we could not but deeply respect the method of government by the First Consul and able men like Cretet, Daru, etc. . . . We cannot therefore saddle the Empire with the responsibility for the obvious change which has overtaken the French character during this first half of the nineteenth century.

I need not press my investigation further; the reader will, on reflection, be well able to reach his own conclusions . . .

THAT YOU SHOULD BE MADE A FOOL OF BY A YOUNG
WOMAN, WHY, IT IS MANY AN HONEST MAN'S CASE.

The Pirate, Volume III, p. 77

BOOK ONE

I WANT to try and establish exactly what this passion is, whose every genuine manifestation is characterized by beauty.

There are four different kinds of love:

1. Passionate Love. This was the love of the Portuguese nun, that of Heloïse for Abelard, of the captain of Vésel, and of the gendarme of Cento.

2. Mannered Love, which flourished in Paris about 1760, and which is to be found in the memoirs and novels of the period; for example those of Crébillon, Lauzun, Duclos, Marmontel, Chamfort, and Mme d'Epinay . . .

A stylized painting, this, where the rosy hues extend into the shadows, where there is no place for anything at all unpleasant – for that would be a breach of etiquette, of good taste, of delicacy, and so forth. A man of breeding will know in advance all the rituals he must meet and observe in the various stages of this kind of love, which often achieves greater refinement than real love, since there is nothing passionate or unpredictable about it, and it is always witty. It is a cold, pretty miniature as against an oil painting by one of the Carrachi; and while passionate love carries us away against our real interests, mannered love as invariably respects those interests. Admittedly, if you take away vanity, there is very little left of mannered love, and the poor weakened invalid can hardly drag itself along.

3. Physical Love. You are hunting; you come across a handsome young peasant girl who takes to her heels through the woods. Everyone knows the love that springs from this kind of pleasure, and however desiccated and miserable you may be, this is where your love-life begins at sixteen.

4. Vanity-Love. The great majority of men, especially in France, both desire and possess a fashionable woman, much in the way one might own a fine horse – as a luxury befitting a young man. Vanity, a little flattered and a little piqued, leads to enthusiasm. Sometimes there is physical love, but not always; often even physical pleasure is lacking. 'A duchess is never more than thirty in the eyes of a bourgeois,' said the Duchesse de Chaulnes, and the courtiers of that just king Louis of Holland cheerfully recall even now a pretty woman from The Hague who was quite unable to resist the charms of anyone

who happened to be a duke or a prince. But true to hierarchical principles, as soon as a prince came to court she would send her duke packing. She was rather like an emblem of seniority in the diplomatic corps!

The happiest version of this insipid relationship is where physical pleasure grows with habit. Then memories produce a semblance of love; there is the pricking at your pride and the sadness in satisfaction; the atmosphere of romantic fiction catches you by the throat, and you believe yourself lovesick and melancholy, for vanity will always pretend to be grand passion. One thing is certain though: whichever kind of love produces the pleasures, they only become vivid, and their recollection compelling, from the moment of inspiration. In love, unlike most other passions, the recollection of what you have had and lost is always better than what you can hope for in the future.

Occasionally in vanity-love, habit, or despair of finding something better, results in a friendship of the least attractive sort, which will even boast of its *stability*, and so on.[1]

Although physical pleasure, being natural, is known to all, it is only of secondary importance to sensitive, passionate people. If such people are derided in drawing rooms or made unhappy by the intrigues of the worldly, they possess in compensation a knowledge of pleasures utterly inaccessible to those moved only by vanity or money.

Some virtuous and sensitive women are almost unaware of the idea of physical pleasure; they have so rarely, if I may hazard an expression, exposed themselves to it, and in fact the raptures of passionate love have practically effaced the memory of bodily delights.

There are some men who are the victims and instruments of a hellish pride, a pride like that of Alfieri. These men, who are cruel perhaps because like Nero they are always afraid, judge everyone after their own pattern, and can achieve physical pleasure only when they indulge their pride by practising cruelties upon the companion of their pleasures. Hence the horrors of *Justine*. Only in this way can they find a sense of security.

Instead of defining four kinds of love, one might well admit eight or ten distinctions. There are perhaps as many different ways of feeling as there are of seeing, but differences of terminology do not affect the arguments which follow. Every variety of love mentioned henceforth

1. A known conversation between Pont de Veyle and Mme du Deffand, by the fireside.

is born, lives, dies, or attains immortality in accordance with the same laws.[1]

CHAPTER 2: *Concerning the Birth of Love*

HERE is what happens in the soul:

1. Admiration.

2. You think, 'How delightful it would be to kiss her, to be kissed by her,' and so on . . .

3. Hope. You observe her perfections, and it is at this moment that a woman really ought to surrender, for the utmost physical pleasure. Even the most reserved women blush to the whites of their eyes at this moment of hope. The passion is so strong, and the pleasure so sharp, that they betray themselves unmistakably.

4. Love is born. To love is to enjoy seeing, touching, and sensing with all the senses, as closely as possible, a lovable object which loves in return.

5. The first crystallization begins. If you are sure that a woman loves you, it is a pleasure to endow her with a thousand perfections and to count your blessings with infinite satisfaction. In the end you overrate wildly, and regard her as something fallen from Heaven, unknown as yet, but certain to be yours.

Leave a lover with his thoughts for twenty-four hours, and this is what will happen:

At the salt mines of Salzburg, they throw a leafless wintry bough into one of the abandoned workings. Two or three months later they haul it out covered with a shining deposit of crystals. The smallest twig, no bigger than a tom-tit's claw, is studded with a galaxy of scintillating diamonds. The original branch is no longer recognizable.

What I have called crystallization is a mental process which draws from everything that happens new proofs of the perfection of the loved one.

You hear a traveller speaking of the cool orange groves beside the

1. This book is freely translated from an Italian manuscript by M. Lisio Visconti, a most distinguished young man, who has just died at his home in Volterra. On the day of his unexpected death he gave the translator permission to publish his essay on Love, if a way could be found of reducing it to a proper form.   Castel Fiorentino, 10th June 1819.

sea at Genoa in the summer heat: Oh, if you could only share that coolness with *her*!

One of your friends goes hunting, and breaks his arm: wouldn't it be wonderful to be looked after by the woman you love! To be with her all the time and to see her loving you . . . a broken arm would be heaven . . . and so your friend's injury provides you with conclusive proof of the angelic kindness of your mistress. In short, no sooner do you think of a virtue than you detect it in your beloved.

The phenomenon that I have called crystallization springs from Nature, which ordains that we shall feel pleasure and sends the blood to our heads. It also evolves from the feeling that the degree of pleasure is related to the perfections of the loved one, and from the idea that 'She is mine.' The savage has no time to go beyond the first step. He feels pleasure, but his brain is fully occupied in chasing deer through the forest, so that he can eat, keep up his strength, and avoid his enemy's axe.

At the other end of the scale of civilization, I have no doubt that a sensitive woman can feel physical pleasure only with the man she loves.[1] This is the direct opposite of the savage's condition. But then, in civilized countries, the woman has leisure, while the savage is so taken up with his occupation that he cannot help treating his female as a beast of burden. If the mates of many animals are happier, it is only because the male has less difficulty in obtaining his food.

But let us leave the forest and return to Paris. A man in love sees every perfection in the object of his love, but his attention is still liable to wander after a time because one gets tired of anything uniform, even perfect happiness.[2]

This is what happens next to fix the attention:

6. Doubt creeps in. First a dozen or so glances, or some other sequence of actions, raise and confirm the lover's hopes. Then, as he recovers from the initial shock, he grows accustomed to his good fortune, or acts on a theory drawn from the common multitude of easily-won women. He asks for more positive proofs of affection and tries to press his suit further.

1. If men do not display this peculiarity, it is because they have no modesty to sacrifice.
2. Which means that the same subtlety of existence can offer only one moment of perfect happiness; but the passionate man's *manner of being* changes ten times a day.

He is met with indifference,[1] coldness, or even anger if he appears too confident. In France there is even a shade of irony which seems to say 'You think you're farther ahead than you really are.' A woman may behave like this either because she is recovering from a moment of intoxication and obeying the dictates of modesty, which she may fear she has offended; or simply for the sake of prudence or coquetry.

The lover begins to be less sure of the good fortune he was anticipating and subjects his grounds for hope to a critical examination.

He tries to recoup by indulging in other pleasures but finds them inane. He is seized by the dread of a frightful calamity and now concentrates fully. Thus begins:

7. The second crystallization, which deposits diamond layers of proof that 'she loves me.'

Every few minutes throughout the night which follows the birth of doubt, the lover has a moment of dreadful misgiving, and then reassures himself, 'she loves me'; and crystallization begins to reveal new charms. Then once again the haggard eye of doubt pierces him and he stops transfixed. He forgets to draw breath and mutters, 'But does she love me?' Torn between doubt and delight, the poor lover convinces himself that she could give him such pleasure as he could find nowhere else on earth.

It is the pre-eminence of this truth, and the road to it, with a fearsome precipice on one hand and a view of perfect happiness on the other, which set the second crystallization so far above the first.

The lover's mind vacillates between three ideas:

1. She is perfect.
2. She loves me.
3. How can I get the strongest possible proofs of her love?

The most heartrending moment of love in its infancy is the realization that you have been mistaken about something, and that a whole framework of crystals has to be destroyed. You begin to feel doubtful about the entire process of crystallization.

1. What the seventeenth-century novelists called the '*coup de foudre*' (or thunderbolt), which determines the destiny of the hero and his mistress, is a movement of the soul which, for all its debasement by a thousand scribblers, is none the less a fact of nature. It comes from the impossibility of performing this defensive manœuvre. A woman in love finds so much happiness in the feelings she is experiencing that she is unable to pretend; tired of being prudent, she throws caution to the wind and flings herself blindly into the happiness of loving. Where there is mistrust there can be no *coup deoudre*.

I T only needs a very small quantity of hope to beget love. Even when hope gives way to despair after a day or two, love will persist.

In a decisive, bold, and impetuous person, with an imagination whetted by misfortune, the degree of hope can be even smaller and more fleeting, without endangering the love.

If the lover has suffered; if he is sensitive and thoughtful; if he turns from other women in keen admiration of the lady in question, no ordinary pleasure will lure him away from the second crystallization. He will prefer to dream of the slenderest chance of pleasing her, rather than to receive all the favours of any ordinary woman.

It is at this stage, and no later, mark you, that a woman who wishes to crush her lover's hopes should do so cruelly, and heap on his head, in public, insults which will make it quite impossible for him ever to see her again.

Even when the periods between all these stages are prolonged, love can still result.

Cold, prudent, phlegmatic people must hope longer and more deeply before they fall in love, and the same is true of elderly people.

The second crystallization ensures that love will last; for you feel that the only alternatives are to win her love or to die. The very idea of ceasing to love is absurd when your convictions are confirmed moment by moment, until the passing months make love a habit. The stronger your character, the slighter the impulse to inconstancy.

This second crystallization is almost entirely lacking when love is inspired by a woman who yields too soon.

When the two crystallization processes have taken place, and particularly the second, which is far the stronger, the original naked branch is no longer recognizable by indifferent eyes, because it now sparkles with perfections, or diamonds, which they do not see or which they simply do not consider to be perfections.

Del Rosso was talking to a former admirer of his mistress, who described her charms in some detail. Del Rosso saw a particular twinkle in the teller's eye, which at once provided another diamond for his crystalline branch.[1] An idea like this, conceived in the evening, would keep him dreaming the whole night through.

An impromptu remark gives *me*[2] dreams enough to last a whole night through. I see a sensitive, generous, burning spirit – *romantic*[3]

1. I have called this essay a book of ideology. I intended to convey that although it was about *love*, it was not a novel, and was not entertaining in the way that a novel is. I beg the forgiveness of the philosophers for having chosen the word *ideology*; I certainly had no intention of stealing a title that by rights should belong to someone else. If ideology be a detailed description of ideas and of all the parts into which those ideas can be analysed, this book is a detailed and painstaking description of all the feelings which make up the passion called *love*. I then draw certain conclusions from this description; for instance, the way in which love can be cured. I know of no word derived from Greek that would indicate discourse upon feelings, as ideology indicates discourse upon ideas. I might have had a word invented for me by one of my scholarly friends, but I am already quite annoyed enough at having had to adopt the new word *crystallization*, and it may well be that if this essay wins any readers, they will not forgive me the neologism. I agree that literary talent would have avoided it and I tried to do so, but without any success. In my opinion this word does express the principal process of the madness known as love, a madness which nevertheless provides man with the greatest pleasures the species can know on earth. If I had not used the word *crystallization* I should have had to replace it repeatedly by an awkward periphrasis, and my description of what happens in the head and in the heart of a man in love would have become obscure, heavy, and wearisome even to me, the author. I hesitate to guess what the reader would have thought of it.

I therefore urge anyone who is shocked by the word *crystallization* to shut the book forthwith. It is no part of my desire, fortunately, to have a great number of readers. It would make me very happy to please about thirty or forty people in Paris, whom I shall never see but nevertheless love devotedly without ever having met them: some young Madame Roland, for instance, surreptitiously reading a volume which she thrusts into a drawer at the slightest noise, by the workbench in the back of her father's watch-engraving shop. Someone like Madame Roland will, I hope, forgive me not only the word *crystallization*, which I use to express the impulse of folly that makes us see all beauties and perfections in the woman we are beginning to love, but also many bolder ellipses. The only thing to do is to take a pencil and write in the few missing words between the lines.

2. It is for the sake of *brevity*, and in order to depict experience from the inside, that the author, by using the first person singular, brings together a number of feelings quite alien to him. He has had none of his own which are worth mentioning.

3. At first all these actions seemed to me to have the sublimity that immediately sets a man apart and differentiates him from all others. I thought I saw in his eyes that thirst for more sublime happiness, that unavowed

as it is commonly called – who sets above the happiness of kings the simple pleasure of walking alone with her lover at midnight in a secluded wood.

Del Rosso would say that my mistress is a prude; I think his a harlot.

CHAPTER 4

IN the unattached heart of a girl who is living in a secluded château in the depths of the country the least touch of surprise can lead to a mild admiration. When this is followed by even the slenderest hope, admiration leads to love and crystallization.

This kind of love is rather fun at first.

Surprise and hope are powerfully supported by the need for love and the melancholy which characterize the sixteen-year-old. It is a commonplace that sixteen is an age which thirsts for love and is not excessively particular about what beverage chance may provide.

The seven stages of love, then, are as follows:

       1. Admiration.
       2. How delightful . . . etc.
       3. Hope.
       4. The birth of love.
       5. First crystallization.
       6. Doubt creeps in . . .
       7. Second crystallization.

The interval between 1 and 2 may be a year. Between 2 and 3 it may be a month; unless hope follows closely stage 2 is imperceptibly given up, as causing unhappiness; 3 leads to 4 in a twinkling. There is no interval between 4 and 5; only intimacy could possibly come between them.

Depending on the impetuousness and habitual boldness of the individual, several days may elapse between 5 and 6. There is no interval between 6 and 7.

---

melancholy which aspires to something better than we can know here below, and which, for a romantic soul, however placed by chance or revolution,
     . . . Still prompts the celestial sight,
     For which we wish to live, or dare to die.
                (*Ultima lettera di Bianca a sua madre.* Forli, 1817.)

CHAPTER 5

M AN is not free to avoid doing what gives him greater pleasure than any other action.[1]

Love is like a fever which comes and goes quite independently of the will. It is chiefly in this that mannered love differs from passionate love. The charms of your beloved are not a matter of self-congratulation, except as a stroke of luck.

Finally, there are no age limits for love. Look at Madame du Deffand's infatuation with the churlish Horace Walpole, or the more recent and certainly pleasanter example in Paris itself.

The embarrassing consequences of grand passion are the only proofs I will admit in evidence of its existence. Shyness, for instance, is a proof of love; I do *not* mean the awkward shame of a boy leaving school.

CHAPTER 6: *The Salzburg Bough*

C RYSTALLIZATION goes on throughout love almost without a break. The process is something like this: whenever all is not well between you and your beloved, you crystallize out an *imaginary solution*. Only through imagination can you be sure that your beloved is perfect in any given way. After intimacy, ever-resurgent fears are lulled by more real solutions. Thus happiness never stays the same, except in its origin; every day brings forth a new blossom.

If your beloved gives way to her passion and commits the cardinal error of removing your fear by the intensity of her response,[2] then crystallization stops for a moment, but what love loses in intensity – its fears, that is – it makes up for by the charm of complete abandon and infinite trust, becoming a gentle habit which softens the hardships of life and gives a new interest to its enjoyment.

If she leaves you, crystallization begins again, and every act of admiration, the sight of every happiness she could give you, and whose existence you had forgotten, ends in the searing reflection: 'I

1. Where crime is concerned, a good education instils remorse; and foreseen remorse acts as a deterrent.
2. Diane de Poitiers, in the *Princesse de Clèves*.

shall never know that joy again, and it is through my fault that I have lost it!' It is no use seeking consolation in pleasures of another sort; they turn to dust and ashes. Your imagination can paint a physical picture for you, and take you a-hunting on a swift horse through Devon woods;[1] but you are aware at the same time that you could find no pleasure in it. This is the optical illusion which leads to the fatal pistol shot.

Gambling also has its crystallization process, concerned with the use you will make of the money you hope to win.

The intrigues at court, so much mourned by the nobles under the cloak of Legitimism, were only fascinating because of the crystallization they bred. Not a courtier but envied Luynes and Lauzun their swift ascent to affluence; not an attractive woman but saw herself with a duchy as great as that of Mme de Polignac. No rational form of government can possibly recapture that crystallization. There is nothing quite so anti-imagination as the government of the United States of America. We have already seen that among their neighbours the savages crystallization is almost unknown. The Romans had but a bare idea of it, and then only about physical love.

Hatred, too, has its crystallization; as soon as you see a hope of revenge, your hatred breaks out afresh.

If belief in the absurd or unproven tends to bring the most incongruous people to the top, that is another effect of crystallization. It even exists in mathematics (see the Newtonians in 1740), in minds which could not at any given moment grasp simultaneously all the stages of proof in evidence of their beliefs.

Think of the fate of the great German philosophers, whose immortality, so widely proclaimed, never managed to last more than thirty or forty years.

It is because we can never understand the whys and wherefores of our feelings that even the wisest men are fanatical about such things as music.

It is impossible to justify oneself at will against someone who holds an opposite view.

1. Because, if you could imagine happiness there, crystallization would have claimed for your mistress the exclusive right to give you that happiness.

CHAPTER 7: *Concerning the Different Beginnings of Love for the Two Sexes*

A WOMAN establishes her position by granting favours. Ninety-five per cent of her daydreams are about love, and from the moment of intimacy they revolve about one single theme: she endeavours to justify the extraordinary and decisive step she has taken in defiance of all her habits of modesty. A man has no such concern, but a woman's imagination dwells reminiscently on every enchanting detail.

Since love casts doubt upon what seemed proven before, the woman who was so certain, before intimacy, that her lover was entirely above vulgar promiscuity, no sooner remembers that she has nothing left to refuse him than she trembles lest he has merely been adding another conquest to his list.

Only at this point does the second[1] crystallization begin, and much more strongly, since it is now accompanied by fear.

The woman feels she has demeaned herself from queen to slave, and matters are aggravated by the dizzy intoxication which results from pleasures as keen as they are rare. And then again, a woman at her embroidery – an insipid pastime that occupies only her hands – thinks of nothing but her lover; while he, galloping across the plains with his squadron, would be placed under arrest if he muffed a manœuvre.

I should imagine, therefore, that the second crystallization is a good deal stronger in women, because fear is more acute; vanity and honour are in pawn and distractions are certainly not so easy.

A woman cannot fall back on the habit of rational thinking that a man like myself is bound to acquire, working six hours a day at a desk on cold rational matters. Women are inclined, and not only in love, to give way to their imaginations, and to become ecstatic; so their lovers' faults are quickly effaced.

Women prefer emotion to reason. It's quite simple: since in our dull way we never give them any business responsibility in the family *they never have occasion to use reason*, and so never regard it as of any use.

1. This second crystallization does not occur in women of easy virtue, who are far removed from such romantic ideas.

Indeed they find reason a positive nuisance, since it descends upon them only to chide them for their enjoyment of yesterday, or to forbid them the enjoyment of tomorrow.

If you were to hand over the administration of two of your estates to your wife, I wager the accounts would be better kept than by yourself; and then . . . well, you would of course have the *right* to feel sorry for yourself, you pitiable despot, since you lack even the talent to excite love.

As soon as women begin to generalize they are making love without knowing it. They pride themselves on being more meticulous in detail than men, and half the trade across counters is carried on by women, who do better at it than their husbands. It is a commonplace that when you talk about business with them, you must always adopt a very serious tone.

The thing is that they are hungry for emotion, anywhere and at any time: think of the pleasures of a Scottish funeral.

CHAPTER 8

> This was her favoured fairy realm, and here she erected her aerial palaces.
>
> *Lammermoor*, 1, 70.

A GIRL of eighteen cannot crystallize so well as a woman of twenty-eight, and conceives desires too limited by her narrow experience of life to be able to love passionately.

I was discussing this tonight with an intelligent woman who disagrees with me. 'A girl's imagination,' she said, 'hasn't been frozen by unpleasant experience and the first fire of youth is still in full flame. Quite possibly she will create for herself an entrancing picture of some quite ordinary man. Every time she meets her lover she will enjoy, not the man as he really is, but the wonderful inner vision she has created.'

'Later on, when she has been disillusioned about this lover and about other men, her power to crystallize will have been reduced by stern reality, and mistrust will have clipped the wings of her imagination. However outstanding the man, she can never again fashion so compelling an image, and will not be able to love so eagerly as when she was younger. And since in love only the illusion appeals, and she cannot at twenty-eight give her image the sublime and dazzling tones she dreamed of at eighteen, her second love will always seem second-rate.'

'On the contrary, madame,' I replied, 'the very fact that there is mistrust, which was not there at sixteen, will give a new colour to this second love. For the very young, love is like a huge river which sweeps everything before it, so that you feel that it is a restless current. Now a sensitive person has acquired some self-knowledge by twenty-eight; she knows that any happiness she can expect from life will come to her through love; hence a terrible struggle develops between love and mistrust. She crystallizes only slowly; but whatever crystals survive her terrible ordeal, where the spirit is moving in the face of the most appalling danger, will be a thousand times more brilliant and durable than those of the sixteen-year-old, whose privileges are simply happiness and joy. Thus the later love will be less gay, but more passionate.'[1]

In this conversation (Bologna, 9th March 1820) a point which had seemed to me quite obvious is contradicted, and convinces me more and more that a man is almost incapable of saying anything sensible about what goes on in the inmost heart of a sensitive woman; as for a coquette, that's another matter, for men, too, have senses and vanity.

The dissimilarity between the way love is born for the two sexes corresponds with a difference in the nature of hope for man and woman. One is attacking, the other defending; one asks, the other refuses; one is bold, the other shy.

The man wonders: 'Shall I be able to please her? Will she love me?'

And the woman thinks: 'Perhaps he's only joking when he says he loves me. Is he reliable? Does he really know himself how long his love will last?' This is why many women treat a young man of twenty-three as if he were a child; of course if he has fought half a dozen campaigns it's a different matter and he becomes a young hero.

For a man, hope depends simply on the actions of the woman he loves, and nothing is easier to interpret than these. For a woman, hope must be based on moral considerations which are extremely difficult to assess. Most men seek a proof of love which they consider

1. Epicurus said that discrimination is necessary to the achievement of pleasure.

dispels all doubt; women are not lucky enough to be able to find a like proof. It is one of life's misfortunes that what brings certainty and happiness to one lover brings danger and almost humiliation to the other.

In love, men run the risk of suffering secret torments, while women lay themselves open to public jest; in the first place they are shyer, and besides, public opinion means much more to them because 'to be esteemed' is imperative.[1]

They have no sure means of winning public approval by revealing their real selves for a moment.

So they have to be more cautious. Force of habit dictates that all the intellectual processes which constitute the birth of love are gentler, shyer, slower, and more tentative in women; they have a greater disposition to constancy and are undoubtedly less able to halt a crystallization once it has begun.

A woman on seeing her lover reflects swiftly, or surrenders to the joy of loving, but this joy is rudely shattered if he makes the slightest advance, because then defence and not surrender is the order of the day.

The lover's part is much simpler. He just looks into his beloved's eyes; a single smile will give him supreme happiness and he never stops trying to obtain this.[2] A long siege humiliates a man, but ennobles a woman.

A woman in love is quite capable of speaking no more than a dozen words in a whole year to the man she loves. In the depths of her heart she keeps note of the number of times she has seen him; twice he has taken her to the theatre, twice they have met at dinner, and he has greeted her three times when she was out walking.

One evening at a party he kissed her hand; and you will observe that since then she has been careful, even at the risk of appearing odd, to allow no one else to kiss her hand.

---

1. Compare the maxim of Beaumarchais: Nature says to a woman, 'If you can, be beautiful; if you like, be wise; but whatever happens, be respected.' In France, no respect means no admiration and therefore no love.

2.   *Quando legemmo il disiato riso*
                     Esser baciato da cotanto amante,
                     Questi che mai da me non fia diviso,
                     La bocca mi bació tutto tremante.
                              Francesca da Rimini. Dante.

Léonore used to say that this sort of behaviour in a man was 'feminine love'.

CHAPTER 9

I AM trying extremely hard to be *dry*. My heart thinks it has so much to say, but I try to keep it quiet. I am continually beset by the fear that I may have expressed only a sigh when I thought I was stating a truth.

CHAPTER 10

THE following story will suffice as proof of the crystallization principle.[1]

A young woman learns that her cousin Edward, who is about to leave the Army, is a distinguished young man and is in love with her already because of what he has heard of her, even though they have never met; doubtless he wishes to meet her before declaring his love and asking for her hand. She sees a young stranger at church and hears him called Edward. She can think of no one else; she is in love. A week later the real Edward turns up, and he is not the stranger in the church. She turns pale . . . and of course will be utterly miserable for ever if she is made to marry him.

This is what the small-minded call 'one of the follies of love'.

A man shows the greatest kindness and generosity to a girl who is unhappy; he has every virtue and could hardly be more attentive. But he wears a shabby hat, and she notices that he does not ride well. She tells herself with a sigh that she could never marry a man like that.

Another man is paying court to a thoroughly good and honest woman. She finds out that he has suffered from an embarrassing physical misfortune; at once she can no longer stand the sight of him. Not that she ever had the slightest intention of giving herself to him, or that his disabilities detract in any way from his wit and pleasant manners; it is simply that crystallization has become impossible. No matter whether it be in the forest of Arden or at a Coulon ball, you can only enjoy idealizing your beloved if she *appears* perfect in the

1. *Empoli*, June 1819.

first place. Absolute perfection is not essential, but every perceived quality must be perfect. Only after several days of the second crystallization will the beloved appear perfect in all respects. It's quite simple; you only need to think of a perfection to perceive it at once in your beloved.

You see to what extent *beauty* is necessary if love is to be born. Ugliness must not present an obstacle. The lover will soon come to see beauty in his mistress whatever she looks like, without giving a thought to *real beauty*.

If he does see real beauty, one might say that it promises him one unit of happiness, while his mistress's features, whatever they are like, will promise him a thousand.

Before love is born, beauty is necessary as an advertisement; it predisposes to love by evoking praise of the person to be loved. If you admire strongly enough, the least spark of hope will turn it into love.

In mannered love, and perhaps in the first five minutes of passionate love, a woman taking a lover will be more concerned with the way other women see him than with the way she sees him herself.

Herein lies the reason for the success of princes and officers.[1]

Even in his old age, the pretty women at court were in love with Louis XIV.

You must be careful not to allow free rein to hope before you are sure that admiration exists. Otherwise you would achieve only an insipid flatness quite incompatible with love, or at least whose only cure would be in a challenge to your self-esteem.

We have no sympathy with stupidity, nor with the smile for each and everyone. Hence the necessity in 'society' for a veneer of sharpness; it is the hallmark of manners. Not even laughter blooms on too vile a plant. We scorn too easy a victory in love and are never inclined to set much value upon what is there for the taking.

1. 'Those who remarked in the countenance of this young hero a dissolute audacity mingled with extreme haughtiness and indifference to the feelings of others, could not yet deny to his countenance that sort of comeliness which belongs to an open set of features, well formed by nature, modelled by art to the usual rules of courtesy, yet so far frank and honest that they seemed as if they disclaimed to conceal the natural working of the soul. Such an expression is often mistaken for *manly frankness*, when in truth it arises from the reckless indifference of a libertine disposition, conscious of *superiority of birth, of wealth,* or of some other adventitious advantage totally unconnected with personal merit.' *Ivanhoe*, Volume 1, p. 145.

CHAPTER 11

Once crystallization has begun, you delight in each new beauty that you discover in your beloved.

But what is beauty? It is a new potentiality for pleasure.

Each person's pleasures are different, and often radically so, which explains quite clearly why something that is beautiful to one man is ugly to another. (See the conclusive example of Del Rosso and Lisio on 1st January 1820.)

To determine the nature of beauty, we must investigate each individual's idea of pleasure. For instance, Del Rosso insists upon a woman who allows him to risk a gesture or two, and smilingly licenses the most delightful liberties, a woman who keeps him continually aware of physical pleasure and at the same time gives him the opportunity and incentive to display his particular brand of charm.

Apparently for Del Rosso 'love' means physical love, and for Lisio it means passionate love. It is clearly improbable that they will agree about the meaning of the word 'beauty'.[1]

Since the beauty a man discovers is a new capacity for arousing his pleasure, and since pleasures vary with the individual, each man's crystallization will be tinged with the colour of his pleasures.

The crystallization about your mistress, that is to say her *beauty*, is nothing but the sum of the fulfilment of all the desires you have been able to formulate about her.

CHAPTER 12: *Crystallization Continued*

Why does one enjoy and delight in each new beauty discovered in the beloved?

It is because each new beauty gives us the complete fulfilment of a desire. We want her to be sensitive: behold! she *is* sensitive. Then we would have her as proud as Corneille's Emilia and, though the two qualities are probably incompatible, she acquires in a trice the soul of a Roman. This is the reason why, on the moral plane, love is the

---

1. *Beauty*, as I intend it here, means the promise of a quality useful to my soul, and transcends physical attraction; the latter is only one particular kind. 1815.

strongest of the passions. In all the others, desires have to adapt themselves to cold reality, but in love realities obligingly rearrange
themselves to conform with desire. There is therefore more scope for
the indulgence of violent desires in love than in any other passion.

There are cetain general conditions for happiness which govern the
fulfilment of all particular desires:

1. She seems to be your property, because you alone can make her
happy.

2. She is the arbiter of your merit. This condition was most important in the chivalric courts of François I and Henri II, and at the
elegant court of Louis XV. Under a constitutional and rational
government women are entirely deprived of this means of influence.

3. If you have a romantic heart, the more sublime the soul of your
beloved the more heavenly will be the pleasure you find in her arms,
and the freer from any taint of vulgarity.

Most young Frenchmen of eighteen are disciples of J.-J. Rousseau,
and tnis condition for happiness is important for them.

In the midst of activities so frustrating to the desire for happiness,
people lose their heads.

From the moment he falls in love even the wisest man no longer
sees anything *as it really is*. He underrates his own qualities, and over-
rates the least favour bestowed by his beloved. Hopes and fears at once
become *romantic* and WAYWARD. He no longer admits an element of
chance in things and loses his sense of the probable; judging by its
effect on his happiness, whatever he imagines becomes reality.[1]

An alarming indication that you are losing your head is that you
observe some hardly distinguishable object as white, and interpret
this as favourable to your love. A moment later you realize that the
object is really black, and you now regard this as a good omen for
your love.

This is the time when, overwrought by doubt, you feel great need
of a friend; but for the lover there can be no friend. That was well
known at court. Here is the origin of the only kind of indiscretion
that a well-bred woman can forgive.

1. There is a physical cause, an incipient madness, a rush of blood to the
brain, a disorder of the nervous system and the cerebral centres; compare the
fleeting courage shown by stags and the colour of a soprano's thoughts. In
1922, physiology will provide us with a description of the physical basis of
this phenomenon. I recommend it to the attention of Mr Edwards.

THE most surprising thing of all about love is the first step, the
violence of the change that takes place in a man's mind.

Society, with its brilliant parties, helps love by making this *first step*
easier.

The beginning is the change from simple admiration to tender
admiration. (What a pleasure to kiss her . . . etc.)

A whirling waltz in a drawing-room lit by a thousand candles will
set young hearts afire, banish shyness, bring a new awareness of
strength, and in the end give *the courage to love*. Because in order to
fall in love it is not enough just to see a lovely person; on the contrary,
extreme loveliness deters the sensitive. You have to see her, if not in
love with you, at least stripped of her dignity.[1]

Imagine falling in love with a queen, unless she made the first
advances![2]

The ideal breeding-ground for love is the boredom of solitude,
with the occasional long-awaited ball; wise mothers of daughters are
guided accordingly.

Genuine 'high society', such as was to be found at the French
court,[3] but which I think ceased to exist in 1780,[4] was hardly propitious to the growth of love, since *solitude* and leisure were almost impossible to obtain there, and both of these are necessary for the
crystallization process.

Court life trains you to perceive and express a great number of
different *shades of meaning*, and a subtly expressed nuance may be the
beginning of admiration and then passion.[5]

1. Hence passions may be of artificial origin; and like that of Benedick and
Beatrice (Shakespeare).

2. cf. the Loves of Struenzee in *The Courts of the North*, by Brown, 3 vols.
1819.

3. See the *Letters* of Madame du Deffand and of Mademoiselle de Lespinasse,
the *Memoirs* of Bezenval, of Lauzun, and of Madame d'Epinay, *le Dictionnaire
des Etiquettes* by Madame de Genlis, the *Memoirs* of Dangeau and of Horace
Walpole.

4. Unless it be at the court of St Petersburg.

5. See Saint-Simon and *Werther*. However sensitive and fastidious a solitary
man may be, he is distrait, and part of his imagination is engaged in anticipating
society. Force of character is one of the charms which most appeals to the truly

When love's troubles are mixed with others (those of *vanity*: when your mistress offends your proper pride, your sense of honour or of personal dignity; those of health, money, or political persecution, etc. . .) it is only superficially that love is increased by the difficulties. Since they engage the imagination elsewhere, they prevent the crystallizations of hopeful love and the growth of little doubts in requited love. The sweetness and the madness of love return when these difficulties are removed.

Note that misfortune favours the birth of love in superficial or unfeeling people. Love is also helped by misfortunes which precede it, for the imagination then recoils from the outside world which offers only sad pictures, and throws itself wholeheartedly into the task of crystallization.

CHAPTER 14

MANY people will disagree with what I have to say now, but I shall confine myself to addressing those who have been, shall I say, unhappy enough to love passionately for many years, unrequitedly and against hopeless odds.

The sight of anything extremely beautiful, in Nature or the arts, makes you think instantly of your beloved. This is because, on the principle of the bejewelled bough in the Salzburg mine, everything sublime and beautiful becomes a part of your beloved's beauty and the unexpected reminder of happiness fills your eyes with tears on the instant. In this way a love of the beautiful, and love itself, inspire each other.

One of life's misfortunes is that one cannot remember distinctly the happiness of seeing and speaking to the beloved. Apparently you become too emotionally upset to notice the cause of the circumstances. You are aware only of your own sensations. Perhaps it is because you cannot wear out these pleasures by deliberate recollection that they are so strongly renewed by anything which diverts you from

feminine; hence the success of very serious young officers. Women are very clever at distinguishing between strength of character and the violences of passion, which they themselves feel potentially in their hearts. The finest women are sometimes taken in by a little charlatanism of that kind. This can be used quite safely as soon as crystallization is seen to be well under way.

the sacred inner contemplation of your beloved and recalls her more vividly by some new relevance.[1]

A dried-up old architect used to meet Léonore evening after evening in society. In the course of conversation, and without paying much attention to what I was saying,[2] I one day waxed eloquent in his praise. She laughed at me, and I was too cowardly to tell her it was because he saw *her* every evening.

This feeling is so powerful that it extends even to an old enemy of mine who is often with Léonore. Whenever I see this other woman, however much I want to hate her, I cannot, because she recalls Léonore so strongly to my mind.

You might say that by some strange quirk of the heart, your beloved communicates more charm to her surroundings than she herself possesses. The picture of a distant town[3] where you once glimpsed her for a moment throws you into a deeper and sweeter reverie than even her actual presence could evoke. This is because of the hardships you have suffered.

The reverie of love defies all attempts to record it. I find that I can re-read a good novel every three years and enjoy it as much every time. It arouses feelings in me which are related to whatever tender interest is engaging me at the time, or, even if it makes me feel nothing, it gives variety to my thoughts. I can also listen to the same music over and over again, but memory must not play any part here – only imagination. If you enjoy an opera more at the twentieth hearing, it may be that you understand the music better, or simply that it recalls the occasion when it was first heard.

As for the new light which a novel is supposed to throw on human nature . . . well, I am very conscious of my original views and like to come upon the marginal notes which I wrote about them at a previous reading. But this sort of pleasure only holds good for the novel's function of furthering my knowledge of man, and not for its chief function of inducing reverie. This reverie cannot be imprisoned in a marginal note. To do so is to kill it for the present, since one begins to analyse pleasure philosophically. It is also to kill it for the

1. Scents.   2. See note 2 on p. 49.
3. . . . *Nessun maggior dolore*
   Che ricordarsi del tempo felice
   Nella miseria
                    Dante, *Francesca*

future, because nothing paralyses the imagination like an appeal to memory. If I come upon a marginal note describing my feelings as I read *Old Mortality* in Florence three years ago, I immediately plunge into my life story, into a comparison of my happiness then and now, in a word, into deep philosophy; and so a long farewell to the indulgence of tender feelings.

Every great poet with a lively imagination is shy; in other words he is afraid of men because they can interrupt and disturb his exquisite reveries, and he trembles for his ability to concentrate. Men with their coarse pursuits come to drag him from the gardens of Armida, and thrust him into a foetid mire; and they can scarcely make him notice them without irritating him. It is because he is emotionally nourished upon reverie, and because he hates vulgarity, that a great artist is always so close to loving.

The more a man has the gifts of a great artist, the more he should aspire to titles and decorations as a protective rampart against the world.

CHAPTER 15

THERE are moments in violent and unrequited love when you suddenly think you are not in love any more. It is like coming across a spring of fresh water in the middle of the sea. You no longer enjoy thinking of your mistress, and even though you are prostrated by her harshness you think yourself unhappier still to have lost interest in everything. A thoroughly miserable and depressed blankness follows a state of mind which, despite its agitation, nevertheless saw all Nature fraught with novelty, passion, and interest.

What has happened is this: the last time you saw your mistress you were placed in a certain situation from which, on some previous occasion, you had reaped a full harvest of sensation. For instance, after a period of coldness she shows a little more warmth, and you conceive just the same degree of hope, based on precisely the same external symptoms, as on some occasion in the past; she may be quite unaware of all this. The imagination finds its progress barred by the ominous warnings of memory, and crystallization[1] stops dead.

1. I have been advised in the first place to dispense with this word, or, if I cannot do that, to include frequent reminders that by *crystallization* I mean a

CHAPTER 16

*In a little seaside village, whose name
I do not know, not far from Perpignan,
25th February 1822*[1]

IT has been borne upon me this evening that perfect music has the same effect on the heart as the presence of the beloved. It gives, in fact, apparently more intense pleasure than anything else on earth.

If everyone reacted to music as I do, nothing would ever induce men to fall in love.

But I noticed last year in Naples that perfect music, like perfect pantomime,[2] makes me think about whatever is preoccupying me at the moment. It inspires me with excellent ideas . . . At Naples it was how best to arm the Greeks.

Now this evening I must admit that I have the misfortune OF BEING TOO GREAT AN ADMIRER OF MILADY L.

And perhaps the perfect music I have just had the pleasure of hearing after two or three music-starved months, despite nightly visits to the Opéra, has merely had an effect I already knew; that of inspiring livelier thoughts about my preoccupation of the moment.

4th March, a week later
I dare neither strike out nor approve what I have just written. Certainly I wrote it as I read it in my heart. If I seem doubtful about it now, perhaps it is because I have forgotten today what I could see so clearly last week.

The habit of listening to music and the state of reverie connected with it prepare you for falling in love. If you are sensitive and unhappy

---

certain fever of the imagination which translates a normally commonplace object into something unrecognizable, and makes it an entity apart. Among those who can only achieve happiness through vanity, the man who wishes to excite this fever must take great pains with his cravat and be constantly on the watch over a thousand details, none of which must be neglected. Women in society admit the effect and at the same time deny, or fail to see, the cause.

1. Copied from Lisio's journal.
2. *Othello* and *The Vestal*, ballets by Vigano, danced by La Pallerini and Molinari.

you will get great pleasure from a tender sad melody, not dramatic enough to goad into action, but evocative only of love's reverie. For example, the long clarinet solo at the beginning of the quartet in *Bianca e Faliero*, or la Camporesi's recitative half way through it.

The lover who has won his lady will delight in the famous duet from Rossini's *Armida e Rinaldo*, which illustrates so well the little doubts of happy love, and the moments of joy which follow reconciliations. The orchestral passage in the middle of the duet, when Rinaldo is trying to run away, is strikingly representative of the conflict of passions, and the lover will feel his heart stirred almost physically by its influence. I dare not tell you what I feel when I hear it; Northerners would think me quite mad.

CHAPTER 17: *Beauty Usurped by Love*

IN a box at the theatre, Albéric meets a woman more beautiful than his mistress. Let me express this mathematically. This woman gives promise of three units of happiness as compared with his mistress's two. And let us assume that four units might be promised by perfect beauty.

It is hardly surprising that he should prefer his mistress, whose features, *to him*, offer a hundred units. Even little facial blemishes on other women, such as a smallpox scar, touch the heart of a man in love and inspire a deep reverie; imagine the effect when they are on his mistress's face. The fact is, that pockmark means a thousand things to him, mostly delightful and all extremely interesting. He is forcibly reminded of all these things by the sight of a scar, even on another woman's face.

Thus *ugliness* even begins to be loved and given preference, because in this case it has become beauty.[1] There was once a man passionately in love with a thin pockmarked woman; she died. Three years later, in Rome, he was introduced to two women, one as fair as the dawn, the other thin and pockmarked, and in consequence shall we say unprepossessing. At the end of a week, during which he blotted out her

---

1. Beauty is only the promise of happiness. The happiness of a Greek differed from the happiness of a Frenchman in 1822. Consider the eyes of the Medici Venus, and compare them with those of the Magdalen of Pordenone (at M. de Sommariva's).

ugliness with his memories, I saw that he was in love with the ugly one. Of course, with pardonable coquetry, she whetted his appetite a little, which helped the whole process along.[1] A man may meet a woman and be shocked by her ugliness. Soon, if she is natural and unaffected, her expression makes him overlook the faults of her features. He begins to find her charming, it enters his head that she might be loved, and a week later he is living in hope. The following week he has been snubbed into despair, and the week afterwards he has gone mad.

CHAPTER 18

SOMETHING of this sort happens in the theatre to actors idolized by the public. The audience ceases to care whether they are ugly or handsome. Le Kain, in spite of his ugliness, aroused the passions of thousands; and so did Garrick. There were several reasons for this, chief among them that one no longer remarked the degree of real beauty in their features and actions, but only saw a product of the imagination, something which had become accepted as theirs in recognition and memory of all the pleasure they had already given. In the same way a comic actor can get a laugh merely by walking on to the stage.

A young woman visiting the Théâtre Français for the first time might easily find Le Kain repulsive throughout the first scene, but he would soon make her tremble or weep, and she would never be able to resist the characters of Tancred[2] or Orosman. If she were still a little aware of his ugliness, it would soon be eclipsed by the surging enthusiasm of the whole crowd and the nervous tension it produced in her young heart.[3] There was nothing left of ugliness except the

1. If one is sure of a woman's love, one looks to see whether she is beautiful or not; if one is doubtful of her heart, there is no time to inspect her face.

2. cf. Mme de Staël, in *Delphine*, I believe. This is the artifice of plain women.

3. It is to this nervous sympathy that I am tempted to attribute the prodigious and unaccountable effect of fashionable music (at Dresden, for Rossini, 1821). As soon as it is out of fashion – and it is none the worse for that – it no longer has any effect on the guileless hearts of young girls. It may have appealed to them because it stirred the emotions of young men.

Mme de Sévigné (Letter 202, 6th May 1672) wrote to her daughter: 'Lully had made a final effort with the whole of the King's orchestra; the lovely

word, and indeed not even that, for one could hear women, fans of
Le Kain, shouting 'Isn't he beautiful!'

Let us remember that *beauty* is the visible expression of character,
of the moral make-up of a person; it has nothing to do with passion.
Now *passion* is what we must have, and beauty can only suggest
probabilities about a woman and about her self-possession. But the
eyes of your pockmarked mistress are a wonderful reality which
makes nonsense of all possible probabilities.

CHAPTER 19: *Beauty's Limitations Further Discussed*

SENSITIVE, intelligent women are sometimes shy and mistrustful,
and after an evening out will agonizedly go over and over what
they may have let slip or implied. For such women a lack of good
looks in men doesn't matter for long; they soon get used to it and fall
in love in spite of it.

By the same token, if your adored mistress is severe towards you,
how beautiful she is no longer matters. You stop crystallizing, and if
a well-meaning friend tells you she is not really very pretty, you
almost agree, and he thinks he is well on the way to curing you.

My good friend Captain Trab told me tonight what he once felt
on seeing Mirabeau.

No one who laid eyes on that great man ever felt an unpleasant
sensation, in other words, ever found him ugly. Carried away by his
electrifying words one only noticed – and enjoyed noticing – what
was beautiful in his face. As practically none of his features could have
been called *beautiful* by the standards of the sculptor or painter, what
one noticed was beauty of another kind[1] – the beauty of expression.

Miserere was still more augmented, and there was a *Libera* that filled all eyes
with tears.'

One can no more doubt the truth of this effect than question Mme de
Sévigné's intelligence or subtlety. The Lully music that delighted her would
frighten people away nowadays. At that time such music encouraged crystallization, but today it makes crystallization impossible.

1. This is the advantage of being in fashion. Setting aside the facial defects
already known which no longer stimulate the imagination, one concentrates on
one of the three following kinds of beauty:

   1. Among the common people: the idea of wealth;
   2. In society: the idea of material or moral elegance;
   3. At Court: the idea 'I want to please the ladies.'

Your attention carefully shut out all that was ugly, pictorially speaking, and at the same time concentrated enthusiastically on the smallest tolerable details. His hair, for instance, his abundant, 'beautiful' hair . . . really, if he had had horns on his head you would have found them beautiful.[1]

The nightly appearances of a pretty dancer compel the attention of those blasé unimaginative souls who adorn the circle at the Opéra. With her graceful, bold, and strange movements she awakens physical love, and encourages perhaps the only kind of crystallization they can still manage. In this way an ugly woman, who could not attract a glance in the street, especially from the jaded, can succeed in being expensively kept, simply by frequent appearances on stage. Geoffroy used to say the theatre was woman's pedestal. The more celebrated

---

Almost everywhere there is a mixture of these three ideas. The happiness associated with the idea of wealth combines with the subtle pleasures which derive from the idea of elegance, and the whole is applied to love. In one way or another the imagination reacts enthusiastically to what is new. Thus a woman can become interested in a very ugly man without noticing his ugliness,* and in the long run his ugliness becomes beauty. Madame Vigano, a dancer and the fashionable woman of the day in 1788, was pregnant, and very soon the ladies began to sport little tummies à la Vigano. By the same reasoning in reverse, there is nothing so frightful as an outmoded fashion. Bad taste consists in confusing fashion, which survives by change, with lasting beauty which is the outcome of such and such a government in such and such a climate. A 'fashionable' building is out of date in ten years' time. It will be less displeasing two hundred years later when the fashion has been forgotten. Lovers are quite crazy to think about dressing well; when one meets the beloved there are many things to do besides thinking about her toilette. As Rousseau says, you look at your lover, you don't examine her. If examination does occur, it is no longer a case of passionate love but of mannered love. Beauty which dazzles is almost offensive in the one you love; you are not concerned with her beauty but wish to see her tender and languishing. In love, fine clothes only make a difference in the case of young girls, who, because strictly confined to their fathers' houses, often reach passion only through the eyes.

Remarks by L., 15th September 1820.

*Little Jermyn, in the *Memoirs* of Grammont.

1. Either for their polish, or their size, or their shape. It is in this way, or by the association of feelings (see above, concerning smallpox scars) that a woman in love becomes accustomed to the defects of her lover. The Russian princess C. has become quite used to a man who, to put it bluntly, has no nose. This miracle has been wrought by a mental picture of courage, of a loaded pistol ready for suicide in despair at this misfortune, combined with pity at the depth of the disaster and the idea that he will recover – that, in fact, he had already begun to recover.   Berlin, 1807.

and faded a dancer is, the higher she is rated; hence the backstage saying: 'You can sometimes sell what you can't give away.' These women derive part of their passion from their lovers, and are very liable to fall in love *from pique*.

Suppose you watch an actress for a couple of hours every night while she registers noble sentiments; suppose her appearance is in no way unpleasant, and you know nothing of her private life, it is then extremely hard not to associate generous or lovable feelings with her. When you are finally admitted to her presence, her features recall such pleasant associations that her real and often mean surroundings glow with a romantic interest.

'In my early youth,' said my friend the late Baron de Bottmer, 'I was a great admirer of tedious French tragedy.[1] When I was lucky enough to have supper with Mademoiselle Olivier, I kept realizing with surprise that I respected her, and spoke to her as if she were a queen. Bless me if I know now whether I *was* in love with a queen or just with a pretty girl.'

CHAPTER 20

PERHAPS men who cannot love passionately are those who feel the effect of beauty most keenly; at any rate this is the strongest impression women can make on them.

The man whose heart has leapt at the glimpse of his beloved's white satin hat in the distance is surprised at his own indifference to the greatest society beauty. When he sees how much others are moved by the latter, he may even feel a little sorry.

Really lovely women are less startling the second day. This is a pity because it does not encourage crystallization. Since their excellence is visible to all, they are bound to have more fools in their lists of lovers: princes, millionaires, and suchlike.[2]

---

1. An unseemly phrase, copied from the *Memoirs* of my good friend the late Baron de Bottmer. It is by the same artifice that Feramorz pleased Lalla-Rookh; see this delightful poem.

2. Clearly the author is neither prince nor millionaire. I did not wish the reader to think of this remark before I did!

EVEN the most ingenuous women,[1] if they have any imagination, are sensitive and *suspicious*. They may be mistrustful without knowing it; after all, life has been full of disillusionment! So everything formal or commonplace in their first encounter with a man scares their imagination, and the likelihood of crystallization is deferred. In a romantic situation, on the other hand, love conquers at first sight.

The process is simple: you are surprised, and as a result you ponder over the event that surprised you. You are already half way to the state of mind in which crystallization takes place.

As an example, take the beginning of Seraphine's love affair in the second volume of *Gil Blas*. Don Fernando is describing his flight from the *sbirri* of the Inquisition: 'It was quite dark, and the rain was pelting down; I had crossed several alley-ways and suddenly came upon the open door of a drawing-room. I went in, and at once became aware of the magnificence of the place . . . on one side I saw a door a little ajar. I half opened it and could see a vista of rooms, the last of which was lighted. I wondered what to do next . . . Overcome with curiosity I crept forward through the rooms until I reached the light, which proved to be a candle in a gilt candlestick, standing on a marble table. Then I noticed a bed, whose curtains were partly drawn aside because of the heat, and my attention was riveted by the sight of a young woman who lay asleep, in spite of the thunderclap which had just shaken the house . . . I moved a little closer . . . I felt overpowered . . . While I was standing there, dizzy with the pleasure of looking at her, she awoke . . .

'Imagine her surprise at seeing in her room, at dead of night, a man she had never set eyes on before. She gave a great start, and uttered a cry . . . I tried to reassure her, and went down on one knee. 'Please',

---

1. Miss Ashton, the Bride of Lammermoor. A man of experience will have more memories of *loves* than he can choose from. But as soon as he wishes to write, he no longer knows which to give as examples. Anecdotes about particular communities in which he has lived are unknown to the public, and it would require a vast number of pages to relate them with the necessary nuances. This is why I quote novels, as being universally known; but the ideas I put before the reader are based on no such empty fictions, which for the most part strive after effect rather than truth.

I said, 'don't be afraid . . .' She called to her maids . . . A little emboldened by the presence of her little serving-maid, she asked me with spirit who I was . . . etc., etc.'

Here is an example of 'first sight' which it is not easy to forget. In contrast, what could be more idiotic than our custom nowadays of introducing a girl to her 'intended', formally and also a trifle sentimentally! Legalized prostitution; a mere mockery of modesty.

Chamfort relates how, on the afternoon of 17th February 1790, he attended a 'family ceremony', as it is called. That is to say, respectable folks, reputedly honest, had gathered together to witness and applaud the happiness of one Mademoiselle de Marille, a lovely, witty, and virtuous young woman, who was being privileged to become the wife of M. R—, an unhealthy, repulsive, doltish, but wealthy old man. She had seen him for the third time that very day at the signing of the contract.

'If anything can be said to characterize this infamous century,' Chamfort continues, 'it is that such a matter should be cause for rejoicing; that joy should be mocked; and, in the long view, that these same people should behave with icy contempt and heartless prudery at the least imprudence of a lovesick young woman.'

Since it is essentially artificial and predetermined, anything which smacks of ceremony or demands *seemly behaviour* paralyses the imagination and allows it to dwell only on the undignified and irrelevant; hence the magical effect of a joke at such a time. The poor girl, painfully shy and modest during the introduction to her future husband, can think only of the part she is playing, and this is another certain way of stifling imagination.

It is a far greater sin against modesty to go to bed with a man only twice seen, after three words of Latin in a church, than to surrender despite oneself to a man adored for two years. But of course I am talking nonsense.

The prolific source of the vice and misery which follow marriage nowadays is Popery. It makes freedom impossible for girls before marriage and divorce impossible afterwards, when they find they have made a mistake – or rather a mistake has been made for them – in the choice of a husband. Look at Germany, that country of happy homes, where that charming princess, Madame la Duchesse de Sagan, has just got most respectably married for the fourth time. What is more, she invited to the wedding her three former husbands, with whom she remains on the best of terms. This is of course overdoing it; but a single divorce that puts paid to a husband's tyrannies can prevent thousands of unhappy homes. The joke of it all is that Rome is one of the places where divorces are most frequent.

A prerequisite of love is that a man's face, at first sight, should reveal something to be respected, and something to be pitied.

CHAPTER 22: *Concerning Infatuation*

HIGH breeding is often marked by curiosity and prejudice, and these ominous symptoms are generally apparent when the sacred flame – the origin of all the passions – has gone out. Schoolboys entering society for the first time are also a prey to infatuation. In youth and age, too many or too few sensibilities prevent one from perceiving things as they really are, and from experiencing the true sensations which they impart.

Some people, over-fervent, or fervent by starts – loving on credit, if I may put it that way – will hurl themselves upon the experience instead of waiting for it to happen. Before the nature of an object can produce its proper sensation in them, they have blindly invested it from afar with imaginary charm which they conjure up inexhaustibly within themselves. As they come closer they see the experience not as it is, but as they have made it. They take delight in their own selves in the mistaken belief that they are enjoying the experience. But sooner or later they get tired or making the running and discover that the object of their adoration is *not returning the ball*; then their infatuation is dispelled, and the slight to their self-respect makes them react unfairly against the thing they once overrated.

CHAPTER 23: *Concerning 'Thunderbolts'*

THAT ridiculous word ought to be changed – but nevertheless the thing 'love at first sight' does exist. I remember the charming and noble Wilhelmina, despair of the beaux of Berlin; she scorned love and laughed at its follies. Her youth, wit, and beauty dazzled the eye, as did her happiness in every way. Boundless wealth, in giving her full scope to develop her qualities, seemed to conspire with nature to show the world a rare example of perfect happiness in a person who perfectly deserved it. She was twenty-three, and had been at court long enough to have rejected the homage of the greatest in the realm. She was held up as a paragon of modest but unshakable virtue; even the most eligible began to despair of ever pleasing her, and aspired only to win her friendship. One night she went to a ball at Prince Ferdinand's, and danced for ten minutes with a young captain.

'From that moment,' she wrote later to a friend,[1] 'he was the master of my heart and of myself, to an extent that would have filled me with terror had the joy of seeing Herman left me time to consider anything else. I could think of nothing but whether he would notice me.

'The only consolation I can find today is the illusion that I and my reason were overwhelmed by some superior force. Words cannot begin to express the full extent of the chaos into which my whole being was thrown at the mere sight of him. I blush to think of the surging violence with which I was thrust towards him. If, when he did at last speak to me, his first words had been "Do you adore me?" I should honestly not have had the strength to avoid saying "Yes!" I had no idea that a feeling could affect one so suddenly and so unexpectedly. Things had reached such a pitch that at one time I feared I was being poisoned.

'Unfortunately, my dear, you and the world know that I loved Herman. Well, he was so dear to me after a quarter of an hour that since then he has not, in fact could not, become dearer. I saw all his faults and forgave him everything, provided he would love me.

'Shortly after I had danced with Herman, the king left, and Herman, who was on royal escort duty, was obliged to go with him. As he left, everything in Nature disappeared. I cannot describe the depths of empty boredom to which I dropped the moment I could no longer see him. They were equalled only by the keenness of the desire I felt to be alone with myself.

'At last I was able to leave. No sooner was I in my room, with the door double-locked, than I tried to fight against my passion. I thought I had conquered it. Oh, my dear, I paid dearly that evening and through the days which followed, for the satisfaction of thinking myself virtuous!'

What you have just read is the exact account of an event which was

1. Translated literally from Bottmer's *Memoirs*.

the talk of the day, for after a month or two poor Wilhelmina's unhappiness was so great as to betray her feelings. A long series of misfortunes followed, culminating in her untimely and tragic death, poisoned either by her own hand or by that of her lover. We couldn't see much in the young captain ourselves, beyond that he danced well, was gay, self-assured, radiated goodwill, and consorted with wantons. For the rest, his lineage barely passed muster; he was extremely poor and did not frequent the court.

An absence of mistrust is not enough; there must be a weariness of mistrusting, and, as it were, courage must be impatient with the hazards of life. You are unconsciously bored by living without loving, and convinced in spite of yourself by the example of others. You have overcome all life's fears, and are no longer content with the gloomy happiness which pride affords: you have conceived an ideal without knowing it. One day you come across someone not unlike this ideal; crystallization recognizes its theme by the disturbance it creates, and consecrates for ever to the master of your destiny what you have dreamt of for so long.[1]

Women who might experience this misfortune are too fine in spirit to love other than passionately. If they could descend to mere gallantry they would escape it.

Since the 'thunderbolt' is the result of a secret weariness of what the catechism calls virtue, and of the boredom which comes from the monotony of perfection, I imagine it falls most often on those whom society labels good-for-nothing. I very much doubt whether the Cato type has ever brought down a thunderbolt.

If, when you fall in love in advance like this, you have the least suspicion of what is happening, there is no thunderbolt, and this is what makes them so rare.

A woman made wary by misfortune will not experience this soul-shaking upheaval.

The likelihood of a thunderbolt is greatly increased if other people, particularly women, praise the man who is to be the object of the passion.

Some of the funniest adventures in love are the result of the pseudo-thunderbolt. An insensitive woman who is bored can believe throughout an evening that she has at last found love for a lifetime. She is filled with pride at the thought that she is now undergoing one of the

1. Several sentences are borrowed from Crébillon, Vol. III.

great experiences that her imagination had been craving. But the next day she is hard put to it to hide her confusion and avoid the poor unfortunate fellow whom she adored the night before.

Quick-witted people can recognize these thunderbolts, and so profit by them.

Physical love also has its thunderbolts. Not long ago the prettiest and most accessible woman in Berlin was seen to blush suddenly as we were out riding in her carriage. The handsome Lieutenant Findorff had just gone by. Soon she was deep in thought, and looked worried. That evening, from what she admitted at the theatre, I gathered that she was crazed, delirious, and could think of nothing but Findorff, though she had never even spoken to him. If she had dared, she told me, she would have sent for him. Her pretty face gave every sign of the most violent passion, which persisted through the next day. But after three days Findorff made a fool of himself, and she stopped thinking about him. A month later she couldn't stand the sight of him.

CHAPTER 24: *Journey Into an Unknown Country*

I RECOMMEND most of you, if you were born in the North, to omit this chapter. It is an obscure dissertation concerning certain phenomena relating to the orange-tree, a plant which only grows, or at least only attains full stature, in Italy or Spain. To make myself intelligible elsewhere, I should have had to *prune* the facts.

I would certainly have done so had it ever been my intention to write a generally pleasant book. However, since heaven has denied me literary skill, I have only tried to describe (with all the dourness of science, but also with all its precision) certain facts of which I have been an involuntary witness during my prolonged stay in the country of the orange-tree. Frederick the Great, or some other distinguished Northerner who never had the opportunity of seeing the orange-tree growing in its native soil, would doubtless have disputed, and disputed in good faith, the statements which follow. I have a prodigious respect for good faith; I can see the point of it. Since this sincere declaration may savour of pride I shall interpose an observation:

We each write at random what seems to us to be true, and yet we give the lie to each other. I think of our books as so many lottery tickets; they are really not worth much more. Posterity, in forgetting some and reprinting others, declares the winning tickets. So those of us who have expressed, as best we can, what we believe to be true, are hardly justified in laughing at our fellows, unless our satire has style, in which case there is every justification, particularly for those who write like M. Courier to Del Furia.

After this preamble I shall proceed boldly to the examination of certain facts of which I feel sure that Paris has seldom seen the like. But then in Paris – which is, of course, a city above all others – there are no flourishing orange-trees as there are at Sorrento. And it was at Sorrento, the birthplace of Tasso, on the gulf of Naples, climbing up a slope above the sea and more picturesque than Naples itself, but where they do not read *le Miroir*, that Lisio Visconti observed and wrote down the following facts:

When you are to meet your beloved in the evening, the anticipation of such immense happiness makes the intervening minutes quite unbearable.

In a consuming fever you try twenty different occupations and as quickly drop them. You are for ever looking at your watch, and you think it's wonderful if you can let ten minutes slip by without a look. At last the hour you have been waiting for strikes – and there, on the doorstep, about to knock, you would be just as glad if she were out. You know you would be sorry later, on reflection; but the fact is that *waiting* to see her gives rise to a disagreeable sensation.

This is the sort of thing that makes ordinary people say that lovers are mad.

What has happened is that the imagination has been violently wrenched from the contemplation of happiness, where every step was new delight, and grim reality now has to be faced.

If you are sensitive you know very well that, in the contest about to begin as soon as you see her, the least negligence, the least lack of attention or of courage will be punished by a snub which would poison your imagination for some time, and indeed would be humiliating outside the realm of passion, if you were tempted to withdraw there. You reproach yourself for lack of wit or boldness; but the only way to show courage would be to love her less.

In early conversations with your beloved, the mere scrap of attentiveness you divert from the crystallization reverie fails to prevent you making the sort of remark which either has no meaning or means the direct opposite of what you feel. Or even worse, you exaggerate your own feelings and they sound ridiculous, even to you. You are vaguely aware that you are not paying enough attention to what you are saying, and at once impose a mechanical control on your utterance. But you cannot stop, because silence is an agony when you can think about her even less. You therefore bring forth sententiously a medley of words which do not express your feelings, and which you would be at a loss to remember afterwards. You obstinately deny yourself her real presence, in trying to be more closely with her in mind. When I was first in love, this paradox in myself made me wonder if it were love at all.

I understand cowardice and the way that conscripts master their fear by throwing themselves into the thick of the firing. I despair at the thought of how many idiotic remarks I have made in the last two years, just for the sake of saying something.

Here indeed is a clear distinction which women can draw between passionate love and mere gallantries, between the sensitive and the prosaic.[1]

At these critical moments the one gains where the other loses; the prosaic soul acquires just that hint of warmth which it usually lacks, while the sensitive soul loses its wits from excess of feeling, and from trying to hide its folly, which is even worse. Wholly occupied in attempting restraint, it has none of the sangfroid required to gain an advantage and is therefore utterly routed where the prosaic person would have made good headway. As soon as the too poignant interests of his passion are at stake, the proud, sensitive person loses the gift of eloquence in the presence of his beloved; failure would hurt too much. The prosaic person calculates the chances of success regardless of the painful risk of defeat, takes a pride in his coarseness and laughs at sensitiveness, which for all its intelligence is always too ill at ease to say the simple things which are bound to succeed.

If you are sensitive, far from being able to snatch anything by force, you must be content to receive nothing but *charity* from your beloved. If she herself is capable of genuine feeling, you will certainly regret having tortured yourself by talking to her of love. You look shamefaced; you look frozen; you would even look untruthful were it not that your passion betrays itself in other ways. To express moment by moment what you feel so strongly is a self-imposed duty which comes from reading novels, for if you behaved naturally you

1. So Léonore used to say.

would never undertake such a painful task. Instead of describing how you felt a quarter of an hour earlier and trying to make this an interesting and coherent story, you have a naive idea of expressing your feelings as they occur. So you do yourself an injury for the sake of a smaller success. What you say lacks the ring of genuine feeling; your memory is in chains, and you say ridiculous and humiliating things under the impression that they are appropriate.

After an hour or so of this confusion you achieve the extremely painful withdrawal from the enchanted gardens of the imagination, so that you can enjoy the presence of your beloved in all simplicity; but by then it is generally time for you to leave.

All this may seem fantastic, but I can go one better. A friend of mine loved a woman beyond idolatry. On goodness knows what pretext of lack of delicacy or something – I never did find out the details – she condemned him to visit her only twice a month. These visits, so rare and so eagerly awaited, were pinnacles of utter madness, and it required all Salviati's force of character to conceal this madness from the outside world.

From the first, the idea that the visit must end mars the pleasure. You talk a lot without noticing what you say, and what you say is often the opposite of what you think. You embark on involved arguments which you have to cut short because they sound silly, as you would recognize if only you could wake up and listen to them. The strain is so great that you give no sign of warmth and love is concealed by its own abundance.

When you were far away from her your imagination was lulled by the thought of entrancing dialogues, and you were in a state of tender ecstasy. So for ten or twelve days you thought you were brave enough to talk to her, but a couple of days before the 'happy' one, fever set in, and grew worse and worse as the awful moment was upon you.

As you enter her drawing-room, you can but clutch at a vow of silence to prevent yourself saying or doing the most unbelievably idiotic things. You can also look at her, in order at least to have some recollection of her face. No sooner are you in her presence than your eyes are afflicted as by a kind of drunkenness. You are seized with a mad impulse to do odd things. It is as if you had two beings, one to act and the other to reproach you for acting. In some confused way you feel that to concentrate upon the idiocies will cool your blood for a moment, and banish the thought of the end of the visit and the pain of leaving her for a fortnight.

If some old bore happens to be present, droning out a dull anecdote, the poor lover in his inexplicable madness is all ears, as if he were particularly anxious to fritter away these rare moments. The hour of delight he had promised himself passes like a searing flash, and yet he is bitterly conscious of all the little things which tell him how much he has become estranged from his beloved. He is one among a crowd of indifferent visitors, and finds that he is the only one who does not know the little day-to-day details of her life. At last he goes, and as he bids her a frigid farewell, he is racked by the thought of the fort-night which must elapse before he may see her again. He would certainly suffer less if he were never to see her. He is even worse off than the Duke of Policastro, who used to travel a hundred leagues to Lecce every six months for a quarter of an hour with his adored but jealously-guarded mistress.

It is easy to see from this that the will has no control over love. Outraged by your mistress and yourself, how gladly you would rush headlong into indifference. The visit is only worth while for one thing: it renews the treasured crystallization.

Salviati's life was divided into fifteen-day periods, and each period was coloured by the evening when he was allowed to visit Mme —; for instance, on 21st May he was madly happy while on 2nd June he dared not return home lest he blew out his brains.

I decided that night that novelists haven't dealt very adequately with the moment of suicide. 'I'm thirsty,' Salviati told me quite simply, 'I think I'd better drink this glass of water.' I did nothing to dissuade him, but said goodbye; then he broke down and began to weep.

Since the utterances of lovers cause them so much anxiety, it would be unwise to jump to conclusions from any single detail of their con-versation. Only in chance remarks are their feelings reflected; then the heart itself cries out. Apart from this, one can only draw conclu-sions from an analysis of the whole pattern of the conversation be-tween the lovers. It should be remembered that a person under the stress of strong emotions seldom has time to notice the emotions of whoever is causing them.

I AM lost in admiration of the shrewdness and sure judgement with which women grasp certain details. A moment later I see them praising folly, moved to tears by mawkishness, and gravely weighing mere affectation as a trait of character. How they can be so silly is beyond me. There must be some law of nature I haven't heard about.

They concentrate on *one* quality, *one* detail in a man, and are so taken up with it that they have no eyes for the rest. All their nervous fluid is engaged in enjoying this one quality so that there is none to spare for perceiving others.

I have seen really first-rate men being introduced to highly intelligent women, but it is always the same: a trace of prejudice, and the consequences of a first meeting are decided in advance.

Let me be personal for a moment, and I will tell you how the charming colonel La Bédoyère was about to meet Madame Struve from Koenigsberg, a really fine woman. We were all wondering, 'Fara colpo?' (would she succumb to him?) and a bet was laid. I went to Madame de Struve and told her that the colonel wore his cravats two days running, and turned them inside out on the second day. If she looked, I said, she would notice the vertical creases on his cravat. The whole story was manifestly untrue.

Just as I finished, the good colonel himself was announced. The most insignificant little ass in Paris would have called forth more response from the lady. Mind you, Madame de Struve was in love; she was a sincere person, and there could never have been a light-hearted affair between them.

Never were two characters more fitted for each other. Madame de Struve was accused of being 'romantic', and the only thing that could touch La Bédoyère was virtuousness carried to its most romantic extreme. It was for her sake that he shot himself, while he was still quite young.

Women are very clever at feeling the imperceptible changes in the human heart, and at distinguishing nuances of affection or the least flicker of pride. They have a sense-organ for this, that men have not; watch them tending a wounded man.

But perhaps at the same time they do not see the thing called intelligence, a moral compound. I have seen some of the best women merely passing the time of day with an intelligent man (not myself, by the way) while at the same time, and indeed almost in the same breath, they were lost in the admiration of utter fools. I have stood fascinated, like an expert who sees the finest diamonds mistaken for paste, while paste ones, being larger, are preferred.

I argued from this that where women are concerned one must dare all. Where General Lasalle failed, a captain bristling with oaths and mustachios succeeded.[1] The whole of one side of men's qualities must be completely missed by women.

For my part, I fall back as usual on the laws of physic. The nervous fluid is taken up in men by the brain, and in women by the heart; that's why they are more vulnerable. Men can find consolation in having to get down to some important task in their chosen and accustomed profession; women have nothing to console them but idle distractions.

I was exchanging ideas tonight with Appiani, who believes in virtue only as a last resort. When I expounded the gist of this chapter he said: 'You remember Eponina, who kept her husband alive in an underground cavern so devotedly and heroically? The force of character she showed in keeping up his spirits would have been used to hide a lover from her husband if they had been living quietly in Rome. Strong characters need strong nourishment.'

CHAPTER 26: *Concerning Modesty*

A WOMAN in Madagascar thinks nothing of showing what is most carefully hidden here, but would die of shame rather than exhibit an arm. Clearly, modesty is largely something that is learnt. It is perhaps the only law begotten by civilization which engenders nothing but happiness.

It has been noticed that birds of prey hide themselves when they are drinking, because at the moment when they plunge their heads into the water they are defenceless. Considering what happens in Tahiti,[2] I doubt whether we need seek further for the natural basis of modesty.

1. Posen, 1807.

2. See the travels of Bougainville, Cook, etc. The females of certain species of animals seem to withhold themselves at the very moment of surrender. We must look to comparative anatomy for the most important revelations about ourselves.

Love is civilization's miracle. Among savages and barbarians only physical love of the coarsest kind exists. And modesty protects love by imagination, and so gives it the chance to survive.

Very early in life little girls learn modesty from their mothers, who teach it very zealously, as if from esprit-de-corps; this is because women are fostering in advance the happiness of the lover they will one day possess.

If a shy, sensitive woman allows herself to say or do, in the presence of a man, something for which she feels she should blush, her embarrassment is agonizing. I am sure that a woman with any spirit would rather die a thousand deaths. If the man she loves takes the slightest liberty, in all tenderness,[1] she has a moment of acute pleasure, but if he then looks disapproving or even does not appear to be carried away with joy, it must leave her heart full of bitter doubts. A well-bred woman therefore has everything to gain by behaving with strict reserve. The game is one-sided; against the trace of pleasure or the advantage of seeming just a little more charming, she has to pit the risk of searing remorse and a feeling of shame which would blight her love. This is a heavy price to pay for a carefree evening and one of heedless gaiety. For days afterwards she must hate the sight of a lover with whom she has shared 'mistakes' of this kind. It is hardly surprising to find a habit so ingrained, when the least lapse from it is punished so severely by the blackest shame.

As for the purpose of modesty, it is the mother of love; that is enough to justify it. Its mechanism is extremely simple. The heart becomes filled with shame instead of with desire. Desire is thus inhibited, and desire is what leads to deeds.

It is obvious that every sensitive, spirited woman – and these two qualities seldom exist apart, since they are cause and effect – that every such woman must assume habits of coldness which are labelled 'prudishness' by those whom they disconcert.

Now this accusation is the more specious in that it is extremely difficult to reach a happy mean. If a woman has more pride than intelligence she will soon come to believe that the need for modesty has no limits. Thus an Englishwoman takes offence if certain garments are mentioned in her presence. At a country house she will take care to avoid being seen leaving the room in company with her husband at bedtime, and worse still she thinks it an offence against modesty to

1. Shows his love in another way.

be jolly in the presence of anyone but her husband.[1] Perhaps it is because they are so particular that the English, an intelligent people, are so patently bored with domestic bliss. It is their own fault, so why so much self-righteousness?[2]

Moving swiftly from Plymouth to Cadiz and Seville, I found a different story in Spain. There the warmth of the climate and of the passions resulted in a little too much disregard for propriety. I noticed that remarkably tender caresses were allowed in public, and this did not appeal to me at all; in fact nothing could have been more painful, and I disliked it heartily.

One must resign oneself to the *incalculability* of the habits which women contract in the name of modesty. A common woman, by overdoing modesty, can believe she has become the equal of a fine lady.

The power of modesty is so great that a sensitive woman may betray her feelings to her lover rather by actions than by words.

The prettiest, richest, and easiest woman in Bologna has just confided to me that last night a little coxcomb of a Frenchman – an odd advertisement for his country who is staying here at the moment – took it into his head to hide under her bed. He was apparently determined not to waste a great number of absurd declarations with which he has been plaguing her for a month. But the fine gentleman lacked presence of mind. He waited until Madame M. had dismissed her maid and retired to bed, but he was too impatient to allow time for people to fall asleep. She sprang for the bell and had him ignominiously thrown out, with half a dozen footmen shouting at him and beating him. 'And suppose he had waited a couple of hours?' I asked her. 'Ah, then I should have been in a sorry plight,' she replied; ' "everyone will believe," he would have said, "that I came here because you asked me to." '[3]

After leaving my pretty friend, I called to see a woman more worthy of love than any other I know. Her extreme delicacy of feeling exceeds, if that be possible, her touching beauty. I found her alone,

---

1. See the admirable description of this tedious way of life at the end of *Corinne*; Mme de Staël has dealt more than kindly with it.

2. Both the Bible and the aristocracy take a cruel revenge on those who believe they owe everything to them.

3. I am advised to withhold this detail. 'You must think me an extremely light woman, to dare tell me such things.'

and told her the story of Madame M. We discussed it. 'Just a moment,' she said, 'if this woman already liked the man who chose to do such a thing, she would forgive him, and later on fall in love with him.' I must admit that I was astounded at the unexpected light this threw upon the depths of the human heart. After a pause, I said: 'But when a man is in love, is he brave enough to resort to violent extremes of that kind?'

This chapter would have been a good deal more to the point if it had been written by a woman. Only on hearsay evidence can I offer any comment on matters relating to feminine pride and vanity, the habit of modesty carried to excess, and certain *refinements of feeling* exclusive to women, which depend solely on interrelated sensations,[1] and often have no natural basis.

In a moment of philosophical frankness a woman once told me something like this: 'If I were ever to give up my liberty, the man I should ultimately choose would set a higher value on my feelings because I had always been sparing of even the lightest preference before.' A charming woman may thus treat a man now with extreme coldness, because she is saving herself for a future lover whom she may never even meet. This is the prime excess of modesty; the second comes from women's vanity; and the third from the vanity of their husbands.

It seems to me that this potential love is often present in the most virtuous women's daydreams, and rightly so. When heaven has endowed you with a soul made for love, not to love is to deprive yourself and others of great happiness. It is as if an orange-tree dared not flower for fear of committing a sin. And remember that a soul made for love can never be satisfied with any other kind of happiness. After its first taste of the much-vaunted pleasures of the world, it finds them intolerably dull, and though it often believes itself fond of Art and the sublimities of Nature, these merely lead the soul back to love, and more intensely than before, if that be possible. The soul soon realizes that it is being reminded of a happiness it has forsworn.

1. Modesty is one of the sources of good taste in dress; a woman promises either more or less by some slight arrangement of it. That is why fine clothes are out of place when a woman is no longer young.

A woman from the provinces, if she attempts to follow Paris fashions, seems pretentious and laughable. When she first arrives in Paris she should start by dressing as if she were thirty.

The one thing I have against modesty is that it encourages untruthfulness; only in this have light women the advantage of sensitive ones. A woman of easy virtue can say: 'My dear, as soon as you please me I'll tell you, and I shall be as happy as you about it, for I have a great respect for you.'

Look at the keen satisfaction of *Constance* after her lover's victory, when she exclaimed: 'Oh, how glad I am that I have never given myself to anyone in the eight years since I quarrelled with my husband.' However absurd the reasoning in this, its joy strikes me as thoroughly refreshing.

I really must tell you here about the regrets of a certain lady of Seville, jilted by her lover. I must ask you to remember that in love everything is significant. Above all, please make allowances for my style.[1]

*

With a man's eyes, I think I can see nine characteristics of *modesty*.

1. A woman is staking much against little. Hence her extreme reserve and often affectation; she does not, for instance, laugh at the things which are in fact the most amusing. Hence also her need for a high degree of intelligence to achieve just the right degree of modesty.[2] Many women fall short on this score at small informal gatherings, or rather they do not insist enough that the stories they hear are at first decently veiled, and become more explicit only as the party becomes more bacchanalian.[3]

Is it a result of modesty and its deadly tedium for some women that most of them seem to admire men's effrontery more than anything else? Or do they perhaps mistake effrontery for character?

2. Second law: My lover will respect me the more for it.

3. Force of habit enforces modesty even at the most passionate moments.

4. Modesty both pleases and flatters a lover, for it lays stress on the laws which are being transgressed for his sake.

1. Note 3, p. 84.
2. Compare the tone of society in Geneva, particularly among the *best* families; function of a Court to counteract by ridicule any prudish tendencies; Duclos telling stories to Mme de Rochefort: 'Really, you think us women much more respectable than we are!' There is nothing more boring than false modesty.
3. Really, my dear Fronsac, the story you're beginning is twenty bottles ahead of what we're talking about now.

5. It must make women's pleasures more *intoxicating*: the stronger the habit these pleasures have to overcome, the greater the turmoil they produce. If the Comte de Valmont finds himself in a pretty woman's bedroom at midnight, why, that happens to him every week, but to her perhaps only once in two years. Rarity and modesty combined in this way must offer women infinitely keener pleasures.[1]

6. The one drawback of modesty is that it invariably leads to untruthfulness.

7. Modesty carried to excess is harsh, and discourages the sensitive and shy from loving.[2] Just the ones, in fact, who were made for the purpose of giving and enjoying the delights of love.

8. If a sensitive woman has had but few lovers, modesty is an impediment to ease of behaviour, and she runs the risk of being led to some extent by friends who are not so impeded.[3] Instead of relying on blind habit, she studies each situation on its merits, and her delicate modesty lends a little constraint to all her actions. In fact, by behaving naturally she comes to appear artificial and awkward; but it is an awkwardness akin to the grace of heaven.

If the friendliness of such women sometimes seems like tenderness, it is because, though angels, they are coquettes without knowing it.

1. It is a question of the melancholic temperament as compared with the sanguine: look at a virtuous woman, even one whose virtue is of the business kind as opposed by religions (which promise to repay virtue a hundredfold in Paradise), and at a jaded old roué of forty. Although Valmont in *Les Liaisons Dangereuses* has not yet reached that stage, the Présidente de Tourvel is happier than he is, throughout the novel; and if the clever author had been cleverer still, that would have been the moral of his ingenious work.

2. The melancholic temperament, which might be called love's temperament. I have seen the best of women, those most made for love, give preference to the prosaic, sanguine temperament, just because of sheer lack of wit. The story of Alfred, Grande Chartreuse, 1810.

I know of no idea which tempts me more to keep what is known as low company.

(Here poor Visconti loses himself in the clouds.)

The emotions and passions of all women are basically the same; it is the *forms* of passion which differ. There are differences created by greater wealth, greater culture, the habit of elevated thought and above all, regrettably a more touchy pride.

A remark that annoys a princess may not have the least effect on an Alpine shepherdess, but once they have lost their tempers, the princess and the shepherdess display the same signs of passion.) (*The editor's only note.*)

3. Said by M—.

Reluctant to interrupt their reverie or to take the trouble of finding something pleasant and polite, just polite, to say to a friend, they will lean tenderly upon his arm.[1]

9. This means that when women become writers they rarely achieve sublimity. On the other hand the little notes they write are delightful, because they are never more than half way to frankness. For women frankness is like going out unclothed. A man generally writes entirely under the spell of his imagination, and without a knowledge of what he is driving at.

Summing Up

It is a common mistake to behave towards women as if they were a more generous and emotional kind of men against whom it is not necessary to compete. It is too easily forgotten that in addition to the normal inclinations of humanity, there are two particular and peculiar laws which dominate these creatures of emotion; I mean: feminine pride, and modesty, with the often unaccountable habits born of modesty.

CHAPTER 27: *Concerning Glances*

GLANCES are the big guns of the virtuous coquette; everything can be conveyed in a look, and yet that look can always be denied, because it cannot be quoted word for word.

It reminds me of Comte Giraud, the Mirabeau of Rome. Because of the nice little Government of this part of the world he has developed an original method of communication, using amputated words which mean everything and yet nothing. He conveys his meaning amply, but you cannot compromise him, however much you quote him verbatim. Cardinal Lante accused him of having stolen this accomplishment from women; and I would say that even the most honest woman knows the trick. It is a cruel but just reprisal for the tyranny of man.

1. Vol. *Guarna.*

CHAPTER 28: *Concerning Feminine Pride*

ALL their lives women hear men talking about things that are supposed to be important. Success in finance and in war, deaths in duels, shocking or well-deserved vengeance, and so forth.

Women of spirit realize that they cannot hope to be proud in these important fields since such matters are out of their reach. They know that in their bosoms beat hearts whose emotions are stronger and loftier than their surroundings, yet they see that even the meanest of men are accorded more respect than themselves. They perceive that they themselves can only be proud in little things, or at least in things whose importance is only measurable in terms of feelings, and which an outsider cannot judge.

Tortured by the painful contrast between the paltriness of their lot and the loftiness of their spirit, women determine that their pride shall be respected for the very vehemence of its manifestation or for the implacable tenacity with which they uphold their interdictions. Women of this sort, before intimacy, think themselves fortresses besieged by their lovers. They are irritated by the latters' advances, though these are only marks of love, and the lovers *are*, after all, in love. Instead of enjoying the expressions of their lovers' affection, women grow conceited, and when they do fall in love, however sensitive they may have been before, they have nothing left but vanity.

A generous woman would lay down her life a thousand times for her lover, yet would break with him for ever on a trivial point of pride as to whether a door should be left open or shut. The thing is a point of honour. Even Napoleon fell because he would not abandon a village.

I have known a quarrel of this kind last more than a year. A very wonderful woman was throwing away all her happiness rather than let her lover entertain the smallest doubt about her overweening pride. They became reconciled quite by chance and because the woman was unable to master a moment of weakness. At a time when she thought he was a hundred miles away, she met her lover in a place where he was certainly not expecting to see *her*. She could not conceal her first impulse of joy, and the man was even more moved than she was. They practically fell into each other's arms, and I have never seen such floods of tears; it was the unexpected vision of happiness, and tears are the ultimate smile.

The Duke of Argyll showed great presence of mind in avoiding a conflict with feminine pride during his interview at Richmond with Queen Caroline.[1] The nobler the character of a woman, the more dreadful are these storms:

> . . . As the blackest sky
> Foretells the heaviest tempest.
>> Don Juan

Perhaps the greater a woman's day-to-day delight in the distinguished qualities of her lover, the more she seeks revenge, in those moments of cruelty when sympathy seems inverted, for seeing him usually as better than other people. She is afraid she may be grouped with the others.

It is a long time since I read that boring book *Clarissa Harlowe*; I seem to remember, though, that it was feminine pride which made her pine to death rather than accept the hand of Lovelace.

Lovelace was gravely at fault; but since she was a little in love with him she should have found it in her heart to forgive a crime committed in love's name.

Monime, on the other hand, strikes me as a moving symbol of feminine delicacy. To hear an actress worthy of the part recite these lines must bring a flush of pleasure to all but a few:

> *Et ce fatal amour, dont j'avais triomphé,*
>
> . . . .
>
> *Vos détours l'ont surpris et m'en ont convaincue,*
> *Je vous l'ai confessé, je le dois soutenir;*
> *En vain vous en pourriez perdre le souvenir;*
> *Et cet aveu honteux, où vous m'avez forcée,*
> *Demeurera toujours présent à ma pensée.*
> *Toujours je vous croirais incertain de ma foi;*
> *Et le tombeau, seigneur, est moins triste pour moi*
> *Que le lit d'un époux qui m'a fait cet outrage;*
> *Et, qui, me préparant un éternel ennui,*
> *M'a fait rougir d'un feu qui n'était pas pour lui.*
>> Racine.

1. *The Heart of Midlothian*, Vol. III.

I can see future generations finding here a justification of monarchy[1] in that it produced characters of this sort and their images in great art.

However, even under the medieval republics, I can find an excellent example of this delicacy which seems to refute my theory of the influence of governments upon passions; but in all fairness I must include it. I refer to these moving lines by Dante:

> *Deh! quando tu sarai tornato al mondo,*
>
> . . . .
>
> *Ricorditi di me, che son la Pia:*
> *Siena mi fe': disfecemi Maremma;*
> *Salsi colui, che innanellata pria,*
> *Disposando, m'avea con la sua gemma.*
>
> *Purgatorio,* c.v[2]

The woman who speaks here with so much restraint had suffered in secret the fate of Desdemona, and could by a word have revealed her husband's crime to her friends still on earth.

Nello della Pietra married Madonna Pia, sole heiress of the Tolomei family, the richest and noblest in Siena. Her beauty was the envy of all Tuscany, and her husband became excessively jealous of her. His jealousy, envenomed by false report and ever-recurrent suspicion, led him to plan a dreadful crime. It is difficult to determine today whether his wife was entirely innocent, but certainly Dante would have us think so.

Her husband took her to the Maremma, the marshy salt flats near Siena, which were then, as now, notorious for the effects of their *aria cattiva* (noxious vapours). He would never explain to his unfortunate wife why she was exiled in so dangerous a place; his pride never condescended to complaint or accusation. He lived alone with her in a solitary tower, whose ruins I have visited by the sea-shore; and there he maintained a disdainful silence, refusing to answer the questions of his young wife or to listen to her prayers. He waited coldly for the pestilential atmosphere to take effect, and it was not long before the miasma of the marshes began to play havoc with those features reputed to be the loveliest of the century. Before many months had passed she was dead. Some chroniclers of those far-off

---

1. Monarchy without Charter or Parliament.
2. Alas, when you return to the world of the living, remember me. I am Pia; Siena gave me life, and I found death in the Maremma. He who gave me his ring in marriage knows my story.

days suggest that Nello used a dagger to hasten her departure, but even her contemporaries were uncertain about the manner of her death beyond that she died horribly, out in the marshlands. Nello della Pietra lived on and passed the rest of his days in unbroken silence.

Nothing could be nobler and more discreet than the way the young Pia speaks to Dante. She asks to be remembered to the friends on earth she had left behind so early; but in speaking of herself and her husband she makes not the least complaint of unspeakable and irreparable cruelty, only suggesting that her husband knows the truth about her death.

I think it is only in Mediterranean countries that pride is so steadfast in its vengefulness.

In Piedmont I once became the involuntary witness of a similar case, but at the time I didn't know the full story. I had been despatched with a force of twenty-five dragoons into the woods along the banks of the Sesia to prevent smuggling. We reached this wild and lonely area towards evening, and I saw through the trees the ruins of an old castle. I moved nearer and found to my surprise that it was occupied. A local nobleman lived there, a sinister-faced fellow, forty years old and six feet tall. With a very bad grace he gave me two rooms, where I used to play music with my quartermaster. After some days we discovered that our host had a woman there whom we laughingly nicknamed Camille; but we had no suspicion of the dreadful truth. Six weeks later, she died. I had a morbid urge to see her in her coffin, and bribed a monk who was watching over her to admit me to the chapel in the middle of the night, on the pretext of sprinkling holy water. She had one of those superb faces that are lovely even in death, with a fine aquiline nose whose noble and tender contour I shall never forget. I left that gloomy spot soon afterwards. Five years later, when a detachment of my regiment was escorting the Emperor to his coronation as King of Italy, I had the whole story related to me. I learned that Count . . . , the jealous husband, had one morning found, hooked upon his wife's bed, an English watch, the property of a young man who lived in their little town. That very day, he took her to the ruined castle in the Sesia woods. Like Nello della Pietra, he never spoke a word. When she begged him for some favour, he would coldly and silently show her the English watch, which he always carried with him. In this way he lived alone with her for almost three years. In the end she died of despair, while still in the full bloom of life. Her husband tried to knife the owner of the watch, failed, took ship from Genoa and has never been heard of since. His estate has been divided up.

If, in the presence of women with feminine pride, you accept insults gracefully—an easy matter for anyone accustomed to army life—the proud beauties are irked. They take you for a weakling, and soon begin to insult you themselves. These haughty characters practically throw themselves into the arms of men who are thoroughly intolerant of others. This is, I think, the only line to take, so that you often have to pick a quarrel with your neighbour to avoid one with your mistress.

Miss Cornel, the celebrated London actress, once saw her rich and extremely useful colonel entering her rooms unexpectedly. She was entertaining some little nonentity of a lover who was just pleasant company. In a trembling voice she introduced him to the colonel. 'Mr So-and-so has called to look at that pony I want to sell.' 'I have called for no such thing!' exclaimed the little man. She had been bored with him, but from the moment he made this spirited rejoinder she began to love him all over again.[1] Such women share in their lovers' pride, instead of pitting their own spirited dispositions against it.

The personality of the Duke of Lauzun – the 1660 duke, that is[2] – would have appealed to women of this kind, provided they could initially excuse his lack of social graces. The finer points of greatness elude them, and they mistake for coldness the cool gaze which sees everything and is not troubled by petty details. I have even heard the

1. I always return from visiting Miss Cornel full of admiration and deep thoughts about passion in the raw. She has an imperious way of giving orders to her servants which is not despotism but the result of a clear and swift appraisal of what has to be done. Angry with me at the beginning of my visit, she has forgotten all about it by the end. She explains the whole pattern of her passion for Mortimer: 'I like meeting him in company much better than alone.' A woman of the greatest genius could do no more, because she dares to be perfectly *natural* and is not hampered by theories: 'I am happier as an actress than I would be married to a peer.' A great woman, whose friendship I must cherish for my own edification.

2. Hauteur and courage in little things, but a passionate regard for those little things; the vehemence of the bilious temperament; his conduct with Madame de Monaco (Saint-Simon, v. 383); his escapade beneath Madame de Montespan's bed, when the king was with her. Without a regard for little things, this kind of character cannot be understood by women.

court ladies at Saint-Cloud maintaining that Napoleon was pretty dry and prosaic.[1] A great man is like an eagle; the higher he goes the less you can see of him, and loneliness is the price he pays for being great.

Feminine pride gives rise to what women call *breaches of delicacy*. I think these are not unlike what kings call lèse-majesté, a crime all the more perilous since it may be committed quite unsuspectingly. The most devoted lover may be accused of offending delicacy if he lacks sparkle, or, sadder still, if he dares to indulge in love's greatest delight: that happy state of being perfectly natural with the beloved and of not listening to what is said to him.

These are the kinds of thing that no gentleman would ever dream of suspecting. You must have suffered it to believe it, because you are so used to dealing fairly and squarely with your friends of the male sex.

You must always remember that you are dealing with creatures who think themselves, however mistakenly, your inferiors in strength of character, or rather, may think that you so regard them.

Surely a woman's pride should really be founded on the strength of the feelings she can inspire. The wife of François I had a lady-in-waiting, who was for ever being teased about the fickleness of her lover. It was said that he hardly cared for her at all. A little later he fell ill, and when he reappeared at court was quite dumb. A couple of years after this, someone expressed surprise that she should still be in love with him, whereupon she turned to her lover and said: 'Speak!' And he spoke.

1. WHEN MINNA TOIL HEARD A TALE OF WOE OR OF ROMANCE, IT WAS THEN HER BLOOD RUSHED TO HER CHEEKS, AND SHEWED PLAINLY HOW WARM IT BEAT NOTWITHSTANDING THE GENERALLY SERIOUS, COMPOSED AND RETIRING DISPOSITION WHICH HER COUNTENANCE AND DEMEANOUR SEEMED TO EXHIBIT. (*The Pirate*, 1. 33.)

Ordinary people suppose that people like Minna Toil are dull, because they do not consider ordinary events worthy of their emotion.

> I tell thee, proud templar, that not
> in thy fiercest battles hadst thou
> displayed more of thy vaunted
> courage, than has been shewn by
> woman when called upon to suffer
> by affection or duty.
>
> *Ivanhoe*. Vol. 3.

I RECALL coming across the following sentence in a history-book: 'All the men lost their heads; at moments like this women are incontestably their superiors.'

Their courage has a greater *reserve* than that of men. In a dangerous situation their self-respect is piqued, and they are so pleased to pit themselves against the men who have so often wounded them with patronizing protectiveness and strength, that the momentum of this pleasure carries them over whatever fear weakens men at such a time. A man too, if he were thus helped in a similar situation, would overcome all odds, for the fear is never part of the danger; it is within ourselves.

Not that I am trying to minimize women's courage. I have occasionally seen women braver than the bravest men. Only they must have a man to be in love with, for then they feel only through him, and thus react to direct and personal danger of the most deadly kind as if it were a flower to be plucked in his presence.[1]

I have also seen women who are not in love display the coolest and most surprising fearlessness and nerve. I did think at the time, though, that they were only brave because they did not know how beastly a wound could be.

As for moral courage, which so much exceeds the other kind, the resolve of a woman who will not surrender to her lover passes all admiration. Any other mark of courage is a mere trifle by comparison with so painful and unnatural a struggle. Perhaps they find strength in the habit of sacrifice which modesty compels.

It is one of the misfortunes of women that the proof of this courage must always remain secret, and is almost incommunicable.

1. Mary Stuart, speaking of Leicester, after her fatal interview with Elizabeth.

A still greater misfortune is that this courage must always be used against their own happiness; the Princesse de Clèves should have said nothing to her husband and yielded to M. de Nemours.

Perhaps women are chiefly sustained by their pride in a well-conducted defence, and imagine that their lovers in trying to win them are seeking to satisfy a point of vanity. A mean and petty idea, this, that a passionate man should plunge from lightheartedness into a series of situations where he makes a fool of himself, and yet have time to think about points of vanity! It's like the monks who think they are cheating the devil, and reward themselves by taking a pride in their hair shirts and mortifications of the flesh.

I think that if Madame de Clèves had reached the ripe old age when one looks back on life and sees how empty were the pleasures of pride, she would have repented. She would have preferred to have lived like Madame de la Fayette.[1]

I have just re-read a hundred pages of this essay. I seem to have given a remarkably poor idea of true love, the love which pervades the whole consciousness and fills it with pictures, some wildly happy, some hopeless, but all sublime; the love which blinds one to everything else in the world. I am at a loss to express what I can see so clearly; I have never been so painfully aware of my lack of talent. In what intelligible terms can I convey the simplicity of gesture and bearing, the deep earnestness, the look which expresses the precise nuance of feeling so exactly and so candidly, and above all, I repeat, the ineffable unconcern about everything but the woman one loves. A *yes* or a *no* spoken by a man in love has a *warmth* and *grace* not to be found elsewhere, nor even in the same man at other times. This morning (3rd August) at about nine o'clock I rode past the Marquis of Zampieri's English garden. It is set on the last slopes of the heavily-wooded hills which back Bologna, overlooking a magnificent view of Lombardy, rich and green, the most beautiful countryside in the world. As I passed Zampieri's garden, on my way to the falls of the Reno at Casa-Lecchio, in a laurel glade which overlooked the road I saw Count Delfante, in profound reverie, and although we had spent the previous evening together until two o'clock in the morning,

1. It is common knowledge that this celebrated woman, with M. de la Rochefoucauld, lived the story of *La Princesse de Clèves* in real life, and that the two authors passed the last twenty years of their lives together in perfect friendship. This is exactly love *à l'Italienne*.

he barely answered my salutation. I went on to the falls and crossed the Reno. At least three hours later, on my way back, I saw him again, still in Zampieri's laurel glade, exactly as he had been before, leaning against a tall pine which soared above the laurels. I am afraid the reader may find this anecdote too simple, proving nothing; but Delfante came up to me, tears in his eyes, and begged me not to tell the story of his immobility. I was touched and suggested we went back together the way I had just come, to spend the rest of the day in the country. Two hours later he had told me everything; his was a fine soul, and the pages you have just read are cold by comparison with what he told me!

In the second place, he thought his love was *not returned*; here I disagree with him. The lovely marble face of Countess Ghigi, with whom he had passed the evening, is quite inscrutable, yet occasionally a sudden little blush which she cannot control betrays the feelings of a soul torn between strong emotion and the most exalted feminine pride. The blush tinges her alabaster neck, and what can be glimpsed of those lovely shoulders worthy of Canova. She is expert at averting her dark eyes from the penetrating scrutiny of those whom her feminine delicacy fears to encounter; but last night I saw her blush all over when Delfante said something to which she took exception. Her proud soul found him the less worthy of her because of it.

But when all is said and done, even if I am mistaken about Delfante's good fortune, I think he is happier than I who am indifferent, although in appearance and reality I am in a very fortunate condition.

Bologna, 3rd August 1818

CHAPTER 30: *A Strange and Sorry Spectacle*

WOMEN, with their feminine pride, revenge themselves upon men of intelligence for having to suffer fools, and upon generous hearts for the dullness of wealthy, insolent bores. You must admit that this is a pretty sorry state of affairs.

Some women have been made unhappy by petty considerations of pride and social convention, and have been placed in an intolerable position by the pride of their relatives. In generous compensation for all their misfortunes, Destiny decreed that they should know the bliss of loving and being loved with passion. But there comes a day when they borrow from their enemies that same insensate pride which had made them unhappy, only to destroy the unique happiness left to them, and to bring misfortune upon themselves and those who love them. Some women friend, who may have had a dozen affairs, perhaps more than one at a time, will persuade them gravely that if they fall in love they will be dishonoured in the eyes of the public. And yet this noble public, whose aspirations never rise above the most base, generously credits all women with a new lover each year because, says the public, 'that is the way things usually happen!' Hence the saddening and curious spectacle of a tender and supremely fastidious woman, and angel of purity, fleeing on the advice of some unscrupulous trollop from the one matchless happiness within her reach, to appear, radiantly dressed in white, before some great lout of a judge, notoriously blind these hundred years, who shouts at the top of his voice: 'She is wearing black!'

CHAPTER 31: *Extract from Salviati's Diary*

> Ingenium nobis ipsa puella facit.
> Propertius, 2. 1.

Bologna, 29th April, 1818

Love has reduced me to a condition of misery and despair, and I curse my very existence. I can take no interest in anything. The weather is gloomy and wet, and a late cold spell has plunged all Nature back into sadness just when, after a long winter, everything was thrusting towards spring.

Schiassetti, a colonel on half-pay, a cool, rational friend, came and spent two hours with me. 'You ought to give up loving her.' 'But how can I? Can you give me back my enthusiasm for soldiering?' 'It's a great pity you ever met her.' I almost agreed with him, I felt so dejected and low-spirited; so much has melancholy taken posses-sion of me. Together we mused upon what her friend had to gain by speaking ill of me to her, and we could find no answer but the Neapolitan proverb: 'When youth and love leave a woman she takes offence at anything.' One thing is certain, anyway: this woman friend is *rabidly* against me; the word was used by a friend of hers. I could get my revenge in the most beastly way, but I haven't the slightest defence against her hatred. Schiassetti left, and I went out into the rain wondering what would become of me. My lodgings, this sitting-room where I lived during the first days of our acquaintance when I used to see her every day, have now become unbearable. Every print on the wall, every stick of furniture, reproaches me for the happiness I dreamed of in this room, and which is now lost for ever.

I strode through the streets under a cold rain; chance, if you can call it chance, led me past her windows. Night was falling, and as I walked by, my tear-filled eyes fixed upon the window of her room. Suddenly the curtain was lifted for a moment, as if for a glimpse of the square outside, and then it quickly fell back into place. I felt a spasm at my heart. I could no longer hold myself up, and took refuge in a neighbouring portico. My feelings were running riot; it might of course have been a chance movement of the curtain; but suppose it had been her hand that lifted it!

There are only two miseries in life; the misery of unrequited passion, and that of the DEAD BLANK.

In love, I have the feeling that boundless happiness beyond my wildest dreams is just round the corner, waiting only for a word or a smile.

Without a passion like Schiassetti's, through dull days, I can find no happiness anywhere, and begin to doubt whether it is in store for me at all; I am growing sour. It would be better not to have strong passions and to be only a little curious or vain.

It is now two o'clock in the morning, and I saw her curtain move at six last night. I have paid ten calls and been to the theatre, but I was silent and moody everywhere, and spent the evening brooding over this question: 'After being so angry, and with so little cause – for after all, did I mean to give offence, and what is there in this world that intention cannot palliate? – after her anger, did she feel a moment of love?'

Poor Salviati, who wrote these words in his copy of Petrarch, died a short time afterwards. He was a close friend of mine and of Schiassetti's; we were privy to all his thoughts, and I have drawn upon him for the more depressing side of this essay. He was imprudence personified, and the woman for whom he did so many foolish things is the most interesting person I have ever encountered. Schiassetti used to tell me that Salviati's unhappy passion had really been a blessing in disguise. For in the first place Salviati had just suffered a severe financial setback, which obliged him to live very modestly, though his youth had been dazzling. In any other circumstances he would have been beside himself with anger at his misfortune, but as it was he didn't think of it once in a fortnight.

Secondly, and this too was important in another way for the kind of mind he had, his passion was the first real course in logic he had ever taken. That may seem odd in a man who had been at court, but the answer lies in the man's supreme courage. For instance he never flinched that day in 18. . when all his hopes were destroyed. He was surprised, as he had been before in Russia, that he did not feel anything out of the ordinary, and it is a fact that he has never been sufficiently afraid of anything to think about it two days running. Instead of being thus heedless he now sought every moment to have courage; hitherto he had never been aware of danger.

When, as a result of his imprudence and of his confidence that people would not misconstrue things,[1] Salviati was condemned to see only twice a month the woman he loved, we occasionally saw him mad with joy, apostrophizing her the whole night through, because she had received him with that noble candour for which he adored her. He maintained that he and Mme — were two souls quite outside the common run, who should understand each other at a glance. He could not grasp that she might pay the least attention to parochial, small-minded misconstructions which could make him appear criminal. His reward for this generous confidence in a woman surrounded by his enemies was to have the door shut in his face.

'Where Mme — is concerned,' I used to tell Salviati, 'you forget your principles, and also that one should never believe in great-heartedness except as a last resort.' 'Do you think,' he replied, 'there could be anyone else in the world whose heart is so much akin to hers as mine is? Admittedly I am paying for my particular kind of passion, which makes me see an angry Léonore in the skyline of rocks at Poligny, and the price is that all my undertakings in real life are dogged by misfortune – a misfortune caused by a lack of assiduity and a rashness resulting from the strength of momentary impressions.' This is verging on sheer madness.

For Salviati life was divided into fortnightly periods which took on the hue of the last audience he had been granted by his beloved. But I noticed more than once that the happiness he was given by a wel-

1. *Sotto l'usbergo del sentirsi pura.* Dante.

come apparently less frigid than usual was considerably less intense than his misery after a cold reception.[1] Also Mme. . . . was not always frank with him, and these are the only two criticisms I have ever dared to offer him. Apart from his most intimate distress, which he always took care to withhold even from his dearest and least envious friends, he regarded a cold reception from Léonore as a victory of prosaic and calculating natures over frank and generous ones. At such times he lost his faith in virtue and even in glory. He would only talk to his friends about sorrowful ideas whose truth his passion led him to assert, but which did have some philosophical interest. I observed his peculiar personality with curiosity; passionate love is normally found only in rather simple, rather German people.[2] Salviati, on the other hand, had one of the soundest and keenest minds I have ever known.

I believe he was only satisfied, after these cold visits, when he had found some justification for Léonore's severities. If he felt that she had been in any way at fault in ill-treating him, this made him unhappy. I should never have believed that love could be so free from vanity.

He never tired of sounding love's praises. 'If some supernatural power said to me: "Break this watch-glass and Léonore will revert to what she was three years ago – a mere acquaintance," I do not believe that I should ever have the courage to break it.' He seemed so frantic as he argued this that I never dared to draw his attention to the foregoing criticisms.

He added: 'Just as Luther's Reformation shook society to its foundations at the end of the Middle Ages and thus renewed and rebuilt the world on a rational basis, so a generous person is renewed and restored by love.

'Only then does he put away all the childish things of life. Without love's upheaval he would always suffer in some way from heaviness or theatricality. It is only since I fell in love that I have learned how to be noble, because our "military college" education is so hopeless.

'Although I behaved myself, I was a mere child at Napoleon's court and in Moscow. I did my duty, but I was unaware of the heroic simplicity which comes from entire and whole-hearted self-sacrifice. For instance, it is only within the last year that I have come to

1. This is something I have often thought to see in love, this tendency to draw more misery from unhappy things than joy from happy ones.

2. Don Carlos, Saint-Preux, and Hippolyte and Bajazet in Racine.

understand the simplicity of Livy's Romans. Previously I found them dull by comparison with our own dashing colonels. What they did for their Rome, I find in my heart for Léonore. If I were fortunate enough to be allowed to do something for her, my first impulse would be to keep it a secret. The conduct of a Regulus or a Decius was something settled in advance, and so could give them no surprise. I was petty-minded, before I fell in love, precisely because I was occasionally tempted to consider myself great. I was conscious of the effort I was making and congratulated myself upon it.

'And in the sphere of the affections, love is all-important. After the chance experiences of early youth, one's heart closes up against sympathy. Death or distance estranges you from childhood companions, and you are thrown upon the company of associates quite indifferent to you, and who, foot-rule in hand, are for ever calculating in terms of self-interest or vanity. Gradually all that is sensitive and generous withers from lack of nurture, and before you reach thirty you have become impervious to sweet or tender sensations. In the midst of this arid desert, love makes a spring burst forth, brimming with feelings sweeter and more abundant than those of early youth. Then there was hope, vague, crazy, and easily distracted;[1] there was no devotion to anything, no deep constant desires; youth, always fickle, craved for novelty, adoring one day what it neglected the next. But nothing is more contemplative, more mysterious, more eternally single in its aim than love's crystallization. Once it was only pleasant things which had the right to please, and the pleasure they gave was no more than momentary; but now all that has any bearing on the woman one loves, even the most irrelevant object, moves one deeply. Once when I arrived in a large town a hundred miles from Léonore's home, I discovered that I was trembling with shyness, quaking at every street corner, lest I should meet Alviza, her intimate friend whom I did not even know by sight. Everything seemed to have taken on a mysterious and sacred glow; my heart pounded as I spoke to an elderly scholar. If anyone mentioned the city gate near the house where Léonore's friend lives, I blushed scarlet.

'The very harshness of the beloved is infinite grace, which is not to be found in any other woman even at her best. In just the same way the great shadows in Correggio's pictures are unlike those of other painters. Usually shadows are necessary to give value to highlights

1. Mordaunt Merton, 1st vol. of *The Pirate*.

and to throw faces into relief, and are otherwise not particularly pleasing; but Correggio's shadows have magical grace in their own right and enwrap one in sweet reverie.[1]

'Yes, half of life, its most wonderful half, is hidden from the man who has never loved passionately.'

It needed all Salviati's argumentative powers to stand up to the wisdom of Schiassetti, who repeatedly told him: 'If you want to be happy, be content with a life free from care and a little good fortune every day. Don't be drawn into the gamble of a grand passion.' And Salviati would reply: 'Lend me a little of your inquisitiveness, then.'

I think there were days when Salviati would have liked to follow the advice of our wise old colonel. He resisted a little and thought he was succeeding, but it was a quite unequal struggle in spite of all his tremendous force of character.

When, far down the street, he saw a white satin hat that looked like the one Mme. . . . wore, his heart missed a beat, and he had to lean against the wall for support. Even in his saddest moments, the happiness of meeting her always left him intoxicated for some hours despite the effects of all his misfortunes and of every attempt to reason with him.[2] In conclusion it must be said that when he died,[3] after two years

1. Since I have mentioned Correggio I might say that you will find the lineaments of happy love in the head of an angel sketched on the tribune of the Florence gallery; and the downcast eyes of love in the Madonna Crowned by Jesus, at Parma.

2.   *Come what sorrow can,*
                 It cannot countervail the exchange of joy
                 That one short moment gives me in her sight.
                                      Romeo and Juliet.

3. A few days before he died he wrote a little ode which has the merit of expressing exactly the feelings about which he had been telling us.

L'ULTIMO DI
anacreontica
A ELVIRA

Vedi tu dove il rio	Odi d'un uom che muore
Lambendo un mirto va,	Odi l'estremo suon
Là del riposo mio	Questo appassito fiore
La pietra surgerà.	Ti lascio, Elvira, in don.
Il passero amoroso,	Quanto prezioso ei sia
E il nobile usignuol,	Saper tu il devi appien;
Entro quel mirto ombroso	Il di che fosti mia,
Raccoglieranno il vol.	Te l'involai dal sen.

of this boundless and generous passion, his character had assumed
nobility in several ways, and in this respect at least he had judged
himself correctly. If he had lived, and if circumstances had helped him
a little, he would have got himself talked of. Perhaps, though, by its
very simplicity, his merit would have passed unnoticed on this earth.

> *O lasso!*
> *Quanti dolci pensier, quanto disio,*
> *Menò costui al doloroso passo!*
> *Biondo era e bello, e di gentile aspetto;*
> *Ma l'un de' cigli un colpo avea diviso.*[1]
>
> Dante

CHAPTER 32: *Concerning Intimacy*

THE greatest happiness love can offer is the first pressure of hands
between you and your beloved.

The particular pleasures of gallantry are, on the contrary, much
more real and much more frequently the subject of witticisms.

In passionate love, intimacy is not so much the perfect happiness,
but the last step on the way to it.

But how can we describe happiness, if it leaves no memories?

Mortimer was returning from a long journey, in a state of agitation.
He adored Jenny, but she had left his letters unanswered. No sooner
was he back in London than he rode to her country house to find her.
When he arrived, she was out walking in the grounds. He ran to her,

> Vieni, diletta Elvira,
>   A quella tomba vien,
>   E sulla muta lira,
>   Appoggia il bianco sen.
> Su quella bruna pietra,
>   Le tortore verran,
>   E intorno alla mia cetra,
>   Il nido intrecieran.
> E ogni anno, il di che offendere
>   M'osasti tu infedel,
>   Faro la su discendere
>   La folgore del ciel.
>
> Simbolo allor d'affeto,
>   Or pegno di dolor,
>   Torno a posarti in petto,
>   Quest' appassito fior.
> E avrai nel cuor scolpito,
>   Se crudo il cor non è,
>   Come ti fu rapito,
>   Come fu reso a te.
>
>   S. Radael

1. Poor wretch! How sweet his thoughts and how constant his desire until
his last hour. He was handsome, with a fine and gentle face, except for a noble
scar which broke the line of an eyebrow.

his heart pounding. They met, and she gave him her hand and greeted him in some confusion; he saw that she loved him. As they strolled along the paths, Jenny's dress caught upon a prickly acacia bush. Later Mortimer gained his heart's desire, but Jenny was unfaithful to him. I maintain that she never loved him, but he says that the way she received him on his return from the Continent is proof enough of her love. Yet he cannot recall a single detail of their meeting. He is, however, visibly shaken by the sight of an acacia, and this is really the only distinct memory he has preserved of the happiest moment in his life.[1]

A former knight, who is both sensitive and frank, told me about some of his love-affairs this evening, as we crouched in the bottom of our boat in rough weather on Lake Garda.[2] I shall not betray his confidences to the public, but I think I may be allowed to draw from them the conclusion that the moment of intimacy is like those lovely days in May, a critical time for the finest flowers; a time which can be deadly and wither the brightest hopes in a moment.

. . . .[3]

Unaffectedness is extremely important. It is the only coquetry permissible in something as serious as a love like that of *Werther*, when all sense of direction is lost. At the same time, by a happy coincidence, it is the best tactic. All unsuspectingly, a man who is really in love says the most delightful things, and speaks in a language unknown to him.

Woe betide the man who shows even a trace of affectation! Even when he is in love, even if he be supremely intelligent, he loses three quarters of his advantage. If you give way to affectation for a moment, you will be met with curtness a minute later.

The whole art of loving seems to me, in a nutshell, to consist in saying precisely what the degree of intoxication requires at any given moment. In other words, you must listen to your heart. You must not

1. *Vie de Haydn*, p. 228.   2. 20th September 1811.

3. 'The first time they quarrelled Madame Ivernetta dismissed poor Bariac who, being really in love, was in despair; but his friend Guillaume Balaon, whose life I am writing, helped him greatly, and so well that the haughty Ivernetta was pacified. Peace was restored and reconciliation was accompanied by such exquisite circumstances that Bariac swore to Balaon that the first favours granted him by his mistress were less sweet than those of this voluptuous forgiveness. This speech so turned Balaon's head that he would fain experience the pleasure his friend had described. . . etc. . . , etc.' *Vie de Quelques Troubadours*, Nivernois, Vol. 1, p. 32.

think this is easy; if you are truly in love and your lover says things which make you happy, you will lose the power of speech.

You are thus deprived of the actions to which your words would have led,[1] and it is better to keep silent than to say tender things at the wrong moment. What was apt ten seconds earlier does not remain so, and will be inept ten seconds later. Whenever I failed to obey this rule,[2] and said something that had come into my head three minutes before and which sounded pretty, Léonore was sure to punish me. Afterwards, as I left, I would say to myself: 'She's right; that sort of thing must be thoroughly shocking for a well-bred woman, it's an indecency of feeling.' Like speechifiers of indifferent taste, they would rather permit a certain weakness or coldness. Their only concern is lest their lover be false, so that the least insincerity in the smallest detail, however innocent, immediately annuls their happiness and puts them on the defensive.

Honest women are averse to what is vehement or unexpected, even though these are symptoms of passion; besides, vehemence alarms modesty and they recoil from it.

After your blood has been cooled by some intimation of jealousy or displeasure, you can generally engage in the sort of conversation likely to promote that intoxication in which love thrives, and if after the first two or three stages of the discussion you seize the opportunity to say exactly what comes into your mind, you will give your beloved keen satisfaction. Most people make the mistake of trying to bring in some remark which they consider pretty, witty, or moving, instead of relaxing from conventional weightiness into a natural intimacy which allows them to say unaffectedly whatever they feel at the time. If you have the courage to do this your reward will be in the nature of a reconciliation.

It is this swift and unsolicited reward for the pleasure you give your beloved that raises love so high above the other passions.

If you are perfectly natural there will be a complete fusion of the

1. This kind of shyness is conclusive proof of passionate love in a man of intelligence.

2. A reminder that if the author occasionally uses the first person singular, it is in an attempt to bring some variety into the form of this essay. He has no intention whatsoever of inflicting his own private feelings upon his readers. He seeks to impart with as little monotony as possible what he has observed in other people.

happiness of both of you.[1] Because of fellow-feeling and various other laws which govern our natures, this is, quite simply, the greatest happiness that can exist.

It is easy to define what we mean by *being natural*, that necessary condition for happiness in love.

We call an action *natural* when it does not differ from the habitual mode of action. It goes without saying that not only must you never tell a lie to your beloved, but you must refrain from the least embellishment of truth which could impair its purity. For the act of embellishment occupies your attention, which can no longer respond unaffectedly, like the keys of a piano, to the feelings which show in her eyes. She soon realizes it, through goodness knows what sense of coldness, and then she in turn falls back upon coquetry. Isn't this the hidden reason why we find it impossible to love women whose intelligence is markedly inferior? In their presence we can pretend with impunity, and since pretence is easier, from force of habit, we yield to the temptation not to be natural. Love thenceforth is no longer love, but shrinks to one of the common affairs of life; the only difference is that instead of money we gain pleasure or self-satisfaction, or a mixture of both. But it is difficult not to feel a shade of contempt for a woman whom you can hoodwink with impunity, and in consequence she is thrown over as soon as a better one appears on the scene. Habit or vows may hold things together; but I am talking about the inclination of the heart, which turns directly towards the greatest pleasure.

To come back to this word *natural*: to act naturally and to act habitually are two different things. If you take them as one and the same, then clearly the more sensitive you are the less easy it is to be natural, because your behaviour is less dominated by habit and your whole personality is more to the fore in your response to each situation. Every next page in the life story of a passionless man is the same as the previous one; take him today, take him yesterday, he is still the same block of wood.

A sensitive man, once his heart is stirred, loses all memory of habit as a guide to action; how can he keep on the track when he has lost the scent?

He is aware of the enormous weight attaching to every word he speaks to his beloved, and feels that a word may decide his fate. He

1. Which will depend upon the same actions.

can hardly avoid trying to express himself well, nor help feeling that he *is* speaking well. From that moment candour is lost. There must, therefore, be no pretensions to candour, which is a characteristic of those who are not turned in upon themselves. We are what we succeed in being, but we are conscious of what we are.

I think we have now reached the last essence of natural behaviour to which, in love, the most fastidious soul can lay claim.

As a last anchor against the storm, the passionate lover can only cling to a pledge to read his heart accurately and never to alter one jot of the truth. If the conversation is lively and frequently interrupted, he can expect several good spells of being natural; if not, he will succeed in being natural only when his love is at a little less than fever pitch.

In your beloved's presence even *physical movements* almost cease to be natural, although the habit of them is so deeply ingrained in the muscles. Whenever I gave my arm to Léonore, I always felt I was about to fall, and I had to think how to walk. The best that can be hoped for is never to show affectation intentionally; convince yourself that failure to be natural is the greatest possible danger to your interests and may easily lead to disaster. Your beloved's heart gets out of harmony with yours and you lose that sharp spontaneous interplay where frankness responds to frankness. This is to lose every means of moving her – I almost said of seducing her. Not that I want to deny that a woman worthy of love can link her destiny with the pretty motto of the ivy: 'With nought to cleave to, I die.' The thing is a law of nature, but for a woman to make her lover happy is always a decisive step to take for her own happiness. It seems to me that a sensible woman is not going to concede everything to her lover until she can no longer defend herself. Now the slightest suspicion about her lover's sincerity immediately renews her strength, at least enough to stave off surrender for yet another day.[1]

Need I add that to make all the foregoing utterly absurd, one has only to apply it to mannered love?

1. *Hoec autem ac acerbam rei memoriam amara dulcedine scribere visum est . . . ut cogitem nihil esse debere quod amplius mihi placeat in hac vita.*
15th January 1819   Petrarch. Marsand's edition.

Always a little doubt to set at rest, that's what keeps one craving, that's what keeps happy love alive. Because the misgivings are always there, the pleasures never grow tedious. This kind of happiness is characterized by extreme earnestness.

CHAPTER 34: *Concerning Confidences*

There is no indiscretion more quickly punished than to tell an intimate friend about your passionate love affairs. Your friend knows that if what you say is true your pleasures are a thousand times greater than his, and that you will be contemptuous of his.

Between women these things are worse still, since their object in life is to inspire passion, and since the confidante, too, has usually displayed her own charms before the same lover's eyes.

On the other hand, when you are in the grip of this fever, there can be no more compelling moral need than for a friend to whom you can confide the fearsome doubts which constantly assail you, for in this terrible passion *whatever you imagine invariably comes to exist.*

Salviati wrote in 1817: 'A major flaw in my character (and in this I differ from Napoleon) is that when we are discussing the pros and cons of a passion and something has been morally proved, I can never use this as a firm basis. In spite of myself, and indeed to my great discomfiture, I keep calling it in question.' It is easy enough to be courageous where ambition is concerned. A crystallization not subject to the desire of the thing sought serves to strengthen courage, but in love it is enslaved by the very thing against which that courage is needed.

A woman risks finding a friend false or bored.

Imagine a princess of thirty-five,[1] bored and plagued by an urge for action, intrigue, and so forth . . ., dissatisfied with her lukewarm lover, yet unable to inspire another. Imagine her at a loss to employ her restlessness, and with no distractions other than occasional bursts of spitefulness. She can easily find herself a pleasant pastime and an aim in life by making a genuine passion miserable, if the passion is

1. Venice, 1819.

misguided enough to be felt for someone other than herself, while her own lover drowses beside her.

This is the only case in which *hatred* can produce happiness; it provides an occupation and something to work at.

At first, when word of it spreads in society, the pleasure of doing something and the *challenge* to succeed make the occupation attractive. Jealousy of the lady is disguised as hatred of the lover; how else is it possible bitterly to hate a man you have never met? All awareness of envy is carefully excluded, for this implies an admission of merit, and there are always flatterers at hand to curry favour with jokes made at the expense of a good friend.

When the treacherous confidante behaves so abominably, she may well believe her only motive is to avoid losing a friendship she values. A woman who is bored will tell herself that even friendship can languish in a heart devoured by love and its mortal anxieties, and that such a friendship can only compete with love by confiding. Now, what could be more hateful to an envious woman than confidences of that kind?

The only confidences likely to be well received between women are those frankly delivered in the following vein: 'My dear, there is an absurd and implacable war waged against us by the prejudices customary among our tyrants. You help me today, and I'll do the same for you tomorrow.'[1]

There is also the earlier exception when true friendship has survived from childhood days and has not since been spoilt by jealousy. . .

Confidences about passionate love are only well received between schoolboys in love with love, and between girls devoured by curiosity, by tenderness seeking an outlet – perhaps already drawn by the instinct[2] which tells them this is the important business of their lives, and the sooner begun the better.

1. *Memoirs* of Madame d'Epinay, Geliotte.
Prague, Klagenfurt, the whole of Moravia, etc., etc. The women there are extremely witty and the men keen hunters. Friendship between women is very common. Winter is the best season there; hunting parties lasting a fortnight or three weeks follow each other at the mansions of the great lords of the province. One of the wittiest of them once told me that since Charles V had been the lawful ruler of all Italy, there was absolutely no point in the Italians trying to rebel. The wife of this noble gentleman used to read the *Letters* of Mlle de Lespinasse.
Znaym, 1816.

2. A moot point. It seems to me that besides education, which begins at the age of eight or nine months, there is a certain degree of instinct.

Everyone must have seen little girls of three very creditably discharging the obligations of gallantry.

Mannered love is stimulated by confidences, while passionate love is cooled by them.

Confidences present difficulties as well as dangers. In passionate love, what you cannot express (because language is too coarse to achieve the required nuance) exists none the less, only it is so fine-drawn that error in observing it is more probable.

And an observer under the stress of emotion observes badly; he fails to give chance her due.

Perhaps the wisest thing is to confide in oneself. Using borrowed names, but including all the relevant details, write down tonight what took place between you and your mistress, and the problems with which you are faced. In a week's time, if you are suffering from passionate love, you will be someone else entirely, and then, on reading your case-history, you will be able to give yourself good advice.

Among men, whenever more than two are gathered together and envy might be aroused, politeness demands that the talk should be confined to physical love. The after-dinner conversation at men's parties is a case in point. Baffo's sonnets[1] are the ones recited, and they give great pleasure, because each person takes his neighbour's praise and enthusiasm literally, though very often the neighbour only wishes to appear gay or polite. French madrigals or the tender charm of Petrarch would be out of place.

CHAPTER 35: *Concerning Jealousy*

WHEN you are in love, no matter what you see or remember, whether you are packed in a gallery listening to political speeches or riding at full gallop under enemy fire to relieve a garrison, you are always adding new perfections to your idea of your mistress, or finding new and apparently ideal ways of making her love you more.

1. There are descriptions of physical love in the Venetian dialect which leave Horace, Propertius, La Fontaine, and all the poets miles behind. M. Burati, of Venice, is now the leading satirical poet in the whole of our sad Europe. He is particularly adept at describing the grotesque physical appearance of his heroes. He is also often in prison; see his *Elefanteide*, *Uomo*, and *Strejeide*.

Each step your imagination takes brings a new delight. Little wonder that this state of mind is enticing.

Though the same habit persists, the moment you become jealous it produces an opposite effect. Far from giving you sublime joy, every perfection added into the crown of your beloved, who perhaps loves another, is a dagger-thrust in the heart. 'This delight,' cries a voice, 'is for your rival!'[1]

And when other things strike you, instead of suggesting new ways of increasing her love, they indicate more of your rival's advantages.

You see a pretty woman galloping in the park,[2] and the rival is immediately famed for his fine horses which can take him ten miles in fifty minutes.

This mood can easily turn to fury. You forget that in love *possession is nothing, only enjoyment matters*. You overrate your rival's success, and the insolence resulting from it. Then you reach the final torment: utter despair poisoned still further by a shred of hope.

Probably the only solution is to observe your rival's good fortune very closely. Often you will find him placidly dozing in the very drawing-room which contains the woman the thought of whom stops your heart beating when you see, far down a street, a hat which might be hers.

If you want him to wake up, just betray your jealousy. You will then perhaps have the privilege of informing him how valuable is this woman who prefers him to you, and you will be the author of his love for her.

Where your rival is concerned there is no middle course; you must either joke with him in the most detached way, or frighten him off.

Since jealousy is the greatest of all ills, you can find a pleasant diversion in risking your life. Because then your thoughts will not be entirely embittered (by the process described above) and you will be able to play with the idea of killing your rival.

On the principle that one should never reinforce the strength of the enemy, you must conceal your love from your rival. Secretly, calmly, and simply, and on some pretext totally unrelated to love, you should say: 'Sir, I do not know why the public chooses to credit me with little Miss So-and-so, and is even so good as to believe me in

1. This is part of love's folly, for the perfection one can see is not a perfection to him.

2. Montagnola, 13th April 1819.

love with her. If you wanted her, why, you could have her with all my heart, were it not that unfortunately I should be made to look a fool. In six months' time you can have all you want of her, but today the honour, which, heaven knows why, attaches to these things, compels me to warn you, to my great regret, that if by any chance you lack the fairness to await your turn, one of us will have to die.'

Your rival is most probably not a passionate man, and may be a very prudent one. Once he is convinced of your resolve he will hasten to surrender the woman upon the first convenient pretext. This is why your declaration must be made lightheartedly and the whole affair shrouded in the utmost secrecy.

What makes jealousy so painful is that you cannot employ vanity to help you bear it, but the method I have explained gives vanity a clear field. You can admire your own bravery, even if you are inclined to despise yourself as an inspirer of love.

If you would rather not be melodramatic, the best thing to do is travel forty leagues and find a dancer to entertain, whose charms should appear to have halted you as you were passing.

Unless your rival has extraordinary insight, he will think you have got over your passion.

Very often the best plan is to wait impassively until your rival, by his own blunders, wears out his welcome with your beloved. Because, barring the case of a grand passion built up stage by stage in early youth, a woman will not love a fool for long.[1] In the case of jealousy after intimacy, you need both apparent indifference and genuine inconstancy, for many women, merely angry with a man they still love, will attach themselves to a man of whom their lover shows jealousy, until suddenly the game becomes a reality.[2]

I have covered this in some detail because in these moments of jealousy one usually loses one's head, and advice written beforehand is a help. Besides, since the important thing is to pretend to keep calm, it is right and proper to learn the right atmosphere from philosophical writings.

Since you are only vulnerable through the proffer or denial of things whose whole value depends on your passion, by managing to sham indifference you disarm your adversaries at one blow.

If there is no action that can be taken, and you can amuse yourself

1. *La Princesse de Tarente*, a short story by Scarron.
2. As in *Le Curieux Impertinent*, a short story by Cervantes.

by seeking solace, you will get some pleasure from reading *Othello*.
Even the most damning appearances will be laid open to doubt, and
you will pause delightedly over the words:

> *Trifles light as air*
> *Seem to the jealous, confirmations strong*
> *As proofs from holy writ.*
>   *Othello*. Act III

I have found consolation in a beautiful view of the sea.

*The morning which had arisen calm and bright, gave a pleasant effect to the
waste mountain view which was seen from the castle on looking to the landward;
and the glorious Ocean crisped with a thousand rippling waves of silver,
extended on the other side in awful yet complacent majesty to the verge of the
horizon. With such scenes of calm sublimity, the human heart sympathizes
even in* HIS *most disturbed moods, and deeds of honour and virtue are inspired
by their majestic influence.*

(*The Bride of Lammermoor*. Vol. I.)

In one of Salviati's manuscripts I found this: '20th July, 1818. – A
little unreasonably, I think, I often apply to life as a whole a feeling
comparable to that of an ambitious man or of a good patriot during a
battle, when he is detailed to look after reserve stores or ordered to
some post away from danger and action. I should have been sorry to
reach forty and to be past the age of loving, without having experienced passion deeply. I should have felt the bitter and degrading pain
of realizing too late that I had been tricked into letting life go by
without living.

'I spent three hours yesterday with the woman I love, in the
presence of a rival whom she wishes me to believe is receiving her
favours. There were admittedly bitter moments when I saw her lovely
eyes gazing on him, and as I left I felt keen pangs of misery and despair. But what a host of new things! What vivid thoughts, and swift
arguments! In spite of my rival's apparent good fortune, I felt with
a rush of pride and delight that my love was far greater than his. I
told myself that those cheeks would grow pale with fear at even the
least of the sacrifices my love would joyfully make. For instance, I
would gladly plunge my hand into a hat to take out one of two
tickets: '*Be loved by her*' or '*Die at once*', and this feeling is so well
established that I was able to make myself agreeable and take part in
the conversation.

'If anyone had told me all this two years ago I should have laughed derisively.'

In the account of the voyage made by Captains Lewis and Clarke in 1806 to the sources of the Missouri, I read this on page 215: 'Though poor, the *Ricaras* are kind and generous, and we stayed some time in three of their villages. Their women are the most beautiful of any tribe we have encountered. Moreover they are disinclined to keep their lovers in suspense. We found a further proof of the saying that to see the world is to discover that nothing is immutable. Among the *Ricaras*, it is a great breach of good behaviour for a woman to grant her favours without the consent of her husband or brother. But, on the other hand, the husbands and brothers are delighted to be able to offer this little courtesy to their friends.

'There was a negro in our party who made a great impression on a people who had never seen a man of that colour before. He was soon the favourite of the fair sex, and we observed that, far from displaying jealousy, the husbands were delighted when he visited their homes. The whole situation was enlivened by the fact that in such ramshackle huts as theirs everything was open to view.'[1]

1. An academy should be established in Philadelphia for the exclusive purpose of gathering material for the study of man in a state of nature. This should be done now, before these strange tribes become extinct.

I know there are such academies, but apparently their regulations are no better than those of our Academies in Europe. (Note and discussion on the Zodiac of Denderah at the Académie des Sciences in Paris, in 1821.) I see that the Academy of Massachusetts, if I am not mistaken, has very prudently requested a member of the clergy, Mr Jarvis, to report on the religion of the savages. This priest cagerly and wholeheartedly refutes a godless Frenchman named Volney. According to the priest, the savages entertain the most exact and noble ideas about the Divinity, and so forth. If he lived in England a report of this kind would earn the worthy academician a PREFERMENT of several hundred pounds and the protection of every noble lord in the county. But in America .... ! The absurdity of this academy reminds me that free Americans set much value on seeing fine coats-of-arms painted on their carriage doors. They have, however, to contend with a lack of education among their coach-painters which leads to frequent errors in heraldry.

CHAPTER 36: *More Concerning Jealousy*

As for the woman you suspect of inconstancy, she is drifting apart from you because you have not stimulated crystallization and perhaps keep your place in her heart merely from habit. She is leaving you because she is too sure of you. You have removed fear, and the little doubts of happy love no longer occur; make her anxious, and above all beware of pointless protestations.

In the length of time you have known her you will no doubt have learned which woman in the town or in society she fears and envies most. Pay your attentions to this woman, but do not broadcast the fact. Try, on the contrary, to conceal it, and try as hard as you can; put your trust in the eyes of hatred to see all and realize all. The profound distaste you will feel for all women[1] for several months should make this easy for you. Remember that, placed as you are, you will spoil everything by showing your passion; so see your beloved but seldom and drink champagne in convivial company.

In judging the quality of your mistress's love, remember that:

1. The more physical pleasure plays a basic part in love and in what initially brought about intimacy, the more liable that love is to inconstancy and, still more, to unfaithfulness. This applies particularly to cases where the crystallization has been abetted by the fires of youth at sixteen.

2. The loves of two people in love with each other are seldom the same.[2] Passionate love has its phases, when first one partner and then the other will be more in love. Often passionate love is answered with mere gallantry or vanity-love, and generally it is the woman who loves to distraction. Whatever kind of love one lover feels, no sooner is jealousy aroused than the other lover is required to fulfil all the conditions of passionate love. Vanity produces all the needs of a tender heart in the jealous lover.

As a matter of fact nothing wearies mannered love so much as passionate love in the partner.

1. One compares the leafless bough to the bough studded with diamonds, and the contrast enhances one's memories.
2. For example, Alfieri's love for that great English lady (Milady Ligonier) who also used to make love with her footman and sign herself, amusingly enough, *Penelope*. Vita, 2.

Quite often an intelligent man courting a woman merely turns her thoughts to love and melts her heart. She welcomes a man who is clever and pleases her, and he begins to entertain hopes.

One fine day this woman meets a man who makes her feel exactly what the clever man had described.

I have no idea what effect a man's jealousy has on the woman he loves. If she is bored with her lover, his jealousy must inspire thorough disgust, which may turn to hatred if the lover is less pleasant than the man of whom he is jealous, for according to Mme de Coulanges we only want jealousy in people of whom we ourselves could be jealous.

If she loves a man who is jealous without the right to be so, a woman's feminine pride – so difficult to recognize and respect – may be shocked. Spirited women, on the other hand, may be pleased by jealousy, as a new way of showing them their power.

Jealousy may please as a new way of proving love; or it may offend the modesty of an over-refined woman.

It may please by showing the mettle of the lover. Note that it is hot blood which is attractive, and not bravery like Turenne's, which may well go with a cold heart.

It follows from the principle of crystallization that a woman should never say *yes* to a lover she has deceived if she wishes to make anything of him.

So great is the pleasure of continuing to enjoy our perfected image of the beloved that, until this fatal *yes*,

> *L'on va chercher bien loin, plutôt que de mourir,*
> *Quelque prétexte ami pour vivre et pour souffrir.*
> —André Chénier.

The story of Mademoiselle de Sommery is well known in France; how, surprised *in flagrante* by her lover, she boldly denied the whole thing. When he pressed her, she cried: 'Oh! I see it all now. You don't love me any more; you'd rather believe your eyes than what I tell you!'

When your adored mistress has been unfaithful, reconciliation means destroying crystallization with dagger-blows, a crystallization perpetually renewing itself. Love has to die, and your heart will be rent by each dreadful stage of the agony. It is one of the unhappiest relationships in love and in life, and it is better to have the strength of mind to be reconciled only as a friend.

WE now come to consider jealousy in women. They are mistrustful, for they are risking infinitely more than we are, and they have sacrificed more for love's sake; they have less to occupy their minds, and above all far less chance of inspecting their lover's actions. A woman feels degraded by jealousy, for it looks as though she is running after a man; she thinks her lover must be laughing at her and mocking her tenderest emotions. She must feel an urge to be cruel, and yet cannot legally kill her rival.

For women, then, jealousy must hurt even more abominably than for men, if that be possible; its impotent rage and self-contempt[1] are as much as the human heart can bear without breaking.

To my knowledge there is no cure for such agonizing suffering except the death either of the one who inspires it or of the one who feels it. For an example of French jealousy see the story of Madame de la Pommeraie in *Jacques-le-Fataliste*.

La Rochefoucauld says: 'We are ashamed to admit that we are jealous, yet we pride ourselves on having been jealous, and on being capable of jealousy.'[2] Women, poor things, dare not even admit that they have suffered this cruel torment, for it makes them look ridiculous. So painful a wound can never quite heal.

If cold reason could withstand the fire of imagination with the shadow of a chance of success, I should say to those unfortunate women made miserable by jealousy: 'There is a great deal of difference between men's unfaithfulness and yours. In your case it is partly a *direct action*, and partly *symptomatic*. Because of our military college kind of education, it signifies nothing in a man. Because of modesty, however, it is the most decisive of all the symptoms of a woman's degree of devotedness. Evil habits make it more or less a necessity for men. Throughout our early youth we follow the example of the so-called *bloods* of the school and take a pride in the number of our successes in this field, regarding them as proof of our merit. Your own education works in the opposite direction.'

1. This contempt is one of the chief causes of suicide. You kill yourself to avenge your honour.

2. Thought no. 495. The reader will have observed several other thoughts from famous writers, without the necessity of my acknowledgement.

I am trying to write history, and thoughts like these are facts.

To illustrate what I mean by the *symptomatic* value of an action, let us suppose that in an angry moment I upset a table on my neighbour's foot. It will hurt him like the devil, but matters are easily mended. However, if I so much as raise my hand to strike him . . .

A man's unfaithfulness is so different from a woman's that a woman in love can forgive an infidelity, while this is quite impossible for a man.

Here is a conclusive way of establishing whether a woman's love springs from passion or *pique*: unfaithfulness practically kills the former and makes the latter twice as strong.

Spirited women cloak their jealousy under haughty pride, and will spend long evenings in icy silence beside the man they adore, whom they tremble to lose, and in whose eyes they think themselves un-attractive. It must be torture for them, and is certainly one of the most fruitful sources of unhappiness in love. To cure a woman like this, who so much needs our respect, we must take some extraordinary and momentous step without appearing to recognize what is happening, such as starting on a long journey with her at twenty-four hours' notice.

CHAPTER 38: *Concerning Wounded Self-Esteem*

PIQUE[1] is a stirring of one's vanity. You do not wish your opponent to get the better of you, yet *you select him as the referee and judge of your merit*. You want to make an impression on him and so go far beyond the bounds of reasonable behaviour. Sometimes, to justify your own extravagance, you go so far as to accuse your opponent of making game of you.

Since *pique* is a *disease of honour* it is most prevalent under monarch-ies and must be less so in countries where actions are habitually judged by their degree of usefulness, such as the United States of America.

Every man, not least a Frenchman, hates to be taken for a dupe. Nevertheless, under the old French monarchy,[2] with its light-hearted looseness of character, *pique* could only play havoc with mannered

1. '*Puntiglio*' in Italian.
2. Three out of every four French noblemen around 1778 would have been liable to criminal conviction in a country where the laws were enforced without respect for persons.

love and gallantry. It was only in monarchies like Portugal or Piedmont, climatically conducive to sombreness of character, that pique
produced really foul enormities.

The French provincial conceives a ludicrous picture of what society
demands in a gentleman and then spends all his life watching to see
whether anyone breaks the rules. In consequence he never behaves
naturally and is incessantly afflicted with pique, which makes even
his love ridiculous. Next to envy, this is the most unbearable thing
about life in small towns, and it is wise to remember this when
you admire some of their picturesque surroundings. The most generous and noble emotions are paralyzed by contact with the meanest
products of civilization. The people in these small towns succeed in
making themselves completely intolerable by their eternal talk of the
corruption in great cities.[1]

Pique has no place in passionate love; either it is feminine pride:
'If I let my lover treat me badly he will despise me and no longer
love me,' or else it is sheer furious jealousy.

Jealousy desires the death of the rival it fears. A man suffering from
pique, on the other hand, wants his enemy to live and above all to
witness his triumph. He would be loth to see his rival give up the
contest, because the rival might be insolent enough to think: '. . . if
I had cared to pursue the struggle I should have got the better of
him . . .'

Pique is not in the least concerned with the achievement of its
apparent goal, but purely with the necessity for victory. This is well
illustrated by the love-affairs of the Opéra girls; their so-called
passion, that was enough to drive them to suicide, dies the moment
their rivals are sent packing.

Unlike passionate love, love through pique is gone in a moment.
It only lasts until the opponent admits defeat in some irrevocable
way. I am a little hesitant to put forward this statement, since I have
only one example to support it, and I am not too sure even of that.
Still here are the facts, which the reader may judge for himself.

Dona Diana was a young woman of twenty-three, the daughter of
one of the richest and proudest citizens of Seville. She was undoubtedly a beauty, though of an obvious type, and she was credited

1. When it comes to love, they are all enviously spying on each other's
activities, so that there is less love in the provinces, and more libertinage. Italy
is more fortunate.

with much intelligence and still more pride. She was passionately in love, to all appearances, with a young officer of whom her family disapproved. This young man went to America with Morillo, and they were for ever writing letters to each other. One day at her mother's house, in front of a crowd of people, some idiot announced that the charming young man was dead. All eyes immediately turned upon her, but Dona Diana merely said: 'What a pity – so young.' That very day we had read an old play by Massinger which ended tragically, but in which the heroine was seemingly unmoved by the news of her lover's death. I saw the mother shudder despite her pride and hatred; the father left the room to conceal his joy. In the midst of all this, while the dumbfounded spectators scowled at the idiot of a tale-teller, Dona Diana, alone unmoved, continued conversing as if nothing had happened. Her mother was frightened and had her daughter watched by a lady's-maid, but there was no apparent change in her behaviour.

Two years later, a very handsome young man paid court to Dona Diana. Again, and for the same reason, that the suitor was not well-born, her parents opposed the match. Dona Diana insisted that she would marry him. She and her father each piqued the other's self-esteem, and the young man was forbidden the house. Dona Diana was no longer taken into the country and hardly ever to church; every possible means of meeting her lover was carefully denied her. The lover used to disguise himself and see her in secret, but only at long intervals. Dona Diana became increasingly obstinate and refused the most brilliant matches, even a title and a high position at the court of Ferdinand VII. The misfortunes of the two lovers and their heroic constancy became the talk of the whole town. At last, when Dona Diana was about to come of age, she told her father that she proposed to exercise her right to marry whom she pleased. The family had no alternative but to start arranging the marriage; but during a formal meeting between the two families, before the arrangements were half completed, the young man broke their engagement, after being constant for six years.[1]

A quarter of an hour later Dona Diana showed no sign that any-

1. Every year there are several cases where women are thrown over just as basely, and I excuse mistrust among decent women.—Mirabeau, *Lettres à Sophie*. Public opinion has no power in countries under despotic rule; all that matters is to be friends with the Pasha.

thing had happened; her heart was mended. Was she in love from pique? Or was she great enough to disdain making a public exhibition of her sorrow?

Passionate love can often reach what I might call happiness only by wounding the beloved's self-esteem. A man thus appears to obtain his heart's desire, so that to complain would seem ridiculous and unwarranted. He cannot admit that he is unhappy, and yet he is continally prodding and testing his unhappiness; the proofs of it are, so to speak, entwined in situations which are both flattering and likely to foster illusions of delight. It is an unhappiness which rears its ugly head at the tenderest moments as if to taunt the lover by showing him, on one hand, the full happiness of being loved by the charming unresponsive creature in his arms and, on the other, that this happiness can never be his. It is perhaps, after jealousy, the most cruel unhappiness of all.

There is a great city[1] where people still remember a gentle, sensitive man, overcome with fury of this kind, who killed his mistress because she only loved him through pique against her sister. He persuaded her to go rowing with him one evening, alone, in a pretty little boat which he had designed himself. When they reached the open sea he touched a spring; the boat sprang a great leak and sank without trace.

I have seen a man of sixty set out to keep the most capricious, irresponsible, lovable, and marvellous actress on the London stage – Miss Cornel. 'And you think she will be faithful to you?' he was asked. 'Not in the least,' he replied, 'but she will love me – and perhaps wildly at that.'

She did love him, for a whole year, and frequently to distraction; for as long as three months in succession she gave him no cause for complaint. He had established a state of pique, by thoroughly shocking means, between his mistress and her daughter.

It is in mannered love that pique triumphs, because here it shapes the whole course of events. It is the best test for distinguishing between mannered and passionate love. Every recruit must have heard the old soldier's proverb that if you are billeted in a house where two sisters live, and you want one of them to love you, you must make eyes at the other one. Generally speaking, among young and willing Spanish women, all you need do is advertise modestly how little interested you are in the particular lady of the house. I had this useful

1. Leghorn, 1819.

precept from my good friend General Lasalle. It is, on the other hand, the most dangerous way of tackling passionate love.

A state of pique can produce the happiest marriages, second only to love matches. Husbands frequently make sure of the love of their wives for many long years by taking a little mistress two months after their marriage.[1] The wives are thus induced to form the habit of confining their thoughts to one man until family ties ensue to make this habit unbreakable.

In the time of Louis XV there was only one reason why a great lady at his court (Madame de Choiseul) was known to adore her husband:[2] he seemed to be extremely fond of her sister, the Duchesse de Gramont.

The most neglected mistress, once she shows a preference for another man, robs us of all peace and stirs our hearts into something very like passion.

The courage of an Italian is a fit of anger, that of a German a moment of intoxication, and of a Spaniard an expression of pride. If there were a nation where courage took the form of a pique of self-esteem between the soldiers of each company and between the regiments of each division, there would be no halting the retreat of such an army if it were once put to rout, without strong support positions in the rear. To foresee the danger and attempt to avert it would be futile with such vainglorious runaways.

'Any account of a journey among the savages of North America,' writes one of the most delightful of French philosophers,[3] 'will be sure to relate the normal fate of prisoners of war. Not only are they burnt alive and eaten, but they are first tied to a stake near flaming logs and tortured for several hours by the most ferocious and refined methods which hatred can imagine. It is worth reading the travellers' accounts of the cannibal joy of those who take part in these frightful scenes, particularly of the fury of the women and children, and their atrocious pleasure as they vie with one another in cruelty. It is worth seeing what they say about the heroic steadfastness and cool self-control shown by the prisoners who, besides betraying no pain, even taunt and defy their executioners with the haughtiest pride, the bitterest irony and the most insulting sarcasm. They sing their own

1. See the confessions of a peculiar man (Mrs Opie's story).
2. *Letters* of Madame Du Deffand; *Memoirs* of Lauzun.
3. Volney, *Tableau des États-Unis d'Amérique*, pp. 491–6.

feats, and name the spectators' relatives and friends whom they have killed, detailing the tortures they inflicted. They accuse all around them of cowardice, weakness, and incompetence as torturers. In the end, torn to ribbons, eaten alive before their own eyes by their frenzied enemies, their voices ring out with a last insult as they die.[1] All this will hardly be believed by civilized nations; our bravest Grenadier captains will regard it as a myth, and posterity will one day question it.'

This physiological phenomenon results from a particular state of mind in which the prisoner undertakes a battle of self-esteem between himself and his torturers; a challenge of vanity against vanity as to who can hold out longest.

Our excellent army surgeons have often noticed that casualties who, had their minds and senses been normal, would have screamed during certain operations, in fact displayed calm strength of character when they were suitably prepared. They had to have their honour impugned; it had to be asserted, at first tentatively and then with annoying insistence, that they were not able to bear the operation without screaming.

CHAPTER 39 (i): *Love at Loggerheads*

WHERE there are quarrels in love these are of two kinds:
   1. When the one who starts the quarrel is in love.
   2. When the quarreller is not in love.

Where one of the lovers has too much advantage over the other in certain qualities which they both value, the other's love will die because sooner or later fear of contempt will abruptly stop the process of crystallization.

Nothing is more hateful to mediocre people than intellectual superiority in others; it is, in our society, the very fountain-head of hatred. If this principle does not breed atrocious hatreds it is only because the people divided thereby are not obliged to live together. But consider what happens in love where natural behaviour is not masked and where the superior partner, in particular, does not conceal his superiority behind social wariness.

1. Someone accustomed to such a spectacle, and who feels that he might be the hero of it, can concentrate his attention upon the nobility, whereupon the whole thing becomes the chief and most intimate of non-active pleasures.

If the passion is to survive, the inferior lover must ill-treat the other, who will otherwise be unable even to close a window without giving offence.

As a superior lover you will create illusions, and not only will your love run no risks, but the very weakness of your beloved will strengthen the bond between you.

For sheer durability, passionate requited love between people of the same calibre takes first place. *Love at loggerheads*, where the quarreller does not love, comes a close second. You will find examples of this in stories about the Duchesse de Berry in the *Memoirs* of Duclos. This kind of love, having as it does something of the coldness of habit which springs from the prosaic and selfish parts of life which follow a man to his grave, may last longer than passionate love itself. In fact it is no longer love but merely a habit caused by love, whose only relation to the original passion is one of memories and physical pleasure. The existence of this habit necessarily presupposes natures of lesser nobility. Every day some little crisis may occur: 'Will he scold me . . . ?' which, as in passionate love, keeps the imagination busy; and every day some new proof of tenderness has to be given. See the anecdotes about Mme d'Houdetot and Saint-Lambert.[1]

Occasionally pride may refuse to stoop to this sort of thing; then, after a few stormy months, pride kills love. But you will find that the nobler passion makes prolonged resistance before it succumbs. A lover who is still in love, despite ill-treatment, will long continue to foster an illusion about 'little tiffs'. A few tender reconciliations can help to make the transition bearable. On the plea of some secret sorrow or stroke of ill-luck, you forgive the person you have loved so much; in the end you become accustomed to a cat-and-dog life. After all, barring passionate love, gambling, and the enjoyment of power,[2] where would you find so rich a source of daily interest? If the aggressor dies, you will notice that the surviving victim is inconsolable. This principle is the successful basis of many middle-class marriages; the scolded ones have to listen all day to their favourite topic.

There is also a kind of love that is pseudo-quarrelsome. I have

1. The *Mémoires* of Madame d'Epinay, I think, or of Marmontel.
2. Whatever some hypocritical ministers of government may say about it, power is the greatest of all pleasures. It seems to me that only love can beat it, and love is a happy illness that can't be picked up as easily as a Ministry.

borrowed my Chapter 33 from the letter of an extremely clever woman:

'Always a little doubt to set at rest – that's what keeps one craving in passionate love. Because the keenest misgivings are always there, its pleasures never become tedious.'

With boorish, ill-bred, or very violent people, this little doubt to be set at rest, this slight anxiety, takes the form of a quarrel.

Unless the beloved possesses that extreme subtlety which results from a careful upbringing, she may find this kind of love more lively, and therefore more enjoyable; and however fastidious she may be she will find it very difficult, when she sees her *furious* lover the first to suffer from his own violent emotions, not to love him the more for it. Perhaps what Lord Mortimer misses most about his mistress are the candlesticks she used to throw at his head. Indeed, if pride will pardon and allow sensations such as these, it must be admitted that they wage a bitter war against boredom, the great affliction of contented people.

Saint-Simon, the only historian France has ever possessed, says: 'After many passing fancies the Duchesse de Berry had fallen deeply in love with Riom, a junior member of the d'Aydie family, the son of one of Madame de Biron's sisters. He had neither looks nor brains; he was fat, short, chubby-cheeked, and pale, and had such a crop of pimples that he seemed one large abscess; he had beautiful teeth, but not the least idea that he was going to inspire a passion which quickly got out of control, a passion which lasted a lifetime, notwithstanding a number of subsidiary flirtations and affairs. He hadn't a penny to bless himself with, and his numerous brothers and sisters were as poor as he. The Duchess's tirewoman and her husband, Mme and M. de Pons, were related to them, and came from the same part of the country. Hoping to make something of the young man, who was then a lieutenant in the dragoons, they invited him to stay with them. No sooner had he arrived than he took the Duchess's fancy and became master in the Luxembourg.

'M. de Lauzun, whose great-nephew he was, laughed up his sleeve about all this. He was overjoyed, and in the young man saw himself all over again, as he used to be at the Luxembourg in the days of the great Mademoiselle. He used to advise the boy what to do, and Riom, who was naturally gentle, polite, and respectful, paid heed to him like the honest lad he was. But very soon he grew aware of the power his charms conferred, with their unique appeal to the unaccountable fancy of the princess. He did not exercise this power unfairly over others and became popular with everyone, though he used to treat his duchess as M. de Lauzun had treated Mademoiselle. He was soon attired in the richest lace and the finest garments, and provided with money, jewellery, and buckles. He would excite but not requite the desire of the princess; he delighted in making her jealous, or pretending to be jealous himself. He would often drive her to tears. Gradually he forced her into the position of doing nothing without his leave, even trifles of no importance. Sometimes, when she was ready to go to the Opéra, he insisted that she stay at home; and sometimes he made her go there against her will. He obliged her to grant favours to ladies she did not like or of whom she was jealous, and to deny favours to people she did like, of whom he pretended to be jealous. She was not even free to dress as she chose; he would amuse himself by making her change her coiffure or her dress at the last minute; he did this so often and so publicly that she became accustomed to take his orders in the evening for what she would do and wear the following day; then the next day he would alter everything, and the princess would cry all the more. In the end she took to sending him messages by trusted footmen, for from the first he had taken up residence in the Luxembourg; messages which continued throughout her toilette, to know what ribbons she would wear, what gown and what other ornaments; almost invariably he made her wear something she did not wish to. When she occasionally dared to do anything, however small, without his leave, he treated her like a servant, and she was in tears for several days.

'This proud princess, whose pleasure was to behave with the greatest arrogance, demeaned herself to attend obscure dinners with him among a crowd of ne'er-do-wells, this woman with whom no one was permitted to sit at table unless he were a prince of the blood. Riglet, a Jesuit whom she had known as a child and who cultivated her, was invited to these private dinner-parties, without shame or embarrassment on either side. Madame de Mouchy was privy to all the strange goings-on; she and Riom would invite the guests and name the days, and she used to patch up the lovers' quarrels. All this was common knowledge in the Luxembourg, where Riom was sought after by everyone; he in his turn took care to be on good terms with everybody, behaving to all others with a respect which he publicly denied only to his princess. Before the assembled company he would give her such brusque replies that everyone lowered their eyes, and the Duchess would blush, though her passion for him was in no way curtailed.'

For the princess, Riom was a sovereign remedy against boredom.

When Bonaparte was a young hero covered with glory and still innocent of any crime against liberty, a famous woman suddenly blurted out to him: 'General, a woman must be either your wife or your sister!' The hero did not understand the compliment, which brought some fine insults upon his head. Women of this kind love to be despised by their lovers and can only love cruel men.

CHAPTER 39 (ii): *Cures for Love*

IN ancient times the Leucadian Leap was an apt image. It is, indeed, almost impossible to find a cure for love. Not only must there be danger, to remind a man forcibly of the need for self-preservation,[1] but, and this is much more difficult to find, it must be a continually pressing danger, yet one which a man can skilfully avoid for long enough to re-acquire the habit of thinking about the need for survival. In my opinion nothing less than a sixteen-day storm as in Don Juan,[2] or M. Cochelet's shipwreck among the Moors will suffice; otherwise you very soon become inured to danger, and in the front line, twenty paces from the enemy, you again begin thinking of your beloved even more devotedly than ever.

We have repeated over and over again that when a man really loves he *rejoices* or *trembles* no matter what he thinks about; and everything in Nature speaks to him of his beloved. Now rejoicing and trembling are interesting activities beside which all others pale.

A friend who wishes to cure lovesickness must in the first place always be on the side of the beloved woman, and yet friends with more zeal than shrewdness never fail to do the opposite. This is simply to attack, with ludicrously inadequate forces, that pattern of exquisite illusion which we have previously called crystallization.[3]

1. The risk run by Henry Morton in the Clyde. *Old Mortality*. Vol. IV, p. 224.
2. By the overrated Lord Byron.
3. Purely for the sake of brevity, and begging forgiveness for the neologism.

The healing friend must always keep in mind that where the lover has a choice between swallowing some absurdity or giving up all that makes life worth living, he will swallow it and use all his intelligence to disprove his mistress's most obvious vices and most blatant infidelities. This is how in passionate love everything is forgiven after a little while.

Men of cold rational temperament will only accept vices in their mistresses after several months of passion.[1]

Far from seeking crudely and openly to distract the lover, the healing friend should rather talk to him *ad nauseam* about both his love and his mistress, and at the same time contrive a whole succession of trivial happenings around him. If travel *isolates* it is no cure,[2] and indeed nothing is more tenderly reminiscent of the beloved than changes of scene. It is in brilliant Paris salons, among the reputedly most charming women, that I have felt the greatest love for my own poor mistress, solitary and sad in her little lodging in the depths of the Romagna.[3]

An exile in a splendid salon, I used to watch the magnificent clock for the exact moment when she would be leaving her lodging on foot, even in the rain, to visit her friend. In seeking to forget her I discovered that changes of scene provided memories, less vivid but far more sublime than those evoked in places where we had once met.

For absence to be of any use, the healing friend must always be on hand to keep commenting as much as possible on the events which have taken place in the love affair, and to ensure that these reflections are long, wearisome, and pointless, so that they begin to sound like commonplace. Tender sentimentality, for example, could be used after a dinner party enlivened with good wines.

The difficulty of forgetting a woman with whom you have been happy is that the imagination tirelessly continues to evoke and embellish moments of the past.

I shall say nothing about pride, a cruel though certain cure, but not one for sensitive people.

The early scenes of Shakespeare's *Romeo* are an admirable illustration. It is a far cry from the man who tells himself sadly: 'She hath

---

1. Madame Dornal and Serigny, in the *Confessions du Comte . . . . . . ,* by Duclos; see his note 4, p. 68; death of General Abdallah at Bologna.

2. I have wept nearly every day (precious words of 10th June).

3. Salviati.

forsworn to love,' to the one who exclaims at the pinnacle of his happiness: 'Come what sorrow can!'

CHAPTER 39 (iii)

> Her passion will die like a lamp for want of what the flame should feed upon.
>
> *Lammermoor*, II.

THE healing friend must beware of empty arguments, for example the mention of *ingratitude*. This will renew crystallization by allowing another victory and a new pleasure.

There is no such thing as ingratitude in love; the pleasure of the moment always seems worth, and more than worth, the utmost sacrifice. The only thing that can be regarded as wrong is a lack of frankness; one *must* be honest and open about one's heart.

In reply to even the mildest frontal attack on love, the lover will tell the healing friend 'To be in love, even if your beloved is angry with you, is as good – to descend to your marketplace metaphor – as having a lottery ticket where the prize is a thousand times more desirable than anything you, in your little world of indifference and selfish interests, can offer me. To be happy just because you are well-received argues a great deal of vanity, small-minded vanity at that. I don't censure men for acting that way in their world. But with Léonore I discovered a world where everything was heavenly, tender and generous. The most sublime and almost unbelievable virtue of your world would have been no more, in our conversations, than a commonplace everyday virtue. At least let me dream of the happiness of spending my life with such a being. Although I realize I have been betrayed by calumny, and have no more hope, at least I can forgo my revenge for her sake.'

It is almost useless trying to stop love except in its very early stages. Besides immediate departure, and the compulsory distractions of high society, as in the case of Countess Kalemberg, there are several other little tricks which the healing friend can bring into play. For example he can draw to your attention, apparently quite by chance, that the woman you love does not, in matters irrelevant to the main issue, accord you the politeness and respect she gave your rival. The most trivial things will suffice, for in love everything is a *symbol*. Perhaps she does not give you her arm when at the theatre you escort her to her box; a trifle like this, taken in tragic earnest by a passionate heart, by joining a humiliation to every judgement which crystallization makes, poisons the very source of love and may destroy it.

The unkind woman may be accused of some embarrassing physical defect which it is impossible to verify; if the calumny could be verified and found true it would very soon be disposed of by the imagination, and forgotten. It is only imagination that can resist imagination, as Henry III well knew when he spoke ill of the celebrated Duchesse de Montpensier.

It is, therefore, most important to control the imagination in a girl if you wish to save her from love. The less commonplace her spirit the more noble and generous her nature; in short, the more worthy she is of our respect the greater the risk she runs.

It is always dangerous for a young woman to allow her recollections to dwell too often and too easily upon any one person. If the ties of memory become strengthened by gratitude, admiration, or curiosity, she is almost certainly on the edge of the precipice. The greater the tedium of her daily life the more deadly are the poisons called gratitude, admiration, and curiosity. Immediate, swift, and energetic distractions then become necessary.

Thus it is that small doses of roughness and unconcern at the beginning, provided the drug be administered in simple manner, are an almost infallible means of gaining the respect of an intelligent woman.

BOOK TWO

ALL kinds of love and all imaginings are coloured in different people by one of the six temperaments:

The sanguine or French, for example M. de Francueil (Madame d'Epinay's *Memoirs*).

The bilious or Spanish, for example Lauzun (Peguilhen in Saint-Simon's *Memoirs*).

The melancholic or German, for example Schiller's *Don Carlos*.

The phlegmatic or Dutch.

The nervous: Voltaire.

The athletic: Milo of Crotona.[1]

If ambition, avarice, friendship, and so on are subject to the influence of temperament, how much more so will be love, where the physical is a necessary component.

Let us suppose that all kinds of love may be classified under the four heads mentioned:

Passionate love as in Julie d'Etanges.

Mannered love, or gallantry.

Physical love.

Vanity-love (a duchess is never more than thirty in the eyes of a bourgeois).

These four types of love must now be qualified by the six varieties corresponding to the habits of imagination induced by the six temperaments. Tiberius did not have the crazy imagination of a Henry VIII.

All the combinations we have now obtained must then be further qualified by the differences of habit which depend on forms of government or national character:

1. Asiatic despotism, such as exists in Constantinople.

2. Absolute monarchy in the style of Louis XIV.

3. Aristocracy masked by a charter, or the government of a nation for the benefit of the rich, as in England, and all according to Biblical morality.

4. The federal republic, or government for the benefit of all, as in the United States of America.

5. Constitutional monarchy, or:

1. See Cabanis, influence of the physical, etc.

6. A state undergoing a revolution, such as Spain, Portugal, or France. This condition in a country inspires everyone with lively passion, induces a more natural way of life, does away with stupidities, conventional virtues, and absurdities of etiquette,[1] makes young people more serious, and causes them to despise vanity-love and to abstain from gallantry.

This state can last a long time, and shape the habits of a generation. In France it began in 1788, was interrupted in 1802, and began again in 1815, to continue until God knows when.

Besides all these general ways of looking at *love* there are the differences resulting from age and, finally, the peculiarities of the individual.

For instance one might say:

In Dresden, I observed in Count Woltstein vanity-love, a melancholic temperament, monarchic habits, the age of thirty, and individual peculiarities.

This method of looking at things is concise and keeps a man's head cool when he is making up his mind about love, which is essential but extremely difficult.

Now just as man has almost no physiological self-knowledge except what is derived from comparative anatomy, so vanity and various other causes of illusion prevent us from having a clear picture of our own passions except through the observation of the weaknesses of others. If by chance this essay of mine serves any useful purpose, it will be to train the mind to make this sort of comparison. With this in view I shall try to sketch certain general patterns exhibited by love in various countries.

Please forgive me if I revert often to Italy; in the present state of civilization in Europe it is the only country where the plant I am describing grows freely. In France, vanity; in Germany a so-called philosophy so crazy that it makes one die of laughter; in England a shy, tormented, resentful pride; all these things torture love, stifle it, or drive it into the strangest paths.[2]

1. The shoes without buckles belonging to the Minister Roland: 'Oh, Sir, all is lost,' cries Dumouriez. During the royal session the president of the Assembly crosses his legs.

2. It will have been only too clear that this treatise is made up of scraps written down as Lisio Visconti on his travels was actually watching the stories taking place. All the anecdotes can be found in full in the journal of his life; perhaps I should have included them here, but they would hardly have been considered proper. The earliest notes bear the date Berlin 1807, and the last are

CHAPTER 41: *Concerning the Love-Life of Nations –*
France

I SHALL try to strip myself of all personal feeling so that I am only a disinterested philosopher.

Frenchwomen, schooled by charming Frenchmen who have nothing to offer but vanity and physical desires, are less active, less energetic, less feared, and above all less loved and less powerful than Spanish or Italian women.

A woman's power lies only in the degree of unhappiness with which she can punish her lover. Now if one is vain every woman is useful but none indispensable; conquest and not conservation is the success that flatters. If your desires are all physical you find wantons, and this is why the wantons of France are attractive while those of Spain are not. In France they can give many men as much happiness as honest women can – happiness without love, that is; and if there is one thing that a Frenchman respects more than his mistress it is his vanity.

A young Parisian treats his mistress as a kind of slave intended chiefly to indulge his vanity. If she fails to obey the dictates of this ruling passion he leaves her, and is even more self-satisfied than ever as he tells his friends how elegantly and pungently he got rid of her.

A Frenchman who knew his country well (Meilhan) said: 'In France great passions are as rare as great men.'

Words cannot express how impossible it is for a Frenchman to play the part of the jilted lover whom the whole town knows to be in despair; nothing is more usual in Venice or Bologna.

To find love in Paris you must go down among those classes where the absence of education and of vanity, and the struggle for bare necessities, have allowed more energy to survive.

To show oneself as having a great but unsatisfied desire is to exhibit an *inferior self*, which is unheard-of in France except at the very bottom of the social scale. It lays one open to the unkindest jokes

---

dated a few days before his death in June 1819. Certain dates have purposely been altered for the sake of discretion, but that is the sum of my emendations; I did not feel entitled to recast the style. This book has been written in a hundred different places; may it be read in as many.

imaginable; hence the exaggerated praise given to wantons by young men who are uncertain of their own hearts. An extreme and vulgar dread of exhibiting an *inferior self* is the active principle in the conversation of provincials. Look at that fellow recently who, on being told that Monseigneur le Duc de Berry had been murdered, replied: '*I know*.'[1]

In the Middle Ages men's hearts were *infused* with an ever-present sense of danger, and here, if I am not mistaken, lies the second reason for the astonishing superiority of the men of the sixteenth century. Originality, nowadays so rare, ridiculous, dangerous, and often affected, was then general and unvarnished. Great men are still born in countries like Corsica,[2] Spain, and Italy, where danger still shows its iron hand often. In climates where burning summers heat the bile for three months of the year it is only the *direction* of drive that is lacking; in Paris I am very much afraid it is the drive itself.[3]

Many of our young men, however brave at Montmirail or in the Bois de Boulogne, are frightened of falling in love, and it is really their faintheartedness which puts them to flight at the sight of a girl they find pretty. When they remember all they have read in novels about what a lover should do, they feel frozen. These uninspired souls have no conception that the hurricane of passion, as it whips up the

1. Historical fact. Many people, although extremely inquisitive, are shocked at learning news; they fear to appear inferior to the person informing them.

2. *Mémoire* by M. Réalier-Dumas. Corsica, which in terms of its population of one hundred and eighty thousand does not equal a half of most of the French *départements*, has recently produced Salicetti, Pozzo di Borgo, General Sebastiani, Cervoni, Abatucci, Lucien and Napoléon Bonaparte, Arena. The *département* of Nord, which has nine hundred thousand inhabitants, can boast no such list. The fact is that anyone who goes out of doors in Corsica risks being shot at, and the Corsican, instead of submitting to this as a true Christian should, endeavours to defend and above all to revenge himself. That is how personalities of Napoleon's calibre are made. This is a far cry from a palace furnished with playfellow nobles and chamberlains, or from a Fénelon obliged to reason himself into respecting *Monseigneur* even while he was talking to *Monseigneur* himself, aged twelve. See the works of this great writer.

3. To be correct in Paris implies attention to a million little details. Nevertheless there is a very strong objection. Far more women commit suicide for love in Paris than in all the cities of Italy combined. This fact puzzles me greatly; I do not for the moment know how to explain it, but it does not change my opinion. Perhaps death is of little consequence to the French at present, so great is the tedium of ultra-civilized life; or more probably one blows out one's brains for the sake of outraged vanity.

waves of the sea, also fills the sails of the ship and gives it the impetus to ride the storm.

Love is an exquisite flower, but it needs courage to pluck it on the brink of a dreadful precipice. Besides ridicule, love is always haunted by the desperate possibility that the beloved will forsake it, leaving nothing but a lifelong DEAD BLANK.

A perfect civilization would unite the delicate pleasures of the nineteenth century with a more frequent presence of danger.[1] The pleasures of private life ought to be augmented to an infinite degree by recurrent exposure to danger. I am not talking simply of military danger. I should prefer perpetual danger of every kind, threatening every interest in life, which was the essence of the life of the Middle Ages. Danger of the sort that our civilization has prepared and dressed up is a fitting companion for the most tedious weakness of character.

In *A Voice from St Helena*, by O'Meara, are these words of a great man:

'If one were to tell Murat: 'go and destroy those seven or eight enemy regiments lying across the plain near that steeple,' he would go like a flash and soon, however little cavalry he could muster, the enemy regiments were broken, killed, wiped out. If you left the man to himself he was no more than a brainless imbecile. I cannot conceive how so brave a man could be so cowardly. He was only brave in the face of the enemy; but there he was probably the boldest and most brilliant soldier in all Europe.

'He was a hero, a Saladin, a Richard Cœur-de-Lion on the battle-field; but crown him king and put him in a council-chamber, and there was nothing left but a poltroon, indecisive and without judgment. Murat and Ney were the bravest men I have ever known.' (O'Meara, Vol. II, p. 94.)

1. I admire the way people lived in the time of Louis XIV. They were constantly leaving the salons of Marly and reaching the battlefields of Senef and Ramillies within three days. Wives, mothers, and mistresses were continually on tenterhooks. See Mme de Sévigné's letters. The presence of danger kept an energy and a frankness in the language which nowadays we should not dare risk; but at the same time M. de Lameth murdered his wife's lover. If a Walter Scott were to write us a novel about the days of Louis XIV we should be greatly amazed.

CHAPTER 42: *More Concerning France*

I BEG leave to say a few more unpleasant things about France. The reader need not fear that my satire will go unpunished; if anyone reads this essay I shall get my insults back a hundredfold, for national honour is a jealous watchdog.

France is important in the pattern of this book because Paris, thanks to the superiority of its conversation and literature, is and always will be the drawing-room of Europe.

Three out of every four notes sent in the morning, whether in Vienna or in London, are either written in French or full of allusions and quotations, also in French[1] – Heaven alone knows what kind!

As regards grand passions, it seems to me that France lacks originality, for two reasons:

1. True honour, or the wish to emulate Bayard, so as to be an honoured member of society and to receive daily satisfaction for our vanity.

2. Foolish honour, or the wish to emulate the 'best people' in Paris society. The art of entering a drawing-room, of treating a rival with pointed coolness, of quarrelling with one's mistress, and so forth. . . .

Foolish honour contributes far more to the pleasures of vanity than true honour. In the first place it is far easier for fools to understand and in the second place it can be applied to daily or even hourly actions. Society is perfectly prepared to accept people with foolish honour but no true honour; the reverse is quite out of the question.

What the 'best people' do is this:

1. They are ironic about anything important. This is quite natural, since those who used really to be the 'best people' were never affected by anything. They had no time. Summers in the country are changing all that. Besides it is flying in the face of nature for a Frenchman to permit himself to *admire* something,[2] because that implies he is inferior not only to the thing admired – that might just about pass –

1. The most serious writers in England think they are being dashing by using French words which for the most part were never French except in English grammar-books. See the contributors to the *Edinburgh Review*; see the *Memoirs* of the Countess of Lichtnau, the mistress of the last King of Prussia but one.

2. There is no objection to fashionable admiration; e.g. that for Hume in 1775 or thereabouts, or for Franklin in 1784.

but also to his neighbour, if the latter chooses to laugh at what *he* admires.

In Germany, Italy, and Spain on the other hand admiration is full of good faith and happiness. There the man who admires is proud of his transports and feels sorry for the censorious – I won't say for the scoffer, since such a person does not exist in those countries where ridicule is reserved for those who have missed their path to happiness, and is not directed against the imitation of a certain mode of being. In the South, mistrust and a horror of having one's keenest pleasures interrupted results in an inborn admiration for pomp and circumstance. Look at the Courts of Madrid and Naples, or a *funzione* at Cadiz – sheer delirium.[1]

2. A Frenchman thinks he is the unhappiest man in the world, and verging on the most ridiculous, if he has to spend his time alone. But what is love without solitude?

3. A passionate man thinks only about himself, while a man seeking to be well thought of thinks only about others. Moreover, before 1789 individual security could only be achieved in France by membership of a *body*, the legal profession for instance,[2] and the consequent

1. Mr Semple's Journey in Spain; he gives a true picture, and his description of the battle of Trafalgar heard from afar is memorable.

2. Correspondence of Grimm, January 1783.
'M. le Comte de N— a substantive captain in Monsieur's Guards, annoyed to find no seats left in the circle the day the new theatre opened, was misguided enough to dispute possession of his place with an honest attorney, one Maître Pernot, who refused to budge. "You've taken my seat." "I am keeping my own." "And who are you?" "I am Monsieur Six-Francs" (the price of the seat). And then sharper words, insults, and jostlings. The Comte de N— carried indiscretion to the point of calling the poor legal gentleman a thief, and finally took upon himself to order the sergeant on duty to apprehend him and take him to the guardhouse. Maître Pernot accompanied the sergeant with great dignity, and on leaving the guardhouse went straight to a magistrate to file his suit. The redoubtable body of which he has the honour to be a member insisted that he pursue the matter to the bitter end, and the case has just been decided before the high court. M. de N— was ordered to settle all costs, to apologize to the attorney, to pay the latter two thousand crowns damages and the interest thereon, to be applied with his consent to the poor prisoners of the Conciergerie; moreover the said Count was expressly enjoined never again to presume upon the King's commission in disturbing the peace of the theatre, etc. . . The incident has been the talk of the town, and great interests were involved; the entire legal profession considered itself insulted by the outrage done to a man who had taken silk, etc. M. de N—, to live it down, has gone to seek new laurels at the camp of Saint-Roch. He could hardly do better by all

protection by other members of that group. Your neighbour's thoughts were therefore part and parcel of your own happiness. This was even more true of the Court than of Paris. It is easy to see how far such manners – which are, to say truth, declining, but will be carried on by the French for another hundred years – encourage grand passions.

I seem to see a man throwing himself out of the window but trying nevertheless to land gracefully on the pavement below.

A passionate man is only like himself, and not like other people, and this in France is the source of all ridicule; moreover he gives offence to others, and ridicule is thereby lent wings.

CHAPTER 43 : *Italy*

IT is the happy privilege of Italy to rely on the inspiration of the moment, a privilege shared to some extent by Germany and England.

Italy moreover is a country where utility, the virtue of the medieval republics,[1] has not been dethroned by honour or virtue adapted for the convenience of kings;[2] and true honour paves the way for

---

accounts, for there is no doubt of his talent for taking a position by frontal attack.' Imagine an obscure philosopher in place of Maître Pernot. Usefulness of duels.

Grimm, Part III, Vol. II, p. 102.

See also p. 496, a sensible enough letter from Beaumarchais refusing a friend of his a private box which had been requested for *Figaro*. When it was believed that this letter was addressed to a duke feelings ran high and there was talk of grave punishment. When Beaumarchais revealed that his letter had been addressed to M. le Président du Paty, everybody laughed. It is a far cry from 1785 to 1822! We no longer understand such feelings. And we are expected to appreciate the same tragedy as moved those people!

1. G. Pecchio nelle sue vivacissime lettere ad una bella giovane inglese sopra la Spagna libera, laquale è un medioevo, non redivivo, ma sempre vivo, dice, pagina 60:

'Lo scopo degli Spagnuoli non era la gloria, ma la indipendenza. Se gli Spagnuoli non si fossero battuti che per l'onore, la guerra era finita colla battaglia di Tudela. L'onore è di una natura bizarra; macchiato una volta, perde tutta la forza per agire. . . L'esercito di linea spagnuolo, imbevuto anch'egli dei pregiudizi dell'onore (vale a dire fatto europeo moderno), vinto che fosse, si sbandava col pensiero che tutto coll'*onore* era perduto, etc.'

2. A man brought honour upon himself in 1620 by incessant and servile

foolish honour; it leads to a habit of wondering what your neighbour thinks of your happiness. And a *feeling* of happiness cannot be the subject of vanity since it is invisible.[1] As a proof of all this, there are fewer love matches in France than in any other country in the world.[2]

Italy has other advantages too. Abundant leisure under magnificent skies tends to sharpen one's awareness of beauty in all its forms. Intense though reasonable mistrust deepens the sense of isolation and doubles the appeal of intimacy. An absence of novel-reading and indeed of almost every kind of reading allows the inspiration of the moment even greater play. A passion for music stirs the spirit in much the same way as love.

Around 1770 there was no mistrust in France; on the contrary it was right and proper to live and die in the public eye; as the Duchess of Luxembourg was intimate with a hundred friends, so there was neither intimacy nor friendship in the true sense of the words.

In Italy, since passion is not infrequent it is not ridiculous,[3] and one hears generalizations about love freely quoted in drawing-rooms. The public knows the symptoms and stages of the disease and takes a great interest in them. When a man is jilted they tell him: 'You will be in the depths of despair for six months but after that you'll recover, like so-and-so, or so-and-so.'

In Italy the judgments of the public are the humble servants of passion. Genuine pleasure wields over them the power which is elsewhere in the hands of society; it is quite simply that society, offering almost no pleasures at all to a people with no time for vanity nor any wish to attract the notice of the pasha, has very little authority. The

---

repetition of the phrase: *The King my master* (see the memoirs of Noailles, Torcy, and all the ambassadors of Louis XIV); it was quite simple: by this turn of phrase he proclaimed his *rank* among the king's subjects. In the latter's consideration and esteem this rank which he held from the king was comparable to that which a man held in ancient Rome by virtue of the opinion of his fellow-citizens who had seen him fighting at Thrasymenus and speaking in the Forum. One can undermine absolute monarchy by destroying vanity, and its outer defences which it calls the *conventions*. The controversy about Shakespeare and Racine is only one of the forms of the controversy between Louis XIV and Magna Carta.

1. It can only be evaluated through unpremeditated actions.

2. Miss O'Neil, Mrs Coutts, and most great English actresses leave the stage to marry money.

3. Promiscuity in women is tolerated, but love makes them look ridiculous, wrote the judicious Abbé Girard in Paris, in 1740.

bored people disapprove of the passionate ones but are themselves derided. South of the Alps society is a despot with no prisons.

In Paris, since honour demands that you defend every admission of interest in matters of major importance, either by the sword, or by verbal sallies if possible, it is much more convenient to take refuge in irony. Many young people have tried a different course by becoming followers of J.-J. Rousseau and of Madame de Staël. Since irony has become a vulgar mannerism it is now necessary to display sentiment. A de Pezai of today would write like M. Darlincourt, and besides, since 1789 events have favoured what is *useful* – individual sensation, rather than what is *honourable* – the realm of public opinion. Parliamentary example teaches discussion of everything, even jokes. The nation is growing serious-minded and gallantry is losing ground.

As a Frenchman I must assert that the wealth of a country does not lie in a few enormous fortunes but in the multiplicity of small ones. Passions are rare in all countries, and gallantry has more grace and finesse, and is consequently happier in France. This great nation, the first of all the universe,[1] is in the same condition in matters of love as it is in intellectual achievement. In 1822, admittedly, we cannot boast a Moore, a Walter Scott, a Crabbe, a Byron, a Monti, or a Pellico; but we have among us more enlightened, pleasant, and well-informed minds than they have in England or in Italy. That is why the debates in our Chamber of Deputies in 1822 are so superior to those of the English Parliament. It also explains why, when an English Liberal visits France, we are surprised to find in him numerous quite feudal opinions.

A Roman artist wrote from Paris:

'I dislike it thoroughly here; I think it is because I have insufficient leisure to love as I please. Here one's sensibility is expended drop by drop as it forms, in such a way as to dry up the source, at least as far as I am concerned. In Rome, where day-to-day events provide so little interest, and where outer existence is so lethargic, sensibility accumulates to the benefit of the passions.'

---

1. *Envy* is the only proof I require of this. See the *Edinburgh Review* of 1821, the German and Italian literary papers, and Alfieri's *Scimiotigre*.

Only in Rome[1] could an honest and wealthy woman descend effusively upon another, a mere acquaintance, and say as I overheard this morning: 'Ah, my dear, don't have an affair with Fabio Vitteleschi; better fall in love with a highway assassin. With his gentle and measured ways he's quite capable of stabbing you to the heart with a dagger, and saying with a smile as he drives it into your breast, "Does it hurt, my little one?" ' And all this was happening in the presence of the second woman's daughter, a pretty girl of fifteen, and wide awake too.

If a Northerner has the misfortune not to be shocked initially by the unaffectedness of this Southern charm, which is simply a consequence of great natural beauty coupled with an absence of 'good form' and a lack of interesting novelty, then the women of all other countries will be unbearable to him after he has been in Rome for a year.

He sees Frenchwomen with their little graces,[2] quite charming, and seductive for the first three days, but boring on the fourth, that fatal day when he discovers that all these graces, carefully studied beforehand and patiently rehearsed, are eternally the same for every occasion and for every person.

He sees German women, on the other hand, so natural, and so enthusiastically carried away by their imaginations, but frequently having nothing to offer, for all their unaffectedness, except sterility, insipidity, and cloying sentimentality. Count Almaviva's remark might have been made in Germany: 'And one fine evening one is quite astonished to find satiety where one was seeking happiness.'

The foreigner in Rome must not forget that while nothing is tedious in a country where everything is natural, evil there is more evil than elsewhere. To speak only of men,[3] you will find in society here a species of monster which does not reveal itself elsewhere, a type of

---

1. 30th September 1819.

2. Besides the fact that the author was unlucky enough not to have been born in Paris, he had only lived there for a short time.—Editor's note.

3.   *Heu! male nunc artes miseras hæc secula tractant;*
        Jam tener assuevit munera velle puer.

                                        Tibullus, I, iv.

man who is passionate, shrewd, and cowardly all at the same time. By an evil chance some such men may be in a position of some standing in relation to a woman; madly in love perhaps, they taste to the full the bitterness of seeing her give preference to a rival. They are there to thwart the more fortunate lover. Nothing escapes them and the whole world knows that nothing escapes them, yet they continue to flout every sentiment of honour by harassing the woman, her lover, and themselves, and no one censures them, *for they are doing something they enjoy*. One evening the lover, at the end of his tether, kicks them in the backside; the following day they are full of excuses, and again begin their continuous, imperturbable annoyance of the woman, the lover, and themselves. One shudders to think how much unhappiness these base spirits need to regale themselves upon daily, and if they were one jot less cowardly they would no doubt be poisoners.

Only in Italy, too, do elegant young millionaires keep dancers from the Theatre in magnificent style, before the very eyes of a whole city full of people with an average income of thirty sous a day.[1] The . . . brothers, fine young men, always hunting, always on horseback, are jealous of a foreigner. Instead of going to him and airing their grievances they secretly spread sly rumours about the unfortunate fellow. In France, public opinion would force such people to prove their statements or account for them to the foreigner. But public opinion and contempt mean nothing in Rome. Wealth is always sure of a welcome everywhere. A millionaire in disgrace, shown the door everywhere in Paris, can quite safely go to Rome; the warmth of his reception will be in direct proportion to the weight of gold in his purse.

CHAPTER 45: *England*

I HAVE spent a good deal of time lately with the dancers from the theatre *Del Sol* in Valencia. I am told that several of them are extremely chaste; their occupation is so tiring. Vigano has them rehearsing his ballet, *The Jewess of Toledo*, every day from ten in the

1. Notice in the manners of the time of Louis XV how the honourable and aristocratic heaped favours upon Mlle Duthé, Mlle la Guerre, and others. Eighty or a hundred thousand francs a year was nothing out of the ordinary; a lesser sum would have demeaned a man in high society.

morning until four, and from midnight to three in the morning; besides this they have to dance the two ballets every evening.

This reminds me of Rousseau who prescribes long walks for Emile. Tonight at midnight, as I walked along the cool beach with the little dancers, it occurred to me that the unearthly sensuous freshness of the sea breeze, under the Valencia sky and those brilliant stars which seem so close, is quite unknown in our dismal foggy countries. That breeze in itself is worth the four-hundred-league journey, and the sensations it induces destroy the power to think. It also occurred to me that the chastity of my little dancers provides a good explanation of the way men's pride, in England, quietly re-establishes the conditions of the seraglio in a civilized country. It is evident that some of these English girls, for all their beauty and the appeal of their features, leave something to be desired in the matter of ideas. Despite liberty, which has only lately been driven out of their island, and despite the admirable originality of the national character, these girls lack originality and interesting ideas. They are often remarkable only for the quaintness of their delicacy. It is all very simple; the modesty of women in England is the pride of their husbands. But, however submissive a slave may be, her company soon grows burdensome. Hence the fact that the men find it necessary to get gloomily drunk every evening,[1] instead of passing the time with their mistresses as in Italy. In England the rich, bored with their homes, and on the plea of necessary exercise, walk four or five leagues every day as though man were created and placed on earth for the purpose of trotting. In this way they use up their nervous fluid through the legs instead of through the heart. After which they make so bold as to talk of feminine delicacy and to despise Spain and Italy.

In contrast, no one could be idler than the young Italians; movement, which might blunt their sensibility, they find tiresome. Now and again they will walk half a league reluctantly for their health's sake; and as for the women, a Roman woman does not cover as much ground in a whole year as an English miss will do in a week.

It seems to me that an English husband's pride very deftly exalts his poor wife's vanity. Above all he convinces her that it will not do to be *vulgar*, and mothers who are training their daughters to catch husbands have an excellent grasp of this idea. Hence a fashion far more

1. This custom is becoming less prevalent in the best circles, which as everywhere are copying the French; but I am speaking of the vast majority.

absurd and imperious in rational England than it is in light-hearted France: Bond Street invented the CAREFULLY CARELESS. In England fashion is a duty; in Paris it is a pleasure. Fashion raises a brazen wall far higher between New Bond Street and Fenchurch Street in London than it does between the Chaussée d'Antin and the Rue Saint-Martin in Paris. Husbands willingly allow their wives to indulge in this aristocratic nonsense as a compensation for the enormous burden of melancholy they impose upon them. I find in the once famous novels of Miss Burney a faithful description of female society in England as shaped by the tight-lipped pride of the men. Since it is vulgar to ask for a glass of water when you are thirsty, Miss Burney's heroines dutifully allow themselves to die of thirst. The flight from vulgarity leads to the most abominable affectation.

I compare the caution of a wealthy young Englishman of twenty-two with the profound suspiciousness of a young Italian of the same age. The Italian needs to be suspicious for his own safety, and lays his suspicion aside or forgets it as soon as he is in intimate surroundings, whereas it is precisely in what appears to be the most friendly company that we see the caution and hauteur of the young English-man redoubled. I once heard: 'For seven months I didn't mention a journey to Brighton.' It was about some forced economy of eighty louis, and the speaker was the young lover of a married woman whom he adored, but in the very fever of his passion his *caution* had not for-saken him; less still had he been foolhardy enough to say to his mistress: ' I shan't go to Brighton, because I can't afford it.'

Remember that the fate of Giannone, Pellico, and a hundred others compels an Italian to be mistrustful, while a young English beau is only driven to caution by the excessive and morbid sensitivity of his vanity. A Frenchman, being expansive with his ideas at any given moment, tells his beloved everything. It is a habit; without it he would not be at ease, and he knows that without ease there can be no grace.

Only reluctantly and with tears in my eyes have I dared to write the foregoing; but since I believe that I should not flatter a king, why should I not say what I think about a country? It may OF COURSE be all quite absurd, simply because the country in question is the birth-place of the most lovable woman I have ever known.

In another form it would be cringing before a monarch. I shall only add that within this whole pattern of custom, among so many

Englishwomen whose intelligence has fallen victim to men's pride, real originality does exist, and it only needs a family brought up free from the gloomy restrictions which mimic the conditions of the seraglio, to produce most charming characters. And how meaningless that word charming is despite its etymology; how trite to convey what I want to express! Sweet Imogen and tender Ophelia have many counterparts alive in England now, but these counterparts are far from enjoying the high esteem unanimously accorded to the standard *accomplished* Englishwoman, designed to comply to the full with all the conventions and to give a husband every opportunity to indulge his most sickly aristocratic pride, and the satisfaction of being bored to death.[1]

In the long fifteen- or twenty-roomed suites, very cool and dark, where Italian women pass their lives reclining languidly on low divans, they hear talk of love or music for six hours a day. In the evenings, hidden in their boxes at the theatre for four hours, they hear talk of music or love.

So besides the climate the very pattern of life in Italy and Spain is as conducive to music and to love as it is discouraging to them in England.

I neither approve nor disapprove; I observe.

CHAPTER 46: *England (continued)*

I AM too fond of England, and have seen too little of it to be able to discuss it. I shall use the observations of a friend.

In Ireland now (1822), for the twentieth time in two centuries,[2] society is in that curious state, so rich in courageous resolution and so contrary to tedium, when people who are breakfasting cheerfully with one another may meet two hours later on the field of battle. Nothing could appeal more directly and forcibly to that state of mind which is most favourable to the tender passions: *unaffectedness*. Nothing could be further from the two great English vices, *cant* and BASHFULNESS (hypocrisy in morality, and proud agonized shyness;

1. See Richardson. The manners of the Harlowe family, transposed into modern terms, are common in England; their servants are more worthy than themselves.

2. Spencer's young child burnt alive in Ireland.

see Mr Eustace's journey to Italy. While this traveller gives a poor
description of the country, he gives us a very precise idea of his own
character; and this character, like that of Mr Beattie the poet (see his
life written by an intimate friend), is unfortunately all too common
in England. For the priest who is honest despite his profession see the
letters of the Bishop of Llandaff[1]).

One might think that Ireland, for two centuries steeped in blood by
the frightened and cruel tyranny of England, was unhappy enough;
but here a horrifying character stalks forth upon the moral scene of
Ireland: the *priest* . . .

For the last two centuries Ireland has been just about as badly
governed as Sicily. A well-informed comparison between these two
islands, in a five hundred-page book, would irritate many people and
make nonsense of many well-worn theories. It is obvious though, that
of the two countries, both governed by madmen for the exclusive
profit of the few, Sicily is the happier. Its rulers have at least left it
love and the pleasures of the senses; they would have taken these like
everything else, but in Sicily, heaven be praised, there is very little
of that moral evil known as law and order.[2]

Laws are made and enforced by old men and priests; this is evident
in the kind of comical jealousy with which the pleasures of the senses
are attacked in the British Isles. The people there might say to their
rulers as Diogenes said to Alexander: 'Keep your sinecures and just
leave me my sunshine.'[3]

By dint of laws, regulations, counter-regulations, and tortures, the
government in Ireland has created the potato, and the population is

1. It seems to me impossible to refute otherwise than by insults the portrait of
a certain class of Englishman as presented in these three works. SATANIC SCHOOL.

2. What I call *moral evil* in 1822 is any form of government which does not
consist of two Houses; the only exception is where the head of the government
is great because of his integrity, a miracle which has occurred in Saxony and
Naples.

3. See in the report of the trial of the late queen of England a curious list of
peers and of the sums they and their families receive from the Crown. For
instance Lord Lauderdale and his family receive £27,000. The half-pint pot of
beer necessary to the scanty meal of the poorest Englishman costs a halfpenny in
tax towards the support of the noble peer. Moreover, what very much concerns
our present argument, both parties are aware of it. Henceforth neither noble
lord nor peasant has time to think of love; instead they are sharpening their
weapons, the one publicly and with haughty pride, the other secretly and with
fury. (The YEOMANRY and the WHITEBOYS.)

far larger than that of Sicily. In other words, several million peasants have been called into existence, degraded, thwarted, crushed by toil and poverty. They drag out a miserable life for forty or fifty years beside the bogs of old Erin, but pay their taxes regularly. The thing is a miracle. With a pagan religion the poor devils might at least have enjoyed one pleasure; but no, they have to worship St Patrick.

You hardly see anyone in Ireland save peasants more unfortunate than savages. But instead of the hundred thousand that Nature intended, there are eight million[1] who enable five hundred absentee landlords to live opulently in London and Paris.

Scotland is socially far more advanced[2] and its government is good in several respects (infrequency of crime, literacy, no bishops, etc.). The tender passions are thus more highly developed there, and we can have done with gloomy thoughts and turn to whimsical ones.

It is impossible not to sense the inner melancholy of Scottish women. In the ballroom this melancholy is particularly attractive, and adds a peculiar poignancy to the warmth and eagerness which they display as they leap in their national dances. Edinburgh has the added advantage of being free from the vile omnipotence of money. In this, as in the strange and savage beauty of its situation, it presents a complete contrast to London. Like Rome, lovely Edinburgh seems rather the abode of quiet contemplation. The restless whirl and anxious cares of active life, with all its assets and liabilities, are in London. It seems to me that Edinburgh gives the devil his due by having a slight disposition towards pedantry. The days when Mary Stuart lived at old Holyrood and Rizzio was murdered in her arms were more favourable to love, all women will agree, than these days of lengthy discussion, even in the presence of ladies, of the relative merits of the Neptunian system as opposed to the Vulcanian ... Conversations about the new uniform given by the king to his guards, or Sir B. Bloomfield's failure to obtain his peerage, which were the topics in London when I was there, seem preferable to a discussion which seeks to determine who is the greatest authority on the nature of rocks, whether Werner or ...

I shall say nothing about the dreadful Scottish Sabbath, compared

1. Plunkett, Craig, *Life of Curran*.
2. Degree of civilization of the peasant Robert Burns and his family; the peasant club with a fee of a penny a session; the questions discussed there. (See Burns' letters.)

to which the London version is a real picnic. This day, intended to
honour heaven, is quite the best picture of hell I have ever seen on
earth. A Scotsman returning from church with a friend of his, a
Frenchman, once said to him: 'Don't go so fast, or people will think
we're out for a walk!'[1]

The one country of the three which has the least degree of hypocrisy (*Cant*: see the *New Monthly Magazine* of January 1822, inveighing
against Mozart and the *Marriage of Figaro*; written in a country where
they perform the *Citizen*. But in all countries it is the aristocrats who
buy and judge literary magazines and literature; and for the last four
years the aristocrats in England have been in league with the bishops)
– the least hypocritical country of the three, it seems to me, is Ireland;
you find, on the contrary, a dizzy and very likeable liveliness there.
In Scotland the Lord's Day is strictly observed, but on Monday they
dance with a joyous abandon utterly unknown in London. Love
thrives among the peasant classes in Scotland. The country was galli-
cized by all-powerful imagination during the sixteenth century.

The besetting sin of English society which daily gives rise to more
unhappiness than does debt and its consequences – more even than
the deadly war of the rich against the poor – may be exemplified by
something I was told this autumn in Croydon, in front of the fine
statue of the bishop: 'No man here wants to press forward, in case he
should be disappointed in the attempt.'

Judge for yourselves what laws such men will impose, in the name
of *modesty*, upon their wives and mistresses!

CHAPTER 47: *Spain*

ANDALUSIA is one of the pleasantest of all the places on earth
where the pleasures of the senses have chosen to dwell. I have
three or four anecdotes which show how true, in Spain, are my
theories about the three or four different acts of folly which together
go to make up love; however, I am advised to sacrifice them to
French delicacy. I have protested in vain that though I am writing in
the French language, I am emphatically not writing *French literature*.
Heaven preserve me from having anything in common with the
respected literary men of today.

1. The same thing in America. In Scotland, the display of titles.

When the Moors withdrew from Andalusia they left their architecture behind them, and a great many of their customs. Since it is impossible for me to refer to the latter in the language of Madame de Sévigné, I shall merely mention the principal feature of Moorish architecture, which is that each house has a little garden surrounded by a narrow and elegant arcade. During the intolerable heat of summer, when the Réaumur thermometer never falls below thirty degrees for weeks on end, these arcades provide a delicious shade. In the middle of the little garden there is always a fountain whose steady and sensuous murmur is the only sound which breaks the quiet of the exquisite retreat. Its marble basin is surrounded by a dozen or so rose trees and oleanders. A heavy tent-shaped awning covers the whole garden, protecting it from the sun and allowing in only the gentle breezes which blow from the mountains towards midday.

Here the charming Andalusian women, lithe and light-footed, live and entertain; a simple black silk dress trimmed with fringes of the same colour, revealing an attractive instep, a pale complexion, eyes which reflect every fleeting nuance of the tenderest and most ardent passions; these are the divine creatures I am forbidden to talk about.

I look upon the Spanish people as the living representatives of the Middle Ages.

They are ignorant of a host of minor truths (whereon their neighbours base a childish vanity) but are profoundly aware of the great truths, and they have enough character and wit to pursue the consequences of these to the uttermost limits. The Spanish character makes a pretty contrast with French *esprit*; hard, abrupt, inelegant, full of untamed pride, never concerned with others, it is precisely the contrast between the fifteenth and eighteenth centuries.

Spain provides me with one extremely useful comparison: the only people who managed to resist Napoleon seem to me to be absolutely free from foolish honour and from what is foolish in honour itself.

Instead of issuing fine military ordinances, changing their uniforms every six months and wearing great big spurs they have a general *no importa*.[1]

1. See the charming Letters of M. Pecchio. Italy is full of people with the same strength; but instead of obtruding themselves they stay quiet: *Paese della virtù sconosciuta.*

CHAPTER 48: *Love in Germany*

THE Italian, for ever torn between hatred and love, lives by his passions, and the Frenchman by his vanity, but the kind and unsophisticated descendants of the ancient Germans live by their imagination. No sooner are they clear of the most basic and vital social functions than one is astonished to see them go off in pursuit of what they call their philosophy, a gentle amiable madness quite free from malice. Not entirely from memory, but from some hasty notes, I am going to quote a work which, though written from the other side, gives even through the author's admiration a clear picture of the military spirit in all its extravagance: it is the *Voyage en Autriche* by M. Cadet-Gassicourt, 1809. What would the noble and generous Desaix have said had he observed the pure heroism of 1795 leading to such execrable egoism?

Two friends were together on a battery at the battle of Talavera; one was the captain in command and the other his lieutenant. The captain was knocked down by a cannon-ball. 'Good,' said the lieutenant, overjoyed, 'now François is dead, and I shall be captain.' 'Oh no, not just yet,' cried François, picking himself up; he had only been stunned. Both the lieutenant and his captain were the best fellows in the world, not at all wicked, only just a little stupid and devoted to the Emperor. But the fury of the chase and the unbridled egoism which the Emperor had been able to engender by honouring it with the name of glory made them forget common humanity.

Amid the grim spectacle of such men on parade at Schoenbrunn, vying with each other for a glance from their master and for the title of baron, this is the way the Emperor's apothecary described German love (p. 288, ibid.):

'No one could be gentler or more obliging than an Austrian woman. For her, love is a cult, and, when she becomes attached to a Frenchman, she adores him in the full sense of the word.

'There are light and capricious women everywhere but, generally speaking, the Viennese women are constant and have nothing of the coquette; when I call them constant, I mean to the lover of their choice, for husbands in Vienna count for much the same as anywhere else.'

7th June 1809

The most beautiful woman in Vienna has been pleased to accept the homage of a friend of mine, M. M—, a captain on the Emperor's headquarters staff. The young man is gentle and witty; but neither his bearing nor his face are anything out of the ordinary.

For the last few days his young lady-friend has been causing more than a mild sensation among our brilliant staff officers, who spend their time ferreting about the remotest corners of Vienna. The thing has become a contest in boldness; every known tactic of war has been employed; the young woman's house has been besieged by the richest and the handsomest. Young staff-officers, dashing colonels, generals in the Guards, even princes, have been wasting their time outside her windows and their money upon her servants. All have been refused admittance. These princes were hardly accustomed to such cruel treatment after Paris or Milan. How I laughed at their discomfiture by this delightful woman. 'But, good Heavens,' she would say, 'surely they know I am in love with M. M—.'

Here is a very strange, and certainly a very indecent story (p. 290, ibid.). 'While we were at Schoenbrunn I noticed that two of the young men on the Emperor's staff never entertained anyone at their lodgings in Vienna. We used to chaff them about this discretion and one of them confided to me one day: "You might as well know what's happening. A young woman from the town has given herself to me on condition she never has to go out and that I don't receive anyone without her consent." I was intrigued (the traveller continues) to know something more of this voluntary recluse, and accepted my young friend's invitation to lunch, my status of doctor – as in the East – giving me an honest excuse. I found a woman very much in love keeping house most carefully,. having no desire to go out of doors despite the inviting weather, and convinced that her lover would take her back to France.

'The second young man, who could no more be found at his lodgings than the first, soon confided a similar story to me. I saw his mistress too; like the first she was fair-haired, very pretty and well-shapen.

'One, eighteen years of age, was the daughter of a wealthy tapestry-maker; the other, who was about twenty-four, was the wife of an Austrian officer campaigning with the army of the Archduke Jean. The second carried her love to the point of heroism, judged by the standards of countries where vanity reigns. Not only was her lover unfaithful to her but he found himself obliged to make a most unsavoury confession to her. She looked after him with perfect devotion and, drawn closer by the gravity of the illness which endangered her lover's life, she loved him all the more for it.

'Since the whole of Viennese high society had withdrawn to its Hungarian estates upon our approach, I as a foreigner and conqueror could naturally not observe love among the upper classes; but I did see enough of it to convince me that it is not the same kind of love as in Paris.

'The Germans regard love as a virtue, a divine emanation, something mystical. It is not eager, impetuous, jealous, and tyrannical as it is in the heart of an Italian woman. It is deep, visionary, and utterly unlike anything in England.

'A few years ago a Leipzig tailor, overcome by jealousy of a rival, lay in wait for him in the public gardens and stabbed him. He was condemned to be beheaded. The moralists of the town, true to German kindness and facile emotion (amounting to weakness of character), argued about the sentence, found it harsh and, drawing a comparison between the tailor and Orosman, were filled with pity at his fate. It was not possible to obtain a reprieve. But on the day of execution all the girls in Leipzig gathered together dressed in white and accompanied the tailor to the scaffold, throwing flowers in his path.

'No one saw anything odd in this ceremony, though in a country which calls itself rational it could be said that they were honouring a kind of murder. But it was a ceremony, and nothing ceremonial can ever be ridiculous in Germany. Look at the ceremonies in the courts of the minor princes; they would make us split our sides with laughter, yet seem most impressive to the people of Meiningen or Cöthen. In the six gamekeepers parading before their petty medalbedizened prince, they see Hermann's soldiers marching against the legions of Varus.

'The Germans differ from all other peoples in that they become exalted by meditation instead of being soothed by it and secondly, that they are always yearning to be people of character.

'While court life is usually propitious to the growth of love, life in German courts stultifies it. You can have no idea of the myriad incomprehensible trifles and meannesses which go to make up what is called a court in Germany,[1] even those of the best princes (Munich, 1820).

'Whenever we were posted with a staff in a German town, by the end of the first fortnight the local ladies had made their selection, once and for all. And I have heard it said that the coming of the French was the undoing of many whose virtue had until then been beyond reproach.'

*

The young Germans I met in Göttingen, Dresden, Königsberg, etc. had been educated among systems claimed to be philosophies, but which were no more than obscure and ill-written poetry, although, morally speaking, of the highest and most sanctified sublimity. My impression is that their heritage from the Middle Ages has been not republicanism, defiance, and dagger-blows, like that of the Italians, but a strong predisposition towards enthusiasm and good faith. This is why they have a new great man every ten years, each greater than the last (Kant, Steding, Fichte, etc.).[2]

Luther once appealed strongly to their moral sense; and they fought for thirty years without a break to satisfy their conscience. A fine word, and worthy of respect, however absurd the belief may be – worthy of respect even for an artist. See, for example, the conflict in the soul of Sand, between the third commandment: *Thou shalt not kill*, and what he believed to be the interests of his country.

A mystical enthusiasm for women and love is to be found even in Tacitus, unless his observations on Rome were entirely satirical.[3]

Before one has travelled five hundred leagues in Germany one will notice a fundamental enthusiasm common to that divided, patchwork country, an enthusiasm gentle and tender rather than burning and impetuous.

If this tendency were not clearly apparent one might re-read three or four of the novels of Auguste La Fontaine, who was made Canon

1. See the *Memoirs of the Margravine of Bayreuth*, and *Twenty Years in Berlin*, by M. Thiébaut.

2. See their enthusiasm in 1821 for the tragedy *The Triumph of the Cross*, which thrusts *William Tell* into oblivion.

3. I had the good fortune to meet a man of the most lively intelligence who was not only as learned as ten German scholars, but was able to convey his discoveries in clear and precise terms. If M. F— ever publishes we shall see the Middle Ages unfold brilliantly before our eyes, and shall love the sight.

of Magdeburg by lovely Louisa, Queen of Prussia, in reward for having portrayed *the peaceful life* so well.[1]

Another proof, as I see it, of this tendency common to all Germans is that in Austrian law, for almost all crimes, the guilty party is required to confess before punishment can be carried out. This law has been designed for a people whose crimes are rare, and rather acts of madness in weak beings than the outcome of courageous and reasoned self-interest in perpetual conflict with society. In this the law is precisely the opposite of what is required in Italy, where efforts have been made to introduce it; but the honest folk who do so are in error.

I have seen German judges in despair in Italy because they had to pass sentence of death or its equivalent, shackles for life, without a confession from the guilty.

CHAPTER 49: *A Day in Florence*

Florence, 12th February 1819

IN a box at the theatre this evening I met a man who had some request to make of a fifty-year-old magistrate. The first thing he asked was: 'Who is his mistress? *Chi avvicina adesso?*' Here all these affairs are completely public; they have their own rules, and there is an approved code of conduct based on justice rather than convention, otherwise one is just a *porco*.

'What's the news?' asked one of my friends yesterday on his arrival from Volterra. After some forceful grumbling about Napoleon and the English he was told in tones of the keenest interest, 'La Vitteleschi has changed her lover: poor Gherardesca is in despair.' 'Whom has she taken?' 'Montegalli, that handsome officer with the moustache who was going about with the Principessa Colonna. There he is in the pit, stuck fast below her box; he's there the whole evening, for her husband won't have him in the house. And you can see poor Gherardesca prowling sadly about in the background counting the glances his lost beloved bestows on his successor. He's changed a good deal, and is in the depths of despair; his friends have tried in vain to persuade him to go to Paris or London. He says that even the thought of leaving Florence makes him feel he is dying.'

1. Title of one of the novels of Auguste la Fontaine, *La Vie Paisible*, another important characteristic of the German way of life; it is the Italian *farniente*, the physiological refutation of the Russian *droski* or the English *horseback*.

There are twenty such cases of despair in high society every year, and I have known some to last three or four years. The poor devils are quite shameless and confide in the whole world. In fact there is very little society here, and when one is in love one avoids it almost entirely. It must be remembered that grand passions and noble spirits are uncommon everywhere, even in Italy; only there hearts more ardent and less etiolated by the thousand little worries of vanity find delicious pleasures even in the lesser varieties of love. For instance I have seen far more furious transports and moments of intoxication caused by a caprice there than were ever brought about by the wildest passion in the longitude of Paris.[1]

I noticed tonight that there are exact words in Italian for hundreds of particular situations in the affairs of love which it would require the most laborious periphrases to describe in French; for example, the action of turning away abruptly, when you have been quizzing from the pit the woman you desire, up there in her box, and suddenly the husband or a servant comes forward and looks over the rail.

The following are the principal characteristics of this people.

1. A power of concentration accustomed to serve deep passion is *quite unable* to move quickly to another topic; this is the clearest distinction between the Frenchman and the Italian. You should see an Italian boarding a mail coach or settling a bill; there's *furia francese* for you; and this is why even the most vulgar Frenchman, provided he is not a grinning nincompoop of the Demasure type, will always seem a superior being in the eyes of an Italian woman. (Princess D—'s lover, in Rome.)

2. Everyone makes love, and not in secret as they do in France; the husband is the lover's best friend.

3. Nobody reads anything.

4. There is no society. For a full and interesting life a man does not rely upon the happiness he derives daily from two hours of conversation and a round of vanities at such and such houses. There is no Italian word for *small talk*. You speak when you have something to say in the cause of a passion, and only rarely for the sake of making random conversation.

5. There is no such thing as *ridicule* in Italy.

1. Of that same Paris which gave the world Voltaire, Molière, and so many men noted for their intelligence; but then one can't have everything, and it would certainly not be intelligent to cavil at that.

In France you and I will both try to imitate the same pattern, and I shall be an expert judge of the way you do it.[1] In Italy I have no idea whether the peculiar act which I observe gives any pleasure to the doer, nor whether it would please me if I did it myself.

Language or manners which are affected in Rome are either good form or else quite meaningless in Florence, a mere fifty leagues away. They speak French in Lyon as they do in Nantes. Venetian, Neapolitan, Genoese, and Piedmontese are spoken languages almost entirely distinct from each other, spoken by people who have agreed only to print in a common language, that of Rome. A comedy whose scene is set in Milan but whose characters speak Roman could hardly be more absurd. The Italian language is far more suitable for singing than speaking, and only music can defend it from the French clarity which is invading it.

In Italy the fear of princes and their spies results in a respect for what is *useful* and there is no such thing as foolish honour,[2] which is replaced by a kind of petty social hatred called *pettegolismo*.

And of course to make anyone look ridiculous is to create a mortal enemy – an extremely dangerous practice in a country where the power and function of governments is limited to the extortion of taxes and the punishment of anything unusual.

6. *Antechamber patriotism.*

The kind of pride that leads people to seek the approval of their fellow-citizens and to harmonize with them was driven out of all noble undertakings around 1550 by the jealous despotism of the petty Italian princes, and has given birth to a barbarous offspring, a monster full of wrath and stupidity, a sort of Caliban – *antechamber patriotism*, as M. Turgot called it, apropos *Le Siège de Calais* (the *Soldat Laboureur* of the day). I have seen this monster stupefying the most intelligent people. For instance a foreigner will incur the disapproval even of pretty women if he be ill-advised enough to find fault with the town's poet or painter. He is earnestly informed in no uncertain terms that it is improper to visit people and then to laugh at them, and a remark by Louis XIV about Versailles is quoted at him for good measure.

1. This habit of the French, daily less and less prevalent, will estrange us from Molière's heroes.
2. All breaches of this honour are *ridiculous* in bourgeois circles in France. (See *La Petite Ville* by M. Picard.)

In Florence they say: 'Our Benvenuti', and at Brescia: 'Our Arrici'; they place a certain restrained but nevertheless ludicrous emphasis on the word our, rather like the Miroir talking unctuously about national music, or about M. Monsigny, the European musician.

Before laughing in the faces of these local patriots, remember that as a result of medieval feuds, envenomed by the abominable politics of the Popes,[1] each town is the deadly enemy of its neighbour, and the name of the inhabitants of the latter is regarded by the former as synonymous with any kind of coarseness. The Popes have succeeded in turning this beautiful country into the fatherland of hatred.

This antechamber patriotism is the great moral disease of Italy; a deadly typhus whose evil effects will be felt long after she has thrown off the yoke of her absurd little princes. One of the manifestations of this patriotism is inexorable hatred for anything foreign. Thus they find the Germans foolish, and are angry if one replies: 'Whom did Italy produce in the eighteenth century to equal Catherine II or Frederick the Great? Where can you show me an English garden to compare with the very least of German gardens; you whose climate makes shade a real necessity?'

7. Unlike the English and the French, the Italians have no political prejudice; La Fontaine's line is well-known there:

Votre ennemi c'est votre Maître.

Aristocracy, supported by the church and the Bible societies, is regarded as so much hocus-pocus to be laughed at. Conversely, an Italian has to live three months in France before he realizes to what extent a draper may be an ultra-royalist.

8. The last characteristic I should mention is their intolerance in argument, their anger as soon as they find themselves bereft of a riposte to fling back at their interlocutors. At such a point they go pale with fury. This is one of the forms of extreme sensitiveness, though not the most pleasant; as such, it is one which I am most willing to allow in proof of its existence.

I have always wanted to see undying love, and this evening I succeeded after a good deal of difficulty in being introduced to the Chevalier C. and his mistress, with whom he has lived for the last fifty-four years. I was much moved by these delightful people when

---

1. See the admirable and strange History of the Church by M. de Potter.

I left their box; here really was the art of being happy, an art unknown to so many young people.

Two months ago I saw Monsignor R—, who received me kindly since I had brought him some copies of the *Minerve*. He was at his country house with the Mme D—, whom he *avvicina*, as they say, and has done so for the past thirty-four years. She is still beautiful, but there is an atmosphere of melancholy in their relationship, said to be due to the loss of a son, poisoned long ago by her husband.

Here being in love is not, as it is in Paris, seeing one's mistress a quarter of an hour in a week, and the rest of the time stealing an occasional glance or a squeeze of the hand. The lover, the fortunate lover, passes four or five hours of every day with the woman he loves. He talks to her of his lawsuits, his English garden, his hunting-parties, his career and so on. This is an intimacy of the most complete and tender kind; he addresses her in the second person singular in the presence of her husband, and indeed everywhere.

A young man from this part of the world, extremely ambitious as he thought, was appointed to an important post in Vienna – no less a post than ambassador. He could not bear being parted, resigned after six months, and returned to the happiness of his lover's box at the opera.

This continuous relationship would be inconvenient in France, where society demands that a certain affectation be displayed and where one's mistress can very well say: 'Mr So-and-So, you are moody tonight. *You are not saying a word.*' In Italy, one can always tell the beloved everything that comes into one's head; in fact one has to think aloud. There is a certain state of mind, resulting from intimacy and from frankness responding to frankness, which can only be reached in this way. But there is one great disadvantage; to make love in this fashion paralyses all other interests and takes all the savour out of every other occupation. This kind of love is the best substitute for real passion.

Our Parisian friends, who are still at the stage of wondering *how anyone can be a Persian*, and not knowing what to say, will denounce this way of life as indecent. In the first place I am no more than a historian, and in the second place I intend one day to prove by weighty argument that in the matter of decency there is fundamentally nothing to choose between Bologna and Paris. These people are still quoting their penny catechism without knowing it.

12th July 1821. In Bologna there are no hateful people in society. In Paris a deceived husband is an odious character; here in Bologna he is no such thing: there are no deceived husbands. The way of life in both places is the same except that hatred is lacking; the man who dances attendance on a woman is always a good friend of the husband, and this friendship, cemented by reciprocal acts of service, often out-lasts other interests. Most of these love affairs go on for five or six years; many last for ever. The lovers finally part when they no longer find it sweet to tell each other everything, and after the first month of separation there is no bitterness.

January 1822. The old custom of squiring, introduced into Italy by Philip II, with the pride and manners of Spain, has entirely lapsed in the great cities. The only exception I know is in Calabria where the elder brother always takes holy orders, solemnizes the marriage of his younger brother, becomes the squire of his sister-in-law and at the same time her lover.

Napoleon did away with libertinage in Northern Italy, and even in these parts (Naples).

The way of life of the present generation of pretty women brings a blush to their mothers' cheeks; they are far more well-disposed towards passionate love. Physical love is much less popular than it was.[1]

CHAPTER 50: *Love in the United States*

A FREE government is one which does its citizens no harm, but rather gives them security and tranquillity. But this is a far cry from happiness, which is something man must make for himself; for his would be a coarse spirit who regarded himself as perfectly happy simply because he enjoyed security and tranquillity. We confuse these things in Europe; accustomed as we are to governments which harm us it seems to us that to be delivered from them would be the acme of happiness, much as a sick man might regard deliverance from acute

1. About 1780 the maxim was:

> *Molti averne,*
> *Un goderne,*
> *E cambiar spesso.*
> Sherlock's *Travels.*

pain. The example of America proves the opposite. There the government fulfils its functions as it should, and harms no one. But, as if fate were bent on confounding and disproving all our philosophy, or rather of accusing it of incomplete knowledge of man (removed as we have been for so many centuries, because of the parlous state of Europe, from true experience) we see that the Americans, without the misfortunes created by governments, feel themselves to be lacking in something. It is as though the springs of sensitiveness had dried up in these people; they are just, they are rational, but they are not at all happy. Is the Bible – or rather the absurd conclusions and code of behaviour that peculiar people have culled from that collection of poems and songs – is this enough by itself to have caused so much unhappiness? The effect seems out of all proportion to the cause.

M. de Volney used to relate how, as he once sat at table in the country house of an American, a fine well-to-do man surrounded by his grown-up children, a young man came into the room. 'Good day, William,' said the American. 'Come and sit down. You're looking well.' The traveller asked who the young man was. 'He's my second boy.' 'And where has he come from?' 'Canton.'

The return of his son from the other end of the world caused him no surprise whatsoever.

All their attention seems to be concentrated on a sensible arrangement of the business of living, and on foreseeing all mishaps. When at last they reach the point of harvesting the fruit of so much care and orderly planning, they find they have no life left with which to enjoy.

One might think the descendants of Penn had never read that line which seems to sum up their own history:

Et propter vitam, vivendi perdere causas.

In winter, which as in Russia is the gay season of the year, young people of both sexes ride over the snow in sleighs, day and night; they race fifteen and twenty miles in high spirits and with no supervision, and nothing untoward ever comes of it.

There is the physical gaiety of youth which is soon gone, as the blood cools, and is all over by twenty-five; but I can see no trace of the passions which make for deeper joy. There is such a *habit of reason* in the United States that the crystallization of love there has become impossible.

I admire their kind of happiness but I do not envy it; it is the happiness of beings of a different and inferior species. I have far greater hopes of the Floridas and South America.[1]

What confirms my conjecture about North America is the total absence of artists and writers. The United States have not yet supplied us with so much as a scene of a tragedy, a single picture, or even a life of Washington.

CHAPTER 51: *Love in Provence, before the Conquest of Toulouse by Northern Barbarians in 1328*

LOVE took a strange form in Provence from 1100 to 1328. There was an established code of laws covering the amatory relationships between the two sexes, as severe and as rigidly followed as the laws which cover the *affair of honour* today. The laws of love, in the first place, took no cognizance of the sacred rights of husbands. They presupposed no hypocrisy. Taking human nature exactly as they found it, these laws must have brought about a great deal of happiness.

There was an official way of declaring that you were in love with a woman and of being accepted as her lover. After so many months of a certain kind of courtship it was permitted to kiss her hand. Society, still young, delighted in formalities and ceremonies which were then a mark of civilization, and which nowadays would bore us to extinction. The same characteristic occurs in the language of the Provençals, in the complexity and interlacement of their rhymes, in their use of masculine and feminine words for the same object, and finally in the infinite number of their poets. Everything *formal* in society, nowadays so insipid, had at that time all the freshness and tang of novelty.

When one had kissed a woman's hand one graduated from stage to stage by merit alone, with no preferment. It should be noted that although husbands were entirely out of the picture the official promotion of lovers did not go beyond what we might call the delights of the most tender friendship between persons of opposite sex.[2] However,

1. See the customs of the Azores: time is fully occupied there by the love of God and the other kind of love. The Christian religion as interpreted by the Jesuits is far less the enemy of mankind in this context than is English Protestantism; it does at least allow dancing on Sundays, and one day of pleasure means a great deal to the labourer who works hard on the six others.

2. Memoirs of the life of Chabanon, written by himself. Knocking on the ceiling with a walking-stick.

after many months or years of trial, when a woman was perfectly sure of the character and discretion of a man, and when that man had all the privileges and outward signs of the tenderest friendship with her, such a friendship must have been a very serious threat to virtue.

I have talked of preferment; a woman might have several lovers, but only one in the higher grades. It would appear that the others could not be promoted much beyond the degree of friendship that allowed them to kiss her hand and see her every day. All that remains to us of this civilization is in verse, verse rhymed in the oddest and most obscure way. It is therefore hardly surprising that the notions we draw from the ballads of the troubadours are vague and inaccurate. Even a marriage contract has been found in verse. After the conquest in 1328 the Popes several times ordered that everything written in the vernacular should be burnt as heretical. Italian shrewdness proclaimed Latin as the only language good enough for such clever people. It would be a most useful measure if we could enforce it again in 1822.

So much publicity and formalism seem at first sight to be little in keeping with genuine passion. If the lady said to her courtier: 'For my love's sake, go and visit the Sepulchre of Our Lord Jesus Christ in Jerusalem. Stay there three years and then return to me,' the lover would depart instantly. A moment's hesitation would be as ignominious as weakness in an affair of honour in our own day. The language of these people has a subtlety delicate enough to define the most fleeting shades of feeling. There is another indication that this way of life was well along the road to true civilization: they were but a step from the horrors of the Middle Ages and of feudalism, where force reigned supreme, yet the weaker sex were less oppressed then than they *legally* are today. The poor weak creatures who have most to lose in love and whose charms soon vanish held in their hands the destinies of the men around them. A three-year exile in Palestine, the transition from the gaiety of civilization to the fanaticism and boredom of a crusaders' camp, must have been a very severe ordeal for all but the most fervent of Christians. But what recourse has a woman against a cowardly lover who abandons her in Paris?

To my way of thinking there is only one answer; no self-respecting woman in Paris takes a lover. Clearly prudence is far more justified nowadays in counselling women against a surrender to passionate love. But does not another prudence (one which I am certainly far from condoning) advise them to revenge themselves through physical love? With our hypocrisy and asceticism[1] we have succeeded, not in paying tribute to virtue (you cannot fly in the face of nature with impunity), but merely in lessening the amount of happiness in the world and almost completely disposing of generous impulses.

When a lover abandoned his poor mistress after ten years of intimacy because he realized she was thirty-two, his honour was lost in fair Provence; there was nothing for it but to bury himself in the solitude of a monastery. Not generosity, but simple prudence, dictated that one should not affect more passion than was really felt.

All this is guesswork, because very few documents remain to give us precise information . . .

The whole pattern of life must be inferred from a few special cases. You know the story of the poet who had offended his lady: after he had been in despair for two years she deigned at last to reply to his numerous appeals, and conveyed to him that he should pull out one of his fingernails and send it to her by fifty lovelorn faithful knights, whereupon she might perhaps forgive him. The poet hastened to undergo this painful operation. Fifty knights wearing their ladies' favours took the fingernail and presented it with all possible solemnity to the offended fair one. It was as imposing a ceremony as that of a prince of the blood entering one of his royal cities. The lover in the garb of repentance followed his fingernail at a distance. The lady, having seen the exceedingly long ceremony to its conclusion, condescended to forgive him and he was reinstated to all the delights of his former happiness. The story goes on to relate that they spent many long and happy years together. Undoubtedly those two years of unhappiness proved that the passion was true, and they would have engendered it if it had not existed so strongly in the first place.

I might quote twenty anecdotes showing the ubiquitous existence of a charming, witty gallantry conducted between the sexes on the principles of justice; I say gallantry because passionate love has always been rather the infrequent and curious exception than the rule, nor will it conform to any rules. Whatever is in essence calculated and rational was, in Provence, based on justice and the equality of rights for the two sexes, and this is what I chiefly admire, in that it tended as far as possible to banish misfortune. Absolute monarchy under

1. Ascetic Principle of Jeremy Bentham.

Louis XV, on the other hand, succeeded in making wickedness and blackheartedness fashionable on the same terms.[1]

Although this attractive Provençal language, so rich in subtleties and so convoluted with rhyme,[2] was probably not that of the common people, the way of life of the upper class had percolated down the social scale to the lower classes, among whom very little coarseness was apparent in those days, for they were very well-to-do. They were enjoying the initial stages of a rich and flourishing prosperity. The people along the Mediterranean coastline had realized (in the ninth century) that the business of risking a few ships on these waters was less arduous and almost as amusing as robbing travellers on the neighbouring highways, in the service of some petty feudal lord. A little later the tenth century Provençals learned from the Arabs that there were sweeter pleasures in life than pillage, rape, and battle.

The Mediterranean must be regarded as the cradle of European civilization. The happy shores of this beautiful sea, blessed by a favourable climate, were doubly so because of the prosperity of the inhabitants, and the absence of all gloomy legislation or religion. The essentially cheerful genius of the Provençals in those days had weathered the Christian religion unscathed.

We get a vivid picture of a similar effect resulting from the same cause, in the Italian cities whose history has come down to us more clearly, and who besides have been fortunate enough to bequeath us Dante, Petrarch, and painting.

The Provençals have left us no great poem like the *Divine Comedy*, reflecting every detail of the way of life of the period. They had, I think, less passion and more cheerfulness than the Italians. They owed this agreeable approach to life to their neighbours the Moors of Spain. In the castles of fortunate Provence love held sway, with merry-making, feasts, and frolic.

At the Opéra, have you ever witnessed the finale of one of Rossini's fine comic operas? The stage is gay, beautiful, magnificently perfect. We are a thousand leagues removed from the uglier side of human nature. The opera ends, the curtain falls, the audience rises to leave, the chandelier goes up, the footlights are put out. A smell of clumsily-

1. One ought to have heard the conversation of the delightful General Laclos, Naples, 1802. If one has not been lucky enough to do so, one can refer to *La Vie Privée du Maréchal de Richelieu*, in nine very pleasantly-written volumes.

2. Born at Narbonne; a mixture of Latin and Arabic.

snuffed lamps pervades the house, and the curtain is half run up again only to reveal ragged urchins running about the stage, gesticulating horribly in the very places occupied a moment earlier by graceful young women.

Such was the effect upon the kingdom of Provence when Toulouse was conquered by the Crusaders. Instead of love, graces, and gaiety, there came the Northern barbarians and St Dominic. I will not blacken these pages with the hair-raising account of the horrors of the Inquisition in all its first fanatical heyday. As for the barbarians, they were our forefathers; they murdered, sacked, and destroyed, for the sheer pleasure of it, whatever they could not loot; a savage fury goaded them to attack everything which bore the stamp of civilization; above all they understood not one word of the lovely language of the Midi, which redoubled their rage. Highly superstitious, and guided by the fearsome St Dominic, they thought they were winning their place in Heaven by killing Provençals. For the latter it was the end – love, gaiety, and poetry were all gone; less than twenty years after the conquest (1335) they were almost as coarse and barbarous as the French[1] our forefathers.

Whence came this delightful form of civilization that brought two centuries of happiness to the upper classes of society in this corner of the world? Apparently from the Moors of Spain.

CHAPTER 52: *Provence in the Twelfth Century*

I AM going to translate a story from a Provençal manuscript. The action of it took place about 1180 and the story was written about 1250;[2] the anecdote is no doubt hackneyed but the essence of the way of life is in its style. I beg to be allowed to translate literally, without any attempt at modern elegance of language.

'My lord Raymond de Roussillon, as you will know, was a valiant baron, and had for wife Madona Marguerite, the fairest woman in the land at that time, and the most gifted with all fine qualities, all

---

1. See *The State of Military Power in Russia*, an authentic work by General Sir Robert Wilson.

2. The manuscript is in the Laurentiana library. Monsieur Raynouard gives an account of it in Volume V of his *Troubadours*, p. 189. There are several mistakes in his text; he gave the troubadours too much praise and too little study.

worthiness, and all graciousness. It so happened that Guillaume de
Cabstaing, the son of a poor knight of the château Cabstaing, came
to the court of my lord Raymond de Roussillon, appeared before him,
and begged, an it pleased my lord, that he might become a varlet of
his court. My lord Raymond, observing him handsome and comely,
bade him welcome and bid him stay at his court. So Guillaume stayed
with him and acquitted himself so well that he was beloved by young
and old alike, and so excelled that my lord Raymond would have him
page to Madona Marguerite his wife, and this was done. At this
Guillaume strove to be yet worthier in words and deeds. But as it is
wont to happen in love, it came to pass that love would have seized
Madona Marguerite, kindling her thoughts. So pleased was she by
the deeds of Guillaume, by his words and by his seeming, that she
must needs say to him one day: "Now tell me, Guillaume, if a woman
made as though to love thee wouldst thou dare love her?" Guillaume,
who had perceived the whole matter, answered her openly:"Aye,
indeed I should, Madame, only provided her pretence were true."
"By St John," quoth the lady, "thou hast replied well, as an honest
man should; but now I would put thee to the test, whether indeed
thou dost know and recognize which pretences are true, and which
not." When Guillaume heard these words, he replied: "Madame, let
it be according to your wish."

'He grew thoughtful, and Love straightway joined battle with
him; and the thoughts Love sends into its own folk entered deeply
into his heart, and from thenceforth he became a liegeman of love
and took to fashioning[1] pretty, gay little couplets, songs for dancing
and songs for singing;[2] and for this he was much admired, not least
by the lady for whom he sang. Now Love, that rewards its servants
when it pleases, wished to give Guillaume his own reward; whereupon it besieged the lady so sorely with thoughts and reflections of
love that she could rest neither by day nor night, for thinking of the
worth and prowess wherewith Guillaume was so greatly filled.

'It happened one day that the lady took Guillaume aside and said
to him: "Now tell me, Guillaume, hast thou now discovered if my
pretences be true or false?" And Guillaume replied: "Madona, so God
help me, from the first moment I became your servant no thought has
entered my head but that you are the best that ever was born, and the
truest in words and seeming. This I believe, and shall believe all my

1. 'Finding'.   2. He invented both music and words.

life." And the lady answered: "Guillaume, I tell you that if God helps me you never shall be deceived by me, nor shall your thoughts be wasted or in vain." And she held out her arms, and sweetly kissed him in that room where they were both sitting, and so they began their dalliance;[1] and it was not long before evil tongues – on whom may God's wrath fall – began to wag and chatter of their love, by reason of the songs Guillaume made, saying his love was for the Lady Marguerite; and round and about they wagged so much that the thing came to the ears of my lord Raymond. At this he was much troubled, and grievously cast down, first that he must needs lose his companion squire, and still more for his lady's shame.

'It happened one day that Guillaume was out hawking with but one squire, and my lord Raymond enquired where he was; a man-servant replied that he was gone hawking, and another who knew added that he was in a certain place. Raymond at once ordered his horse to be brought, and bearing his arms concealed, rode alone to the place where Guillaume was, and rode about till he found him. When Guillaume saw him approach he was much surprised, and was straightway filled with foreboding. He went to meet him, saying:

' "Welcome, my lord. How is it that you are thus alone?"

'My lord Raymond replied: "I came seeking you that I might amuse myself in your company. Have you taken aught?"

' "I have taken little, my lord, for I have found little; and who finds little takes little, as the proverb tells."

' "Let us carry that conversation no further," said my lord Raymond, "but by the faith you owe me, speak to me truly of all I would ask you."

' "By the Lord," said Guillaume, "anything that can be told I shall tell you gladly."

' "I want no riddles," replied my lord Raymond, "but that you should tell me the whole truth of anything I ask you."

' "My lord, as much as you shall please to ask, that I shall tell you truly."

'Then my lord Raymond enquired: "Guillaume, as you value God and Holy Faith, have you a mistress for whom you sing or for whom Love has you in thrall?"

'And Guillaume replied: "Ah, my lord, how could I sing if I were not urged by love? Know the truth, that love has me all in its power."

1. *A far all'amore.*

' "I well believe it," answered Raymond, "else you could not sing so well, but I would know, if you please, the name of your lady."

"Oh, my lord, in the name of God," said Guillaume, "what is it you ask of me? Well you know that a man must not name his lady, and that Bernard de Ventadour says:

> In one thing my reason serves me:[1]
> Never man has asked me my delight
> But I have purposely replied him false.
> To me it seems no proper doctrine,
> But rather folly or a childish act,
> That he who is well treated in his love
> Should to another man confide his heart
> Unless that man can help and serve him.'

'And my lord Raymond replied: "I give you my oath that I shall serve you according to my power."

'This he repeated so often that Guillaume said: "My lord, you must know that I love the sister of my lady Marguerite your wife and think to be loved in return. Now that you know this I beg you will help me, or at least do me no hindrance."

' "Here is my hand upon it," cried Raymond, "for I swear and engage to you that I shall do all that lies in my power for you." And so he gave him his pledge, and when he had given it he said:

' "Let us go to her castle, for it is not far off."

' "With all my heart," said Guillaume, and so they made their way to the chateau of Liet where they were well received by En Robert of Tarascon,[2] who was the husband of the lady Agnes, sister of the lady Marguerite; and also by the lady Agnes herself. And my lord Raymond took lady Agnes by the hand and led her into the bedchamber, and sat with her upon the bed. And my lord Raymond said: "Now tell me, sister-in-law, by the faith you owe me, do you love with a true love?"

' "Aye, my lord," replied she.

' "And whom?" he asked.

' "Oh, I cannot tell you that," she answered, "and how can you talk to me so?"

'In the end he so pressed her, that she said she loved Guillaume de

---

1. Translated word for word from the Provençal verses quoted by Guillaume.

2. *En*, a customary form of address among the Provençals, which we should tender as *Sire*.

Cabstaing; she said this because she saw Guillaume sad and thoughtful, and well knew how he loved her sister, and so she feared lest
Raymond have evil intent towards Guillaume. Such a reply brought
great joy to the heart of Raymond. Agnes related all to her husband,
and the husband said she had done right, and gave her his word that
she might do or say all she could to save Guillaume. Agnes did not
fail to do so. She called Guillaume to her chamber alone, and stayed
so long with him that Raymond believed he must have had love's
pleasure of her; and all this pleased him, and he began to think that
what he had been told of him was untrue, and mere idle talk. Agnes
and Guillaume came out of the chamber, supper was made ready, and
they supped with good cheer. And after supper Agnes had beds for
her two guests made ready outside her chamber, and so well did the
lady and Guillaume carry on from pretence to pretence, that Raymond
believed he had lain with her all night.

'And the day after they dined at the castle with great rejoicing, and
after dinner departed with all the honours of a noble farewell, and so
came to Roussillon. And as soon as it could be done, Raymond left
Guillaume and came to his wife, and told her what he had seen of
Guillaume and her sister, at which his wife sorrowed greatly the
whole night through. And the next day she sent for Guillaume, and
received him coldly, and called him false friend and traitor. And
Guillaume begged her mercy, as a man faultless in that wherewith she
accused him, and told her all that had passed, word for word. And
the woman sent for her sister, and learned of her that Guillaume
spoke the truth. And for this she commanded him to make her a song
that should show he loved no woman but her, and so he made the
song that says:

> That sweet thought
> Which love oft sends me.

And when Raymond of Roussillon heard the song that Guillaume
had made for his wife, he made him come and talk to him far from the
castle, and cut off his head, and put it in a game-bag; he took the heart
from his body and put it with the head. He returned to the castle, and
had the heart roasted and brought to his wife at table, and made her
eat it unawares. When she had eaten it Raymond arose and told his
wife that what she had just eaten was the heart of lord Guillaume de
Cabstaing, and he showed her the head and asked if the heart had

been good to eat. And she heard what he said, and saw and recognized the head of lord Guillaume. She replied that the heart had tasted so good that neither food nor drink should ever drive from her mouth the taste that lord Guillaume's heart had left there. And Raymond ran at her with his sword. She ran away from him, threw herself from a balcony and broke her neck.

'This became known through all Catalonia and throughout the lands of the king of Aragon. King Alphonso and all the barons of that country sorrowed greatly at the deaths of lord Guillaume and of the woman whom Raymond had put to death in so ugly a fashion. They made war on him with fire and sword, and King Alphonso, having seized Raymond's castle, had Guillaume and his lady placed in a monument before the church door of a burgh called Perpignac. All perfect lovers prayed to God for their souls. The king of Aragon took Raymond, put him to death, and gave all his wealth to the parents of Guillaume and the parents of the woman who died for him.'

CHAPTER 53: *Arabia*

IT is beneath the sombre tent of the Bedouin Arab that we must seek the model and the homeland of true love. There, as elsewhere, solitude and a fine climate have brought forth the most noble of all the passions of the human heart, that which can only find happiness by inspiring it as ardently as it feels it.

For love to assume its full stature in the heart of man, it was necessary that the greatest possible equality should be established between the mistress and her lover. In our miserable West there is none of this equality; a jilted woman is either wretched or dishonoured. In an Arab's tent a pledge once given can *never* be broken. Contempt and death are the immediate reward of such a crime.

Generosity is so sacred among these people that they are allowed to *steal* in order to give. Besides, danger is ever-present and life is spent in what might be called a passionate solitude. Even in their gatherings the Arabs speak but little.

For the dweller in the desert nothing changes; everything is eternal and motionless. Their curious customs, which for lack of knowledge I can but faintly outline, probably existed in Homer's day.[1] They were

1. 900 B.C.

described for the first time in about the six hundredth year of our era, two centuries before Charlemagne.

Clearly it is we who were the barbarians when we went to harass the East with our crusades.[1] What is more, we owe what is noble in our own way of life to these crusades and to the Moors of Spain.

When we compare ourselves with the Arabs, proud and prosaic people smile pityingly. Our fine arts are greatly superior to theirs, and our legislations apparently even more so; but I doubt whether we can hold a candle to them in the art of domestic happiness, for we have always lacked good faith and simplicity, and in family relationships the deceiver is the first to suffer. There can be no refuge for him; being always a lawbreaker, he is always afraid.

At the period when the most ancient historical works were written we find the Arabs already divided from time immemorial into a great number of independent tribes wandering in the desert. Their ways of life were more or less elegant according to the ease with which each tribe could obtain the prime necessities of mankind. Their generosity was the same everywhere, but showed itself according to the wealth of the tribe either by the gift of a loin of kid for mere subsistence, or by the gift of a hundred camels on some family or hospitable occasion.

The heroic century of the Arabs, in which those generous spirits shone free from all affectation of wit or refinement, was the one which preceded Mohammed and which corresponds with our fifth century, with the foundation of Venice, and with the reign of Clovis. Let the proud among us consider the love-songs left us by the Arabs, and the noble way of life reflected in *The Thousand and One Nights*, compared with the bloody and disgusting horrors which sully every page of Grégoire de Tours, the historian of Clovis, or those of Eginhard, the historian of Charlemagne.

Mohammed was a *puritan*, who sought to proscribe pleasures which harm nobody; he disposed of love in those countries which embraced Islam,[2] and this is why his religion has always been less practised in Arabia, its birthplace, than in all other Mohammedan countries.

The French brought from Egypt four folio volumes entitled *The Book of Songs*. These volumes contain:

1. The biographies of the poets who wrote the songs.

1. 1095.
2. Way of life in Constantinople. The only way to destroy passionate love is to prevent all crystallization by making love easy.

2. The songs themselves. The poet sings of all that interests him. He praises his swift steed and his bow after he has spoken of his mistress. The songs were often the love-letters of their authors, and offered the beloved a faithful picture of all that the author held dear. Sometimes they speak of nights so cold that they were obliged to burn their bows and arrows. The Arabs are a nation without houses.

3. The biographies of the musicians who set the songs to music.

4. A key to the musical notation. To us this is mere hieroglyphics, for the music is lost to us for ever and, besides, would give us no pleasure.

There is another collection called *History of the Arabs who died of love*.

These strange books are very little known, and the few scholars who could read them have had their hearts desiccated by study and academic pursuits.

To help us find our bearings amid these old works, whose interest lies in their antiquity and in the singular beauty of the way of life they reveal, we must examine a few historical facts.

In all times, but particularly before Mohammed, Arabs have been going to Mecca to walk around the *Kaaba*, or House of Abraham. In London I saw a remarkably accurate model of the holy city. There are seven or eight hundred flat-roofed houses set down in the middle of a sun-scorched desert. At one end of the city is an immense structure roughly in the form of a square; this structure surrounds the Kaaba and consists of a long series of arcades to shelter from the Arabian sun those who make the sacred circuit. These arcades play a great part in the history of Arabian customs and poetry; for centuries they were apparently the only place where men and women were ever in each other's company. They walked slowly round the Kaaba, mingling together, chorally reciting sacred poems; the whole circuit took about three quarters of an hour and was repeated several times a day; and this was the sacred rite for which men and women foregathered from every corner of the desert. It was beneath the arcades of the Kaaba that Arabian customs acquired polish. A conflict soon developed between fathers and lovers; and the love-song quickly became the means by which an Arab revealed his passion to a girl jealously guarded by brothers or father, as they walked together round the sacred circuit. The generous and sentimental habits of these people already existed in their camps, but in my opinion Arab gallantry first came into being around the Kaaba; it was also the birthplace of their literature, which at first expressed passion simply and vehemently as poets felt it. Later a poet, instead of trying to touch the heart of his beloved, thought of writing fine things for their own sake, and thus began the affectedness which the Moors imported into Spain and which even today spoils the books of this people.[1]

I see in their convention for divorce a touching proof of the Arabs' respect for the weaker sex. During the absence of the husband from whom she wished to separate, a wife would strike the tent and then put it up again, taking care that the opening should be on the side opposite where it was before. This simple ceremony separated husband from wife for ever.

FRAGMENTS

Selected & Translated
From an Arabic Collection
entitled
THE DIVAN OF LOVE
compiled by Ben-Abi-Hasdglat
(*Manuscripts from the Bibliothèque du Roi nos. 1461 & 1462*)

Mohammed, son of Jaafar Flawazadi, relates that when Jamil was sick of the sickness of which he died, Elabas, son of Sohail, visited him and found him about to give up the ghost. 'O son of Sohail,' said Jamil, 'what thinkest thou of a man who never drank wine, nor gained aught unlawfully, nor inflicted death upon any living creature whose killing is forbidden by God; one who bears witness that there is no god but God, and Mohammed is his prophet?' 'I think,' replied Ben Sohail, 'that such a man would be saved, and attain to Paradise – but of what man dost thou speak?' 'It is myself,' replied Jamil. Then Ben Sohail said: 'I did not think that thou hadst embraced Islam; besides, for twenty years thou hast made love to Bothaina, praising her in thy verses.' 'I am now at the beginning of the other world,' replied Jamil, 'and at the end of my days in this world; and I desire

---

1. There are a great many Arabic manuscripts in Paris. Those of later date are affected, but never seek to imitate the Greeks or Romans; this is why they are despised by scholars.

that the mercy of our master Mohammed shall not shelter me at the day of judgment if ever I laid a hand upon Bothaina with any improper intent.'

This Jamil and Bothaina his mistress both belonged to the Benou-Azra, a tribe famous for love throughout all the tribes of Arabia. Their way of loving has become a byword, for God never made other creatures who loved so tenderly.

Said, son of Agba, asked an Arab one day: 'What is thy people?' 'I belong to the people who die for love,' answered the Arab. 'So thou art of the tribe of Azra?' pursued Said. 'Even so, by the Master of the Kaaba,' replied the Arab. 'How is it that you love in this fashion?' asked Said. 'Our women are beautiful, and our young men chaste,' answered the Arab.

One day someone asked Arwa-Ben-Hezam:[1] 'Is it true, as people say, that among all men yours have the tenderest hearts when in love?' 'By Allah, that is true,' replied Arwa, 'and I have seen thirty young men of my tribe carried off by death, whose only sickness was that they were in love.'

An Arab of the Benou-Fazarat said one day to one of the Benou-Azra: 'You Benou-Azra think that to die of love is a sweet and noble death, but that is clearly weakness and stupidity; and those whom you regard as great-hearted are no more than senseless weaklings.' 'You would not say so,' replied the Arab of the tribe of Azra, 'if you had seen our women with their great dark eyes flashing half-hidden beneath their long lashes, if you had seen them smile, and the shine of their teeth between brown lips.'

Abou-el-Hassan Ali, the son of Abdulla Elzagouni, relates the following: A mussulman who loved a Christian girl to distraction was obliged to make a journey to a foreign land with a friend who shared the secret of his love. His business kept him abroad for a long time and he was stricken with a mortal illness, whereupon he told his friend: 'Now my end is near, and I shall never again in this world set eyes on the woman I love; indeed I fear that if I die a mussulman I shall never meet her in the next life either.' He became a Christian, and died. His friend sought out the young Christian woman and found her ill. And she said to him: 'I shall never see my loved one

1. This Arwa–Ben–Hezam belonged to the Azra tribe of which mention has already been made. He is famous as a poet, and still more famous as one of the many martyrs to love whom the Arabs claim.

again in this world but I would fain be with him in the next; so now I testify that there is no god but God, and Mohammed is his prophet.' With that she died, and may God have mercy on her soul.*

Eltemini relates that in the Arab tribe of Tagleb there was a wealthy Christian girl who loved a young mussulman. She offered him her fortune and all that was precious to her, yet could not succeed in winning his love. When she had given up all hope, she gave a hundred dinars to an artist who made for her a statue of the young man she loved. When the girl had the statue she put it in a place which she visited daily. There she would begin by kissing the statue and would then sit down beside it and spend the rest of the day in tears. When evening came she would bid the statue goodnight and depart. This went on for a long time until a day came when the young man died. She wished to see his dead body and to kiss it; after this she returned to her statue, greeted it, kissed it as usual and lay down beside it. When morning came she was found there, dead, her hand stretched towards some lines she had written before she died.*

Weddah, from the Yemen, was famous among the Arabs for his beauty. He and Om-el-Bonain, daughter of Abd-el-Aziz son of Merwan, loved each other so much even as children that they could not bear to be separated from one another for a moment. When Om-el-Bonain became the wife of Walid-Ben-Abd-el-Malek, Weddah lost his reason. After a long period of grief and frenzy he made his way to Syria and began to prowl around the dwelling of Walid, son of Malek, without at first discovering a means of reaching his heart's desire. In the end he scraped acquaintance with a girl whose devotion he cultivated by dint of much perseverance. When he thought he could trust her he asked if she knew Om-el-Bonain. 'Of course I do, since she is my mistress,' replied the girl. 'Well,' said Weddah, 'thy mistress is my cousin, and if thou wilt take her news of me she will certainly be pleased.' 'That I will gladly do,' answered the girl, and ran straight to Om-el-Bonain to give her news of Weddah. 'Watch thy words, girl,' cried her mistress, 'Sayest thou that Weddah is alive?' 'Certainly he is,' said the girl. 'Go then and tell him,' ordered Om-el-Bonain, 'that he must not depart before he receives a messenger from me.' At once she took steps to have Weddah smuggled into her apartments, where she kept him hidden in a chest. She allowed him emerge from this, to be with him when she believed it was safe; when someone came who might have seen him she made him go back into the chest.

It happened one day that a pearl was brought to Walid, and he ordered one of his servants to carry the pearl to Om-el-Bonain. The servant took the pearl and without waiting to be announced brought it to Om-el-Bonain at a time when she was with Weddah, so that the servant was able to glance into Om-el-Bonain's private room in an unguarded moment. Walid's servant accomplished his errand and begged Om-el-Bonain for something in return for the jewel he had brought her. She refused him sternly and scolded him. Bitter against her the servant withdrew and, going to Walid, he described the chest into which he had seen Weddah climb. 'Thou liest, thou motherless slave, thou liest!' shouted Walid and ran instantly to Om-el-Bonain. There were several chests in her rooms, and he sat down on the one described by the slave, saying to Om-el-Bonain 'Give me one of these chests.' 'They are all thine, as I am myself,' replied Om-el-Bonain. 'Well,' said Walid, 'I wish to have the one on which I am sitting.' 'That one is full of the things that a woman requires,' said Om-el-Bonain. 'I am not concerned with what is in it,' continued Walid, 'it is the chest that I want.' 'It is thine,' she replied. Immediately Walid had the chest taken out, and called two slaves whom he ordered to dig a trench in the ground to a depth where they should find water. Putting his mouth close to the chest he shouted: 'I have been told something of thee. If I have been told the truth may all trace of thee be banished, and all news of thee buried. If what I have heard be untrue I do no harm by burying a box – it is but a piece of wood.' He then had the chest thrust down into the pit and covered with the earth and stones which had been dug out. From that day Om-el-Bonain was seldom far from the spot, weeping, and it was not long before she was found there lifeless, with her face to the ground.*[1]

1. These fragments are drawn from various chapters of the collection in question. The three marked * are taken from the last chapter which consists of numerous very brief biographies of Arabs who were martyrs to love.

CHAPTER 54: *Concerning the Education of Women*

THE present system of education for girls, which is the fruit of chance and the most idiotic pride, leaves idle their most brilliant faculties, those which hold the richest promise of happiness both for themselves and for us. But where is the man of prudence who has not cried at least once in his life:

> *Une femme en sait toujours assez,*
> *Quand la capacité de son espirit se hausse*
> *A connaître un pourpoint d'avec un haut-de-chausse.*
> Les Femmes Savantes, *Act II, Scene VII.*

In Paris the highest praise for an eligible girl is that 'she has a very gentle nature', and stupid suitors, like sheep, are always greatly impressed by this phrase. Look at them two years later, hat on head, lunching alone with their wives on a dull day, with three tall lackeys standing in the background.

In 1818 a law was enacted in the United States by which any man who taught a Virginian negro to read was liable to receive thirty-four lashes.[1] Nothing could be more logical and reasonable than this law.

Were the United States of America themselves more useful to the mother country as her slaves, or since they have become her equals? If the labour of a free man costs two or three times as much as that of the same man reduced to slavery, why should the same not be true of that man's thoughts?

If we dared we should educate our girls like slaves, and the proof is that the only useful things they know are those we do not wish to teach them.

'But these scraps of education they pick up by mischance, they turn against us,' may argue some husbands. Precisely; and Napoleon too was right to withhold arms from the National Guard, and the ultra-royalists are also right when they forbid Mutual Instruction. Give a man arms and then continue to oppress him, and you will find him perverse enough to turn these arms against you when he has the chance.

Even if we were legally permitted to bring up our girls as idiots,

1. I am sorry I cannot find the official source of this fact in the Italian manuscripts. I hope it can be denied.

with *Ave Marias* and lewd songs as in the convents in 1770, there would still be one or two minor objections:

1. In the case of a husband's death they are required to assume control of the family.

2. As mothers they provide their male children, the young tyrants of the future, with the initial education which forms their characters and gives them a bent to seek happiness in one way rather than another, a matter which is always decided by the age of four or five.

3. For all our arrogant pride, in all those little domestic matters on which our happiness depends, since when passions are lacking happiness is based on the absence of little everyday vexations, the advice of our life's indispensable companion exerts a very great influence, not because we want to let her influence us in the least, but because she repeats the same things for twenty years on end; and where is the man of such Roman mettle that he can resist the same idea reiterated throughout a lifetime? The world is full of easily-led husbands, not because they have any feelings of justice or equality, but because they are weak. Since men will grant things under duress there is always a temptation to be over-insistent, and it is sometimes necessary to be over-insistent in order to protect one's gains.

4. Lastly, as to love, during that period which in Southern climes often lasts twelve or fifteen years – the best years in life – our whole happiness lies in the hands of the woman we love. One moment of misplaced pride can make us unhappy for ever; and if a slave be put upon the throne he can hardly be expected not to abuse his power. This is the origin of false delicacy and feminine pride. My pleadings could hardly be more futile; men are *despots*, and look how much notice other despots take of the most reasonable advice. The man with limitless power heeds only one kind of advice, that which teaches him to extend that power. Where shall girls find themselves a Quiroga or a Riego to give advice to the despots who oppress them, and degrade them only to oppress them further – salutary advice which would earn honours and decorations instead of the gallows which was Porlier's fate?

Such a revolution would only take place over several centuries, because by extremely bad luck all the early experiments would be bound to suggest the opposite of the true facts. Enlighten a girl, shape her character, give her, in fact, a good education in the true sense of the words, and sooner or later she will perceive her superiority over other women and become a prig, the most unpleasant and degraded creature in the world. Not one of us but would prefer a servant rather than a blue-stocking as a life companion.

Plant a young tree in the middle of a thick forest and, deprived of air and light by its neighbours, itsl eaves will be etiolated; it will grow spindly and ridiculous, developing *unnaturally*. The whole forest must be planted at the same time; it is hardly an occasion for pride that a woman should know how to read.

For two thousand years pedants have been telling us that women have quicker wits and men more staunchness; that women have subtler ideas and men more power of concentration. A Parisian who used to go gaping round the gardens of Versailles concluded from what he saw that all trees grow clipped.

I will grant that little girls are less strong physically than little boys; and clearly this must hold good for their intelligence too, since as everyone knows Voltaire and d'Alembert were in their time the chief exponents of the art of fisticuffs. It is generally admitted that a little girl of ten is twenty times as clever as a young hooligan of the same age. Why is it that by the age of twenty she has become a great dolt, gauche, shy, and frightened of spiders, while the little hooligan is then a man of intelligence?

Women only know what we do not wish to teach them, in fact what they learn from experience of life. It is therefore a great disadvantage for them to be born into very wealthy families; instead of mixing with people who behave *naturally* towards them they find themselves surrounded with chambermaids and lady companions who are already corrupted and spoilt by riches.[1] There is no fool like a prince.

Sensing their bondage, girls have their eyes open very early; they see everything but are too ignorant to perceive it correctly. A woman of thirty in France has not the acquired knowledge of a boy of fifteen, nor a woman of fifty the logic of a man of twenty-five. Look at Mme de Sévigné admiring Louis XIV's most ridiculous behaviour. Look at the childish arguments used by Mme d'Epinay.[2]

Women must feed and care for their children: I deny the first statement and grant the second. *They must also keep control of their cook's accounts*: therefore they have no time to be the equals of little boys of fifteen in

1. *Memoirs* of Madame de Staal, Collé, Duclos, the Margravine of Bayreuth.
2. First volume.

terms of acquired knowledge. Men have to be judges, bankers, barristers, merchants, doctors, priests, and so forth. Yet they can still find time to read Fox's speeches and the *Lusiade* of Camoëns.

In Peking, the magistrate who runs early to the Palace to find an excuse for imprisoning and ruining (with the most honourable intentions) a poor journalist who has offended the Under-Secretary with whom he had the honour to dine the night before, is certainly just as busy as his wife who checks her cook's accounts, teaches her little girl to knit a stocking, watches her at her dancing-class and piano lesson, entertains the parish priest who brings her the *Quotidienne*, then goes to choose a hat in the Rue de Richelieu and take a walk in the Tuileries.

In the midst of his noble pursuits the magistrate still finds time to think about that walk his wife is taking in the Tuileries, and if he were on as good terms with the power that rules the universe as he is with the one which rules the State, he would entreat heaven to grant women, for their own good, eight or ten more hours of sleep a day. In the present state of society, leisure, which for men is the source of all happiness and all wealth, is not only a disadvantage for a woman but is one of those ill-starred freedoms from which the worthy magistrate would gladly help to deliver us.

CHAPTER 55: *Objections to Education for Women*

B^UT *women are responsible for the small household tasks* – My Colonel, M. S—, has four daughters brought up in the best traditions, which is to say that they work all day; when I arrive they are singing some music by Rossini which I brought them from Naples; besides this they read the Royaumont Bible, study the stupidities of history, learning chronological tables and the verses of Le Ragois; they know a good deal of geography and execute admirable embroidery. I calculate that each of these pretty little girls could earn by her labours some eight sous a day. For three hundred days that makes four hundred and eighty francs a year: less than the salary of one of their tutors. For four hundred and eighty francs a year they fritter away for ever the time allotted to the human machine for gathering ideas.

If women are to take pleasure in reading the ten or twelve good books annually published in Europe, they will soon cease to look after their children.

– This is as if we feared that by planting trees along the shores of the ocean we should arrest the movement of the waves. This is not the way in which education is all-powerful. Besides, for the last four hundred years the same argument has been used against education of all kinds. Not only has a Parisian woman more virtues in 1820 than in 1720, in the days of Law's system and of the Regent, but the daughter of the pettiest lawyer nowadays receives a better education than did the daughter of the wealthiest farmer-general in those times. And are household duties less well accomplished now? Certainly not. And why? – because poverty, sickness, shame, instinct, all compel their accomplishment. It is as though one were to assume that because an officer had acquired too much charm, he would forget how to ride; the fact is ignored that he would break an arm the first time he took such a liberty.

The good and bad effects of the acquisition of ideas are the same for both sexes. Vanity is always with us, even when there is no conceivable reason for being vain: look at the *bourgeois* of a small town. Let us at least insist that vanity should be based on true merit, a merit useful or agreeable to society.

The not-so-clever, drifting in the wake of the revolution which is changing the face of France, have come to admit over the last twenty years that women can be active, but that they should confine themselves to those occupations proper to their sex, such as tending flowers, making a herbarium, or breeding canaries; all these are classed as innocent pleasures.

1. These innocent pleasures are better than idleness. Let us leave them to foolish women, just as we leave to fools the glory of penning verses in honour of the feast-day of the master of the house. But could we in all good faith suggest to Mme Roland or Mistress Hutchinson[1] that they should spend their time looking after little Bengal rose-trees?

All that this argument boils down to is that one wishes to be able to say of one's slave: 'he is too stupid to be wicked.'

But because of a certain law called *sympathy*, a natural law which in truth vulgar eyes never perceive, the shortcomings of your life's companion do not detract from your happiness by virtue of the direct

1. See the *Memoirs* of these admirable women. I could quote other names, but they are unknown to the public, and besides one must not even mention merit in its own lifetime.

harm they could cause you. I would almost prefer that my wife should try to stab me in an angry moment once a year, than that she should behave ill-humouredly every evening.

Lastly, for people who live together, happiness is contagious.

Whether your mistress has spent her morning, while you were at the Champ de Mars or the Chamber of Deputies, in copying a rose from Redouté's beautiful work, or in reading a volume of Shakespeare, her pleasures will have been equally innocent; but on your return she will soon bore you with the ideas she has culled from her rose, and will moreover be eager to spend the evening in society in search of sensations somewhat more lively. If on the other hand she has read her Shakespeare, she will be as fatigued as you yourself and will have had as much pleasure. She will be happier to take a walk alone with you in the Bois de Vincennes, arm in arm, than to put in an appearance at the most fashionable *soirée*. The pleasures of high society are no pleasure at all for a happy woman.

Ignorant people are the natural enemies of education for women. At present they spend their time with women, make love to them, and are well-treated by them; but what would become of them if women were to tire of playing boston? When people like ourselves return from America or India, sunburnt and with a manner which remains a little outlandish for six months, how could the ignorant counter our stories if they could not say: 'Well, we have the ladies on our side. While you have been in New York, the colour of tilburies has changed; nigger-brown is the fashion now.' And we listen carefully, because information of this kind is useful: such and such a pretty woman won't look at us if our carriage is in poor taste.

These same fools, thinking they owe it to the pre-eminence of their sex to be better-informed than women, would be utterly ruined if women took it into their heads to learn anything. When he sees girls of twelve at a friend's country house, a thirty-year-old fool will say to himself: 'Ten years hence I shall be spending my time with them.' Imagine his protestations and horror if he were to see them studying something useful.

Instead of the company and conversation of effeminate fops, a well-educated woman, if she has acquired ideas without losing the graces of her sex, is sure to inspire among the most distinguished men of her century a consideration which verges on the fanatical.

Women would become men's rivals instead of their companions. – Yes, as soon as you have abolished love by legislation. And in anticipation of this fine law, love will merely grow twice as delightful and exciting. The basis for the establishment of *crystallization* will grow wider; a man will be able to enjoy his ideas to the full with the woman he loves, and all nature will take on new charms before their eyes. And since ideas always reflect something of people's characters they will know each other better and be less liable to act rashly; love will grow less blind and result in less unhappiness.

The desire to attract raises modesty, delicacy, and all feminine graces for ever beyond the influence of any education whatsoever. It is as though one feared lest nightingales were to learn not to sing in springtime.

The graces of women bear no relation to their ignorance; look at the worthy helpmates of your village *bourgeois* or the wives of wealthy merchants in England. The affectation named *pedantry* – (for I call it pedantry, this affectation of irrelevant allusion to a dress by Léroy or a novel by Romagnesi, likewise the affectation of quoting Fra Paolo and the Council of Trent in a discussion upon our gentle missionaries) – this pedantry of dress and fashionable taste, the necessity of saying just the right thing about Rossini, all these destroy the graces of Parisian women; and yet despite the ravages of this contagious disease is not Paris the home of the most charming women in all France? Might it not possibly be that they are precisely the ones into whose heads chance has introduced the greatest number of apt and interesting ideas? Now these are the very ideas I expect books to give me. Not for one moment would I suggest that they should read Grotius or Puffendorf, now that we have Tracy's commentary on Montesquieu.

Women's finesse is a product of the perilous position in which they so soon find themselves, and of their having to spend their lives among cruel though charming enemies.

There are in France perhaps fifty thousand women who are wealthy enough to be exempt from all work. But where there is no work there is no happiness. (The passions themselves drive one to work, and very arduous work at that, which needs all the energy of one's mind.)

A woman with four children and an annual income of ten thousand francs *works* when she knits stockings or makes a dress for her daughter. But it is quite untrue that a woman who has her own coach is working when she is at her embroidery or tapestry-making for chair-covers. Apart from a few glimmers of self-satisfaction the action can hold no interest for her; she is not working.

Her happiness is therefore gravely jeopardized.

And what is more, so is the happiness of the despot, because a woman whose heart has for two months been stimulated by no interest beyond that of tapestry-making will perhaps make so bold as to feel that mannered love, vanity-love, or in the last resort even physical love, offer very great happiness as compared with her customary condition.

A woman must not get herself talked about. – To which I again reply: 'Show me the woman whose ability to read is a matter for gossip.'

And what is to stop women, while they are waiting for their luck to turn, from concealing the study with which they normally occupy themselves, and which provides them with a daily ration of honest happiness? I will let them into a secret, *en passant*: once you have set yourself a goal, for instance to reach a clear understanding of the Fieschi conspiracy in Genoa in 1547, the most insipid book becomes interesting, rather as, when in love, one meets a person of no consequence who has just seen one's beloved; the interest is redoubled month by month until study of the Fieschi conspiracy is done with.

The real setting for a woman's virtues is the sickroom. – But are you earnest in your entreaties that Divine goodness should multiply the occasions of illness in order to keep our womenfolk busy? This is argument from the exception.

Besides, I maintain that a woman should spend three or four hours of each day at leisure in the same way as sensible men spend their own leisure hours.

A young mother whose son has the measles could no more find pleasure, even if she would, in reading Volney's travels in Syria, than could her husband the wealthy banker, in meditating upon Malthus during a run on the banks.

In this way alone can rich women set themselves apart from the common run: by moral superiority. Naturally one has other feelings then.[1]

So you want to turn every woman into an author? – Yes, exactly as you announce your intention of having your daughter sing at the Opéra

1. See Mistress Hutchinson refusing to serve the interests of her family and her husband whom she adored, by betraying certain regicides to the ministers of the forsworn Charles II (vol. II, p. 284).

when you engage a singing tutor. I say that a woman should never write except, like Mme de Staal (de Launay), works to be published after her death. For a woman of less than fifty to go into print is to pit her happiness against terrible odds; if she is fortunate enough to have a lover she will begin by losing him.

I can see only one exception, and that is the woman who writes books for the sake of feeding or educating her family. In this case she must always fall back on economic necessity in speaking about her work. To a cavalry major, for instance, she should say: 'Your profession brings you in four thousand francs a year, and with my two translations from English last year, I was able to devote another three thousand five hundred to the education of my two sons.' In other cases, a woman should publish as did Baron d'Holbach or Mme de la Fayette, whose best friends knew nothing of it. The publication of a book is fraught with difficulties for anyone but a harlot; the vulgar, being able to despise her as they please for her profession, will praise her to the skies for her talent and will even go into raptures about it.

In France, among those whose income is six thousand francs a year, there are many men whose happiness customarily derives from literature even though they have no thought of going into print; to read a good book is one of their greatest pleasures. After ten years they find they are twice as intelligent, and no one will deny that, in general, the greater one's intelligence the less one is subject to passions incompatible with the happiness of others.[1] No more do I believe it would be denied that the sons of a woman who reads Gibbon and Schiller must have greater genius than those of a woman who tells her rosary and reads Mme de Genlis.

A young barrister, a merchant, a doctor, or an engineer can launch themselves in life without any education, for they are teaching themselves every day in the practice of their professions. But what opportunity have their wives to acquire necessary and admirable qualities? The great book of life and of necessity is closed to them, isolated as they are within their households. The three louis which their husbands give them every Monday are always spent in the same way, after a discussion with the cook.

In the interests of the despot I must aver that the least of men, if

1. This is what gives me great hopes of the rising generation among the privileged. I also hope that the husbands who read this chapter will be less despotic for three days.

he be twenty years old and rosy of cheek, is dangerous for a woman who knows nothing, because she is entirely a creature of instinct; while in the eyes of a woman of intelligence he will rightly create no more impression than a handsome footman.

The amusing thing about present-day education is that it teaches girls only those things that they have to forget the moment they are married. It takes four hours a day for six years to learn to play the harp properly; and half that time to learn to execute good miniatures or water-colours. Most girls do not even achieve a competent mediocrity; hence the all too true proverb: 'who says amateur says dunce.'[1]

And even supposing a girl has some talent, three years after her marriage she will not take up her harp or her brushes once in a month. These symbols of so much hard work will have become wearisome unless fate has chanced to endow her with the soul of an artist, which is exceedingly rare and not at all suited to household duties.

Thus it is that on the flimsy pretext of propriety girls are taught nothing which will serve to guide them through the situations they will encounter in life. Furthermore these situations are concealed and denied so that to their own force is added: (i) the element of surprise and (ii) an element of mistrust which regards all education as having misrepresented the truth.[2] I maintain that well-brought-up girls should be informed about love. Who would dare claim in good faith that girls of sixteen in the present day know nothing of the existence of love? And from whom do they gather ideas so important and so difficult to convey effectively? Remember Julie d'Etanges complaining of the knowledge she owed to the woman Chaillot, a chambermaid in the household. We must be grateful to Rousseau for having dared to portray this so faithfully in a century characterized by false propriety.

Since present-day education for women is perhaps the most ludicrous nonsense in modern Europe, women are the less educated in the true sense of the word, and the more highly-prized.[3] Perhaps it is because of this that in Italy and Spain they are so superior to men, and I should even say superior to the women of other countries.

1. The opposite of this proverb is true in Italy, where foreign amateurs in the theatre have the finest voices.

2. Education given to Mme d'Epinay (*Mémoires*, vol. I).

3. I except education in manners; they enter drawing-rooms better in the Rue Verte than they do in the Rue Saint-Martin.

IN France all our ideas about women come from the penny cate-chism, and the amusing thing is that while many people would question the authority of that book in settling some fifty-franc trans-action, they follow it literally and slavishly in dealing with what may matter most to their happiness in our nineteenth-century framework of futile habit.

There must be no divorce, because marriage is a *mystery*, and what mystery? – the symbol of Christ's union with his handmaiden the Church. And what sort of a mystery would it be if the *Church* had happened to be personified in a more masculine way?[1] But enough of these outworn prejudices;[2] let us merely remark the peculiar spectacle of a tree whose roots have been chopped away by the axe of ridicule, yet whose branches continue to blossom. And now to return to the observation of facts and their consequences.

For both sexes one's fate in extreme old age depends upon the way one's youth has been spent; and women experience this earlier. What sort of reception is accorded by society to a woman of forty-five? A rather uncompromising one, and generally less than she deserves; women are flattered at twenty and abandoned at forty.

A woman of forty-five is only of consequence by reason of her children or of her lover.

---

1.   *Tu es Petrus, et super hanc petram*
                Aedificabo Ecclesiam meam.
            See M. de Potter's *History of the Church*.

2. Religion is a matter between each man and the Divinity. What right have you to come between my God and myself? I do not employ an attorney in the pay of the social contract except for affairs I cannot undertake myself.

Why should a Frenchman not pay his priest as he does his baker? If we have good bread in Paris it is because the State has not yet seen fit to declare that the provision of loaves shall be free, and to make all bakers a charge upon the Treasury.

In the United States each man pays his priest, so that these gentlemen are obliged to be worthy, and my neighbour does not see fit to stake his happiness upon saddling me with his priest (Birkbeck's *Letters*).

If I am convinced, as our fathers were, that my priest is the close ally of my wife, what then? In that case, short of a Luther, Catholicism in France would cease to exist before 1850. Only M. Grégoire could have saved that particular religion in 1820, and see how he is treated.

A mother with a talent for the fine arts can only very rarely hand that talent down to her son, in the exceptional case where he is naturally gifted. A mother who is intelligent and cultivated will instruct her young son not only in the purely pleasant talents but also in all the others useful to a man in society, and he will be able to choose for himself. The barbarity of the Turks derives largely from the moral benightedness of the lovely women of Georgia. Young men born in Paris owe to their mothers their incontestable superiority at sixteen over their country cousins of the same age. Between sixteen and twenty-five the tables are turned.

Every day the men who invented the lightning conductor and printing and the art of weaving cloth contribute to our happiness, and the same is true of people like Montesquieu, Racine, and La Fontaine. Now the number of geniuses which a nation produces is proportional to the number of men who are educated to an adequate level of culture,[1] and there is nothing to prove that my bootmaker has not the soul of a Corneille; all he lacks is the education needed to develop his feelings and to teach him how to communicate them to the public.

With the present system of education for girls any genius who happens to be born a *woman* can make no contribution to public happiness; but no sooner does chance provide a means of showing her capabilities than you will see her mastering the most difficult achievements. Take, in our time, Catherine II, who had no education beyond danger and whoring; take Mme Roland, or Alessandra Mari raising a regiment in Arezzo and leading it against the French; take Caroline, Queen of Naples, with a better cure for the epidemic of liberalism than your Castlereaghs and your P. . .s. As for what prevents women from pre-eminence in the works of the mind, you are referred to the chapter on modesty, article 9. What heights might not Miss Edgeworth have reached had the respectability necessary to a young English miss not obliged her from the very beginning to carry the pulpit into her novels?[2]

1. Compare the generals of 1795.

2. In the field of the arts, this is the great defect of a reasonable government and also the only reasonable point in favour of monarchy in the style of Louis XIV. See the literary sterility of America. Not a single ballad like those of Robert Burns or of the Spaniards in the thirteenth century. See the admirable ballads of the modern Greeks, those of the Spaniards and Danes of the thirteenth century, and still better, Arabic poetry of the seventh century.

How many men, married or in love, are fortunate enough to be able to communicate their thoughts as they occur, to the woman with whom they spend their lives? Such a man finds a kind heart to share his troubles, but he must always translate his thoughts into small change if he wants to be understood, and it would be futile to expect sound advice from a mind which requires such a diet to be able to digest ideas at all. The paragon of womankind by present educational standards leaves her partner isolated amid life's dangers and soon risks boring him.

What an excellent counsellor would a man find in his wife if she knew how to think! – a counsellor whose interests are, after all, exactly the same as his own, with but one exception, and that only in the morning of their lives.

One of the finest prerogatives of intelligence is that it commands respect for old age. Consider how Voltaire's arrival in Paris outshone royal majesty. But poor unfortunate women, once the brilliance of their youth begins to wane, have but one sad blessing: the ability to delude themselves about the part they play in society.

The remnants of their youthful talents are now no more than ludicrous, and it would be a blessing for our women nowadays if they could die at fifty. As for real morality, the greater one's intelligence the more clearly one sees that justice is the only road to happiness. Genius is a power, but even more is it a torch which lights the way to the great art of being happy.

There comes a moment in the lives of most men when they are capable of great things, a moment when nothing seems impossible to them. Women's ignorance deprives the whole human race of this wonderful opportunity. At best, nowadays, love teaches one to ride well or to know a good tailor.

I have no time to ward off criticism; if it were in my power to establish systems I should, as far as possible, give girls exactly the same education as boys. As I have no intention of filling this book with irrelevancies I shall not be expected to itemize the absurdity of present-day education for men (they are taught neither of the two most important sciences, logic and ethics). Even taking this education as it is, I say it would be better to give it to girls rather than merely to teach them music, water-colour, and embroidery.

Therefore, teach girls reading, writing, and arithmetic, using Mutual Instruction in central boarding-schools where the intrusion of any man except the schoolmaster would be severely punished. The great advantage of bringing the children together is that, whatever the limitations of the teachers, the children would learn willy-nilly from their little companions the art of living in society and of looking after their interests. A sensible teacher would be there to explain their little quarrels and friendships to the children, and so lead that way to the study of ethics instead of beginning with the *Golden Calf*.[1]

Doubtless within a few years Mutual Instruction will be applied to all subjects of study, but taking things as they are now I should like to see girls learning Latin as do little boys. Latin is valuable because it teaches one to cope with tedium; and with Latin should go History, Mathematics, the study of plants useful as food or medicine, then Logic and the moral sciences, etc. Dancing, music and drawing should be begun at five.

At sixteen, a girl should begin to think of finding a husband, and be given sound ideas by her mother upon love, marriage, and the scant probity of men.[2]

CHAPTER 56 (ii): *Concerning Marriage*

WHERE there is no love, women's faithfulness to the marriage bond is probably against nature.[3]

1. Young man, your esteemed father is fond of you, which is why he gives me forty francs a month to teach you mathematics and drawing, in a word, to earn your living. If you were cold for lack of a little coat your father would suffer. He would suffer because he feels sympathy, etc., etc. But when you are eighteen you yourself will have to earn the money required to buy that coat. Your father is said to have an income of twenty-five thousand francs a year, but since you are one of four children you will have to get used to doing without the carriage you are privileged to enjoy at your father's home, etc., etc.

2. Yesterday evening I heard two delightful little girls of four singing some very lively love-songs as I pushed them in their swing. The chambermaids teach them these songs and their mother tells them that *love* and *lover* are meaningless words.

3. Anzi certamente. Coll'amore uno non trova gusto a bevere acqua altra che quella di questo fonte prediletto. Resta naturale allora la fedeltà.

Coll'matrimonio senza amore, in men di due anni l'acqua di questo fonte diventa amara. Esiste sempre però in natura il bisogno d'acqua. I costumi fanno superare la natura ma solamente quando si può vincerla in un instante: la moglie indiana che si abruccia (21 ottobre 1821) dopo la morte del vecchio

This unnatural condition has been sought after by using the fear of hellfire and religious sentiments; the examples of Spain and Italy will indicate how far this has been successful.

In France public opinion was used to the same end, and it was the only bulwark that might have held; but it has been ill-constructed. It is ridiculous to tell a girl she must be faithful to the husband of her choice, and then to marry her against her will to a tedious old dotard.[1]

But girls are very glad to marry. – This is because, with the restraints of the present educational system, they are intolerably bored by having to submit to the slavery of their mothers' households; besides, they lack enlightenment and, after all, it is the will of Nature. There is but one way to ensure greater faithfulness among women to the bond of marriage, and that is to allow freedom to girls, and divorce for married couples.

In a first marriage a woman invariably throws away the brightest days of youth, and by her divorce invites the malicious gossip of fools.

Young women with many lovers have no use for divorce. Older women who have had many lovers think they can mend their reputations, and indeed in France they always succeed, by an attitude of extreme severity towards misdemeanours which are now past for them. It is left to some virtuous young woman, head over heels in love, to seek a divorce and bring down upon herself the contumely of women who have had fifty lovers.

---

marito che odiava, la ragazza europea che trucida barbaramente il tenero bambino al quale testè diede vita. Senza l'altissimo muro del monistero, le monache anderebbero via.

1. With us everything to do with the education of women is comical, even the minutest details. For instance in 1820, in the reign of those same nobles who proscribed divorce, the Ministry despatched to the town of Laon a bust and a statue of Gabrielle d'Estrées. The statue was destined for the main square, apparently with the intention of popularizing love for the Bourbons among young girls and of exhorting them, if the occasion arose, not to be cruel to charming kings but rather to provide this illustrious family with offspring.

On the other hand this same Ministry refused to supply the town of Laon with a bust of Marshal Serrurier, a fine fellow who was not a ladies' man – a man moreover who had begun his career in a plebeian way as a mere private soldier. (Speech by General Foy, in the *Courrier* of 17th June 1820. Dulaure, in his curious *History of Paris*, section entitled *Loves of Henri IV*.)

CHAPTER 57: *Concerning What is Called Virtue*

For my part I honour with the name of virtue the habit of acting in a way troublesome to oneself and useful to others.

As for St Simeon Stylites, who sat on top of a pillar for twenty-two years and lashed himself, I own that he hardly seems virtuous at all to me, and it is this attitude of mine which lends too free a tone to the present essay.

No more do I respect a Carthusian monk who eats nothing but fish and only allows himself to speak on Thursdays. I confess to a preference for General Carnot, who in his old age would rather put up with the rigours of exile in a small Northern town than descend to commit an act of meanness.

I have a faint hope that this excessively vulgar declaration will induce the reader to skip the rest of the chapter.

This morning at Pesaro (7th May 1819), as it was a feast day and I had to attend Mass, I borrowed a missal wherein I happened upon these words:

Joanna Alphonsi quinti Lusitaniae regis filia, tanta divini amoris flamma praeventa fuit, ut ab ipsa pueritia rerum caducarum pertaesa, solo coelestis patriae desiderio flagraret.

That inspiring virtue preached in the beautiful prose of the *Génie du Christianisme* is therefore merely abstention from truffles for fear of stomach-ache. This is a very reasonable proposition if one believes in hell-fire, but it is a proposition based on the most egoistical and prosaic self-interest. The *philosophic* virtue which so well explains the return of Regulus to Carthage, and has inspired similar symptoms in our own revolution,[1] indicates, on the contrary, a generosity of spirit.

It was simply to avoid being fried in a cauldron of boiling oil in the next world that Madame de Tourvel resisted Valmont. I cannot imagine why the idea of being the rival of a cauldron of boiling oil did not turn Valmont away in disdain.

How much more appealing is Julie d'Etanges, mindful both of her own pledges and of the happiness of M. de Wolmar.

---

1. *Memoirs* of Madame Roland. M. Grangeneuve who went for a walk along a certain street at eight o'clock in order to get himself killed by the Capuchin monk Chabot. It was thought that a death would serve the cause of liberty.

What I have said about Madame de Tourvel may equally well apply to the noble virtue of Mistress Hutchinson. What a woman was there snatched by puritanism from love!

One of the most entertaining delusions of men is the belief that they always know everything which it is unquestionably necessary for them to know. Listen to them talking politics, that complex science, or discussing marriage and society.

CHAPTER 58: *Marriage — The Position in Europe*

So far we have only considered the question of marriage in a theoretical way;[1] now we must look at it in the light of the facts.

In all the world, which country can claim the greatest number of happy marriages? Unquestionably Protestant Germany.

The following extract is quoted from Captain Salviati's journal without the alteration of a single word.

'Halberstadt, 23rd June 1807 ... Nevertheless M. de Bulow is deeply and openly in love with Mlle de Feltheim; he follows her all over the place incessantly, is for ever talking to her, and very often draws her a little way apart from the rest of us. Society here is shocked and riven by this overt preference, which would indeed be regarded as the height of impropriety on the banks of the Seine. The Germans are much less conscious than ourselves of what will disrupt society, and impropriety is hardly more than conventionally frowned upon. M. de Bulow has been paying court to Mina in this way for five years, but has not been able to marry her because of the war. Each young lady in society has her lover, and all the world knows who it is; yet at the same time among all the Germans known to my friend M. de Mermann not a single one but married for love. They include:

'Mermann, his brother George, M. de Voigt, M. de Lasing, etc., etc. He has just named a dozen of them.

'The open and passionate way in which all these lovers court their mistresses would be, in France, the height of impropriety, absurdity, and dishonesty.

'Mermann was telling me tonight, as we came back from *The Green*

---

1. The author had read a chapter entitled *dell' Amore* in the Italian translation of M. de Tracy's ideology. The reader will find in that chapter ideas philosophically quite unlike any he will meet here.

Huntsman, that of all the women in his very numerous family, he believed that not one of them had ever deceived her husband. Even supposing he is wrong by half, it is still a very strange country.

'His scandalous suggestion to his sister-in-law Madame de Muni-chow, whose family is dying out in default of heirs male and whose estate will revert to the prince, was coldly received with "Never speak to me of it again."

'He hinted at it in very guarded terms to the divine Philippina (she has just obtained a divorce from her husband, who quite simply wanted to sell her to the sovereign); the response was unfeigned indignation, moderated rather than exaggerated in the telling: "Have you no respect at all left for our sex? I hope for the sake of your honour that you are joking."

'While they were travelling to the Brocken once, this really beauti-ful woman was sleeping, or pretending to sleep, with her head on his shoulder. All at once she was jolted a little against him, whereupon he put his arm about her waist; immediately she flounced across to the far side of the carriage. He did not think it impossible to seduce her but feared she might kill herself the day after she surrendered. What is certain is that he loved her passionately, that he was loved by her in return, that they were always in each other's company, and that she is beyond reproach. My friends, the sun is wan in Halberstadt, the government fussy, and these two people very cold. Kant and Klop-stock were always present at their most impassioned private discussions.

'Mermann told me that a married man convicted of adultery may be condemned by the Brunswick courts to ten years in prison; the law has fallen into disuse but this does not mean that such affairs are entered into lightly. To be a philanderer is by no means the advantage it is in France, where it is almost unnecessary to deny the fact to a husband just to avoid giving offence.

'Anyone who suggested to my colonel or to Ch— that they had had no woman since they were married would be very ill received.

'A few years ago a woman from hereabouts, in an access of reli-gious fervour, confessed to her husband, a gentleman of the court of Brunswick, that she had been deceiving him for six successive years. The husband, as big a fool as his wife, told the whole story to the Duke; and the lover was obliged to resign from all his posts and leave the country within twenty-four hours, upon pain of legal action by the Duke.'

'Halberstadt, 7th July 1807.

'Here husbands are not deceived, it is true, but great heavens, what women! Statues, great rough-hewn masses. Before they marry they are very attractive, as nimble as gazelles, and with a tender and lively glance quick to discern every hint of love. This is because they are hunting husbands. No sooner is the husband netted than they become nothing but child-bearers, in perpetual adoration before the begetter. In a family of four or five children one of them is always bound to be ill, since half the children die before they are seven, and in this country whenever a toddler is ill the mother stays at home. They seem to me to find inexpressible pleasure in the caresses of their children. Little by little they are shorn of all their ideas. It is rather like Philadelphia. Girls bubbling over with the most innocent gaiety become the most tedious of women there in less than a year. As a last word on the marriages of protestant Germany, women's dowries are negligible because of the fiefs. Mademoiselle de Diesdorff, whose father's income is forty thousand francs a year, may perhaps have a dowry of two thousand crowns (seven thousand five hundred francs).

'M. de Mermann received four thousand crowns with his wife.

'The balance of the dowry is payable in vanity at court. Mermann told me: "By going to the bourgeoisie you could find a match worth a hundred or a hundred and fifty thousand crowns (six hundred thousand francs instead of fifteen). But you could no longer be presented at court and you would be ostracized by all society where there is a prince or princess. It would be *frightful*." These were his very words, and they came from the heart.

'Imagine a German woman with the soul of Phi. . ., with her intelligence, her noble and sensitive face, the fire she must have had at eighteen (she is twenty-seven now); honest and straightforward according to the custom of the country, and with the customary useful little streak of religion. Such a woman would doubtless make her husband extremely happy. But how could one take a pride in remaining constant to so colourless a materfamilias?

' "*But he was married*," she countered this morning, when I condemned Corinne's lover, Lord Oswald, for his four years' silence. She stays up till three in the morning reading *Corinne*; the novel moves her profoundly, – and then she answers with all her appealing candour: "*But he was married*."

'Phi— is so unaffected and naively sensitive that even in this unaffected country she seems a prude to those small minds with petty
souls. Their jokes nauseate her, and she generally shows it.

'When she is in good company she will double up with laughter at
the spiciest jests. It was she who told me the story of the young
princess of sixteen, later so famous, who often used to arrange for the
officer of the guard at her gate to visit her in her apartments.'

Switzerland

I know few happier families than those of the *Oberland*, a part of
Switzerland not far from Berne; yet it is notorious (1816) that the
girls there spend the whole of their Saturday nights with their lovers.

The fools who know the world from having made the trip from
Paris to Saint-Cloud will protest; fortunately I have been able, from
the work of a Swiss writer, to confirm my own observations over
four months.[1]

'An honest farmer was complaining of damage caused in his orchard
and I asked him why he did not keep a dog. "My daughters would
never marry," was his reply, which I did not understand until he
told me that once he had had a dog so fierce that none of the boys
ever dared to climb through his windows.

'Another farmer, who was mayor of his village, told me in praise
of his wife that when she was a girl she had more *kilter* or *veilleurs* (in
other words more young men who spent the night beside her) than
anyone else in the village.

'A highly-respected colonel was once obliged in the course of a
mountain journey to spend the night deep in one of the most secluded
and picturesque valleys in the country. He stayed at the house of the
senior magistrate of the valley, a wealthy and respectable man. As he
entered the traveller noticed a girl of sixteen, a model of grace, freshness, and simplicity; she was the daughter of the house. That night
there was a dance, and the traveller set his cap at the girl, who really
was strikingly beautiful. Finally he summoned up the courage to ask
if he might spend the night with her. "No," she replied, "because of
my cousin: she sleeps beside me. But I will come to you." One may
well imagine the agitation this answer aroused. After supper the
traveller rose and went to his room, followed by the girl carrying a

1. Colonel Weiss, *Philosophical Principles*, seventh edition, vol. II, p. 245.

torch; he thought happiness was awaiting him. "Not yet," she said simply, "first I must ask Mother's permission." He could hardly have been more staggered by a thunderbolt. She left the room, and plucking up courage he tiptoed up to the thin wooden wall of the good people's living-room in time to hear the daughter asking her mother in caressing tones for the desired permission, which at last she obtained. "What do you say, Father?" said the mother to her husband, who was already abed, "You're agreeable to Trineli spending the night with the colonel, aren't you?" "With all my heart," was the reply; "I think I'd lend my wife herself to such a man." "Off you go, then," said the mother to Trineli, "but be a good girl, and don't take off your skirt." At daybreak Trineli, respected by the traveller and still a virgin, rose and arranged the pillows of the bed; she prepared coffee and cream for her companion, and having breakfasted with him, sitting on the bed, she cut off a tiny piece from her *broustpletz* (a velvet cloth covering the bosom). "Take this," she said, "and keep it in memory of a happy night; for my part I shall never forget it; why are you a colonel?" And kissing him for the last time she ran away, and he never saw her again."[1] This is the extreme antithesis of our way of life in France, and something of which I cannot bring myself to approve.

If I were a statesman I should like to establish in France the German custom of evening dances. Three times a week the girls would go with their mothers to a ball which started at seven and ended at midnight, and cost no more than the fiddler's fee and the price of a glass of water. In a nearby room the mothers, perhaps a little jealous of their daughters' happy tuition, would play boston, while in another the fathers could read the papers and talk politics. Between midnight and one o'clock the families would reunite and make their way home to the paternal roof. The girls would learn to know the young men; vaingloriousness and the indiscreetness which goes with it would quickly become odious to them; and lastly *they could choose themselves a husband*. A few girls would have unhappy love affairs, but the number of deceived husbands and unhappy homes would decrease enormously. On such a basis it would be less ridiculous to try and

---

1. I am glad to be able to quote another man's words in relating extraordinary events which I have myself observed. Certainly without M. de Weiss I should not have given an account of this particular custom. I have omitted equally characteristic ones from Valencia and Vienna.

punish unfaithfulness by shame; the law would insist that a young woman having chosen a husband must then be faithful to him. On such a basis I would admit the prosecution and punishment by the courts of what the English call *criminal conversation*. The courts would be able to send a seducer to prison for several years, and impose a fine equal to two thirds of his fortune, which would be used for the benefit of the prisons and hospitals.

A woman could be prosecuted before a jury for adultery. The jury would first have to establish that the conduct of the husband had been irreproachable.

A convicted woman could be condemned to prison for life. If the husband had been absent for more than two years, the woman's maximum sentence would be reduced to only a few years in prison. The public way of life would soon adapt itself to these new laws and bring them to perfection.[1]

Then the nobles and the priests, while bitterly regretting the righteous centuries of Madame de Montespan or Madame Du Barry, would be compelled to allow divorce.[2]

In some village within sight of Paris there would be a haven for

---

1. The *Examiner*, an English newspaper, reporting the Queen's trial (No. 662 of 3rd September 1820), goes on to say:

'WE HAVE A SYSTEM OF SEXUAL MORALITY UNDER WHICH THOUSANDS OF WOMEN BECOME MERCENARY PROSTITUTES WHOM VIRTUOUS WOMEN ARE TAUGHT TO SCORN, WHILE VIRTUOUS MEN RETAIN THE PRIVILEGE OF FREQUENTING THOSE VERY WOMEN WITHOUT ITS BEING REGARDED AS ANYTHING MORE THAN A VENIAL OFFENCE.'

It shows a noble audacity to dare in the land of *cant* to express a truth about this subject, however trivial and obvious; it redounds even more to the credit of a poor newspaper whose only hope of success is to be bought by rich people who regard the bishops and the Bible as the sole safeguard of their fine liveries.

2. Madame de Sévigné wrote to her daughter on 23rd December 1671:

'I do not know whether you have heard that Villarceaux, in speaking to the king about a post for his son, cleverly took the opportunity of telling him that certain people had been suggesting to his niece (Mademoiselle de Rouxel) that his Majesty had some design upon her; that if this were so he begged the king would make use of him, as the affair would be better entrusted to his hands than those of others, and he could bring it off successfully. The king burst out laughing and said: '*Villarceaux, we are too old, you and I to run after young ladies of fifteen.*' And he laughed at him as a gentleman should, and related the whole story to the ladies.' (Vol. II, p. 340.)

Memoirs of Lauzun, Bezenval, Madame d'Epinay, etc., etc. I beg the reader not to condemn me outright without re-reading these memoirs.

unhappy women, a house of refuge where no man other than doctor or chaplain would ever set foot, upon pain of the galleys. A woman seeking divorce would be obliged first of all to submit to incarceration in this haven; she would have to spend two years there without any break at all. She would be able to write letters but not to receive replies.

A commission composed of peers of France and a few respected magistrates would conduct the case for divorce on behalf of the woman and dictate the sum payable to the institution by the husband. A woman who failed in her petition to the courts would be allowed to spend the rest of her life in the haven. The government would contribute a subsidy of two thousand francs to the institution for each woman who took shelter. To be eligible for admission a woman's dowry would have to have exceeded twenty thousand francs. Moral discipline would be extremely severe.

After two years entirely cut off from the world a divorced woman would be permitted to re-marry.

Once this point had been reached, the government might consider whether to give boys twice as large a share as their sisters in the paternal heritage, in order to encourage meritorious emulation between girls. Girls who did not succeed in getting married would receive a share equal to that of their brothers. It might be noted in passing that such a system would gradually eliminate the practice of 'suitable' marriages which are thoroughly unsuitable. The possibility of divorce would render excessive meanness quite futile.

In poor villages scattered throughout France there would have to be established thirty abbeys for old maids. The government would try to cushion these institutions with consideration, in order to palliate the sadness of the unfortunate spinsters living out the rest of their lives there. They would have to be given all the paraphernalia of dignity.

But enough of these fancies.

WHEN a gathering of young men has had a good laugh at the expense of some poor unfortunate lover, and the latter has departed, the conversation generally turns to a debate on the question of whether it is better to approach women in the manner of Mozart's Don Juan or in that of Werther. The distinction would be more precise if I had cited Saint-Preux, but he is such a dull character that I should be wronging the sensitive if I were to choose him as their champion.

The character of a Don Juan demands a greater number of the useful virtues esteemed by the world: fearlessness which commands admiration, resourcefulness, zest, poise, wit, and so forth.

Don Juans are prone to long periods of barrenness and to an extremely cheerless old age. Most men, however, never reach old age.

A man in love cuts a poor figure in a drawing-room in the evening, because one can only exercise skill and power over women to the extent that one regards their conquest in the same way as a game of billiards. Since society is aware that lovers have one chief interest in life, however intelligent the lovers may be they lay themselves open to jest; but when they wake in the morning, instead of being testy until something stimulating or subtle happens to soothe them, their thoughts are wholly about the loved one, and they build castles in Spain wherein dwells happiness.

Love *à la Werther* opens the mind to all the arts, to all sweet and romantic impressions, moonlight, the beauty of the woods and of painting, in a word, to the feeling and enjoyment of the *beautiful*, in whatever form it presents itself, even the humblest. It shows the way to happiness even without riches.[1] People like this do not run the

---

1. First volume of *La Nouvelle Héloïse*, and indeed all the volumes if Saint-Preux had happened to have a trace of character; but he was a true poet, an irresolute chatterbox who only put himself in good heart by speechifying; besides, he was very dull. Such men possess the great advantage of not shocking feminine pride, and they never give their mistresses cause for *surprise*. Let this be given due weight; it perhaps contains the whole secret of the success which dull men achieve with women of distinction. Nevertheless love is only a passion to the extent that it makes one forget one's self-love, and so those women who, like Léonore, insist upon the pleasures of pride, do not feel complete love for a dull man. They are unsuspectingly at the same level as the prosaic man whom

risk of becoming sated like Meilhan, Bezenval, etc., but rather lose their wits in an excessive sensibility like Rousseau. Women gifted with minds of a certain distinction, who once their first youth is past recognize love for what it is when they see it, usually manage to evade the Don Juans, whose conquests generally run to quantity rather than quality. To the detriment of the respect due the sensitive, note that publicity is essential for the triumphs of a Don Juan, just as secrecy is necessary for the triumphs of a Werther. Most professional philanderers come from wealthy homes, which is to say that by virtue of their education and their imitation of those who surrounded them in childhood they are selfish and unfeeling.[1]

Genuine Don Juans even come to regard women as their enemies, and to rejoice in the misfortunes of the opposite sex.

By contrast, the charming Duke delle Pignatelle showed us at Munich the true way to achieve happiness through satisfied desire, even without passionate love. 'I realize that a woman attracts me,' he told me one evening, 'when I find myself tongue-tied in her presence and don't know what to say.' Far from making his self-love blush and cry for revenge because of this awkward moment, he cherished it as the source of his happiness. For this charming young man, mannered love was entirely free from corroding vanity; it was a weaker, though pure and unmixed variant of true love, and he respected all women as delightful creatures to whom we men are most unfair (20th February 1820).

As it is not given to men to choose their temperaments, that is to say their souls, they cannot adopt a superior attitude. Try as they might J.-J. Rousseau and the Duc de Richelieu, for all their intelligence, could not have exchanged their amatory careers with each other. I am inclined to believe that the Duke never experienced moments like those of Rousseau in company with Madame d'Houdetot in the park of la Chevrette, or listening to the music of the *Scuole* in Venice, or at the feet of Madame Bazile in Turin. But neither can

they despise, and who seeks to find in love both love and vanity. They themselves seek love and pride; but love blushes crimson and retreats, for it is the proudest of despots: it is either everything or nothing.

1. See a page of André Chénier, *Works*, p. 370; or even open your eyes wide in society, which is more difficult. 'Generally speaking those whom we call patricians are further removed from loving anything than are other men,' said the Emperor Marcus Aurelius. (*Thoughts*, p. 50.)

he have had occasion to blush for the kind of foolishness which Rousseau perpetrated with Madame de Larnage, and for which he reproached himself to the end of his days.

The role of a Saint-Preux is sweeter and pervades the whole of existence, but it must be admitted that Don Juan's role is far more brilliant. If Saint-Preux alters his tastes half-way through his life, solitary, withdrawn, and habitually meditative, he finds himself at the end of the back row on the stage of life; while Don Juan can boast a magnificent reputation among men, and may even yet win a sensitive woman by giving up all his dissolute tastes for her sake.

Considering all the arguments put forward so far, it seems to me that the question is still left in the balance. What leads me to believe that the Werthers are the happier is that Don Juan reduces love to the level of an ordinary affair. Unlike Werther, for whom realities are shaped by his desires, Don Juan's desires are imperfectly satisfied by cold reality, as in ambition, avarice, and the other passions. Instead of losing himself in the bewitching reveries of crystallization his attitude is that of a general to the success of his tactics,[1] and in brief he destroys love instead of enjoying it more than others, as is commonly believed.

The foregoing seems to me undeniable. Another reason which seems to me just as undeniable. though thanks to the perversity of Providence we must forgive men for not recognizing it, is that a habit of fair-dealing appears to me to be, bar accident, the surest way to happiness; and our Werthers are not rogues.[2]

To be happy in crime one must be entirely without remorse. I do not know whether such a being can exist;[3] I have never met one, and I would wager that the affair of Madame Michelin must have disturbed the repose of the Duc de Richelieu.

1. Compare *Lovelace* with *Tom Jones*.

2. See *La Vie Privée du Duc de Richelieu*, 9 octavo volumes. Why does a murderer not fall dead beside his victim the moment he has killed? Why are there diseases, and if there are diseases why does a man like Troistaillons not die of colic? Why did Henri IV reign twenty-one years and Louis XV fifty-nine? Why is the span of life not directly proportional to each man's degree of virtue? And other *infamous questions*, as the English philosophers would say, questions which certainly reflect no credit on the inquirer; but to which it would be fairly creditable to provide an answer other than by the use of insults and *cant*.

3. See Nero's reaction to the murder of his mother, in Suetonius; and yet with what a fine crop of flatteries he was surrounded!

One would have to be entirely without sympathy, which is inconceivable, or be capable of annihilating the whole human race.[1]

People whose only knowledge of love comes from novels will feel a natural disgust at reading these arguments in favour of virtue in love. This is because the canon of the novel demands that virtuous love be depicted as essentially tedious and uninteresting. Viewed thus from afar, virtue appears to neutralize love and the words *virtuous love* seem synonymous with feeble love. But all this is a weakness in the art of portrayal and quite unrelated to passion as it exists in nature.[2]

Allow me to sketch the portrait of my most intimate friend.

Don Juan disclaims all the obligations which link him to the rest of humanity. In the great market-place of life he is a dishonest merchant who takes all and pays nothing. The idea of equality is as maddening to him as water to a rabid dog; this is why pride of birthright becomes Don Juan's character so well. With the idea of equality of rights vanishes that of justice – or rather, if Don Juan comes of an illustrious stock, such vulgar notions would never have entered his head; and I am ready enough to believe that a man who bears a historic name is more disposed than another to set fire to a city for the sake of boiling himself an egg.[3] He must be forgiven; he is so possessed with self-love that he fails to perceive the harm he causes, and sees none but himself in the universe as capable of joy or suffering. In the fire of youth, when all the passions make us feel the life in our own hearts and banish our mistrust of the hearts of others, Don Juan, rich in sensations and apparent happiness, congratulates himself

1. Cruelty is but ailing fellow-feeling. *Power* is the greatest happiness, after love, only because one believes one is in a position to *command sympathy*.

2. If for the spectator's benefit one depicts the sentiment of virtue in conjunction with the sentiment of love, one finds one has portrayed a heart torn between the two. Virtue in a novel is only there to be sacrificed: Julie d'Etanges.

3. See Saint-Simon, the miscarriage of the Duchess of Burgundy; and Madame de Motteville, *passim*. The princess who was surprised that other women should have five fingers to a hand as she had; the Duke of Orléans, Gaston, brother of Louis XIII, who found it so simple that his favourites should go to the scaffold to please him. See the gentlemen in 1820 pressing for an electoral law that might bring back the Robespierres to France, etc., etc.; see Naples in 1799. (I retain this note written in 1820. List of the great lords of 1778 with notes on their morals by General Laclos, seen at Naples in the house of the Marquis Berio; a highly scandalous manuscript of more than three hundred pages.)

upon his own egoism as he watches other men making sacrifices
at the altar of duty; he believes he has discovered the great art of
living. But in the full tide of his triumph, at hardly more than thirty
years of age, he realizes with surprise that life is passing him by, and
he feels increasing disgust for what once had been his whole pleasure.
In an access of melancholy Don Juan said to me at Thorn: 'There
are less than twenty varieties of womankind, and once one has
sampled two or three of each variety, one begins to grow sated.' I
replied: 'Only imagination can escape once and for all from satiety.
Each woman provides a different interest, and what is more the
same woman will be loved in a different way if chance should offer her
to you two or three years earlier or later in life, provided that chance
decrees you should love her at all. But a sensitive woman, even if she
loved you, would merely chafe your pride with her claims to equality.
Your relationship with women destroys all the other joys in life; that
of Werther multiplies them a hundredfold.'

The dismal drama draws to its close. We see an ageing Don Juan
who blames his satiety upon the world outside him, never upon himself. We see him tortured by the poison that consumes him, moving
restlessly hither and thither, fickle of purpose. But however brilliant
the outward appearances, everything leads to the same end, to a mere
barter of sorrows; he has but one option, the choice between peaceful
boredom and restless boredom.

In the end he himself admits the fatal truth; and from that moment
his opportunities for enjoyment become restricted to the exercise of
his power and the overt practice of evil for evil's sake. This is indeed
the last extreme of chronic unhappiness; no poet has ever dared
present a faithful likeness of it: the picture would be too horrifying.

But there is a chance that a superior man will turn from this fatal
path, for Don Juan's character contains a fundamental contradiction.
I have postulated him as a man of great intelligence, and great
intelligence leads to the discovery of virtue by way of the temple of
glory.[1]

La Rochefoucauld, who after all knew something about *amour-
propre*, although in real life he was nothing but a fool of a literary

---

1. The character of a young man of the privileged class is pretty correctly
represented by the bold Bothwell in *Old Mortality*.

man,[1] said (267): 'The pleasure of love lies in loving, and the passion one feels brings more happiness than the passion one inspires.'

Don Juan's happiness is nothing but vanity, springing, it is true, from circumstances created by a good deal of intelligence and activity; but he must sense that the pettiest general who wins a battle, the most junior *préfet* who keeps his *Département* under control, both experience an enjoyment greater than his own; while on the other hand I believe the happiness of the Duke de Nemours, when Madame de Clèves confessed her love for him, was greater than Napoleon's at Marengo.

Love as understood by Don Juan is a feeling akin to a taste for hunting. It is a craving for an activity which needs an incessant diversity of stimuli to challenge skill.

Love *à la Werther* is like the feeling of a schoolboy who writes a tragedy, though a thousand times better; it is a new aim in life upon which everything focuses, and which changes the appearance of everything. Passionate love spreads all Nature in her sublimity before a man's eyes, like something invented only yesterday. He is surprised never to have noticed the strange sights he now perceives. Everything is new, alive, and pulsating with the most passionate interest.[2] A lover sees the woman he loves in every skyline, and as he travels a hundred leagues to catch a momentary glimpse of her each tree, each rock speaks to him in a different way and teaches him something new about her. Instead of the tumult of these magical visions, Don Juan requires that external objects, which he values only in proportion to their utility, should be given piquancy by some new intrigue.

Love *à la Werther* holds strange pleasures; after a year or two the lover's soul is, as it were, merged with that of his beloved. And strangely enough this happens quite regardless of the success of his love, and despite the harshness of his mistress. At this stage, whatever he does or notices, he asks himself: 'What would she say if she were here with me? What would I say to her about this view of *Casa Lecchio*?' He talks to her, listens to her replies, and laughs at the jokes she tells him. A hundred leagues away from her, in the shadow of her displeasure, he catches himself thinking: 'Léonore was very gay this

---

1. See the *Memoirs* of Retz, and the awkward moment he gave the bishop's coadjutor between two doors in the High Court of Justice.

2. Volterra, 1819. Honeysuckle on the way down.

evening.' He rouses himself. 'Ye gods,' he sighs, 'there are madmen
in Bedlam less crazy than I am!'

'You put me out of all patience,' said one of my friends when I
read him this remark. 'You continually contrast the passionate man
with Don Juan, but that's not the point. You'd be right if one could
work up a passion at will. But suppose one remains indifferent, what
then?' Mannered love, without horrors. Horrors are always the work
of a petty mind which needs to reassure itself about its own merit.

Now let us proceed. The Don Juans must find it very hard to
admit the existence of the mood I was describing a moment ago.
Besides the fact that they can neither see nor feel it, the affront to their
vanity is too great. Their great mistake is to believe they can capture
in a fortnight what a bashful lover can hardly secure in six months.
They argue from experiments carried out at the expense of those poor
wretches who have neither a soul which pleases by revealing its
simplicity to a sensitive woman nor the wits required to play the part
of a Don Juan. They will not see that what they obtain, even if it be
granted by the same woman, is not the same thing.

> *The prudent man is ever full of qualms,*
> *And for this reason lovers not a few*
> *Practise deceit. The ladies, begged for alms,*
> *Long leave those suitors sighing in their rue*
> *Who never in a lifetime were untrue.*
> *Yet of that treasure which at last they grant*
> *None knows the value but the hearts who take;*
> *The more hard-won, the more it doth enchant;*
> *The prize, in love, is equal to the stake.*
>
> Nivernais, *le troubadour Guillaume*
> *de la Tour*, III, 342.

From the point of view of the Don Juan passionate love may be
compared to a strange road, steep and difficult, which at first, it is
true, leads through delightful groves, but soon loses itself among
jagged rocks not in the least attractive to ordinary eyes. Gradually the
road climbs among high mountains and through a dark forest whose
huge trees shut out the light with their thick towering foliage, bringing terror to the hearts of those unaccustomed to danger.

After many painful and humiliating wanderings as if through an
endless, tortuous labyrinth, suddenly one turns a further corner and
comes upon a new world, Lalla-Rookh's wonderful valley in Kashmir.

How can the Don Juans, who never set out along this road, or at most take only a few steps along it, how can they have any idea of the view at journey's end? . . .

'So you see that inconstancy is a good thing:
I must have novelty, be it the last thing on earth.'

Very well, so you make light of promises and fair play. What is one's purpose in being inconstant? Pleasure, apparently.

But the pleasure experienced with a pretty woman who has been lusted after for a fortnight and enjoyed for three weeks is *different* from the pleasure to be found with a mistress desired for three years and enjoyed for ten.

If I do not write 'enjoyed *for ever*' it is because old age, which changes our bodies, reputedly robs us of the power to love; for my own part I do not believe this at all. A mistress, having become an intimate friend, gives you other pleasures: the pleasures of old age. In the morning, in the season of flowers, she is a rose, and in the evening, when roses are no longer in season, she changes into a delicious fruit.[1]

A mistress desired for three years is truly a mistress in the full sense of the word; she is to be approached with fear and trembling, and to the Don Juans I will say this, that a man in fear and trembling is never bored. The pleasures of love are always in proportion to the fear.

The curse of inconstancy is boredom; the curse of passionate love is despair and death. People notice love's despair and talk about it; no one pays any attention to the jaded old libertines, bored to death, who litter the streets of Paris.

'More brains are blown out for love than from boredom.' I can well believe it, for boredom strips away everything, even the courage to kill oneself.

There are people constitutionally unable to find pleasure in anything but variety. But a man who sings the praises of champagne at the expense of the wine of Bordeaux is only saying with a certain amount of eloquence: 'I prefer champagne.'

Each of these wines has its partisans, and both sides are right, if they know their own minds and actively pursue the kind of happiness

1. See Collé's *Memoirs*, his wife.
2. Physiologists who have studied the body will tell you that injustice in the relationships of social existence produces aridity, mistrust, and unhappiness.

best suited to their bodies[2] and their habits. What spoils the party of the inconstant ones is that all the fools join their ranks for lack of courage.

But after all, if he takes the trouble to examine his own mind, each man has his *beau idéal*, and it always seems to me a little absurd to try to convert one's neighbour.

CHAPTER 60: *Concerning Fiascos*

'THE whole realm of love is full of tragic stories,' said Madame de Sévigné, relating her son's misfortune with the celebrated Champmeslé.

Montaigne handles so scabrous a subject with great aplomb.

'I am yet in doubt, these pleasant bonds, wherewith our world is so fettered and France so pestered, that nothing else is spoken of, are haply but the impressions of apprehension, and effects of feare. For I know by experience, that some one, for whom I may as well answer as for my selfe, and in whom no manner of suspition either of weaknesse or enchantment might fall, hearing a companion of his make report of an extraordinary faint sowning, wherein he was fallen, at such a time as he least looked for it, and wrought him no small shame, whereupon the horrour of his report did so strongly strike his imagination, as he ranne the same fortune, and fell into a like drooping: and was thence forward subject to fall into like fits: So did the passionate remembrance of his inconvenience possesse and tyrannize him; but his fond doting was in time remedied by another kinde of raving. For himselfe avowing and publishing aforehand the infirmitie he was subject unto, the contention of his soule was solaced upon this, that bearing his evill as expected, his dutie thereby diminished, and he grieved lesse thereat . . .

'If a man have once beene capable, he cannot afterwards be incapable, except by a just and absolute weaknesse . . . Such a mischiefe is not to be feared, but in the enterprises, where our minde is beyond all measure bent with desire and respect . . . I know some, who have found to come unto it with their bodies as it were halfe glutted elsewhere . . . The minde of the assailant molested with sundry different alarums is easily dismaid . . . Pythagoras his neece was wont to say, that a woman which lies with a man ought, together with her petie-coate, leave off all bashfulnesse, and with her petie-coate, take the same againe.'

This woman was right as regards gallantry, but wrong as regards love.

The first triumph, if all vanity be set aside, is never directly pleasant for any man:

1. Unless he has had no time to desire the woman and submit her to the action of his imagination; in other words unless he takes her in the first moments of his desire. These are the conditions for the greatest possible amount of physical pleasure, because the whole mind is then devoted to perceiving the beauties, without a thought of the difficulties.

2. Or unless the woman in question is of absolutely no importance, a pretty chambermaid for example, one of those women whom one only remembers to desire when one happens to see her. The least trace of passion which then enters the heart sows the seed of potential *fiasco*.

3. Or unless the lover takes his mistress in so unexpected a fashion that it leaves him no time for the least reflection.

4. Or unless there is a dedicated and excessive love on the woman's part which the man does not share to the same degree.

The more distractedly a man is in love, the greater the violence he is obliged to do his own feelings if he dare thus familiarly touch and thereby risk offending a being who, like the Deity, inspires him with absolute love and absolute respect at the same time.

This particular fear and, in mannered love, the false shame which springs from an intense desire to satisfy and from lack of courage, both result in an extremely painful feeling which seems insurmountable and brings a blush to one's cheek. Now if the mind is occupied in feeling shame and trying to overcome it, it cannot be engaged in the experience of pleasure; for any concentration upon pleasure, which is a luxury, is impossible where there is a threat to one's sense of *security*, which is a necessity.

There are people who, like Rousseau, feel a false shame even with prostitutes; they do not frequent them, for such women are possessed but once, and that first experience gives no pleasure.

In order to realize that, vanity apart, the first triumph is very often a painful tribulation, a distinction must be drawn between the pleasure of the adventure and the happiness of the moment which follows it. A man is well content:

1. To find himself at last in that situation which he has so long coveted; to be in possession of a perfect happiness for the future, and to be past the stage of those cruel hardships which made him doubt the love of the beloved.

2. To have managed things so well, and to have escaped a danger; this circumstance prevents the joy from being quite pure in *passionate love*; he does not know what he is doing, but is sure of what he loves; in *mannered love*, which never loses its head, this moment is like the return from a journey, a time for self-appraisal; and if the love is largely based on vanity, the appraisal is concealed.

3. The lewd part of the mind is cock-a-hoop at victory.

However little passion you may feel for a woman, provided your imagination has not run dry, if she be inept enough to say to you one evening, tenderly and bashfully, 'Come tomorrow at noon. I shall be alone,' for sheer nervous agitation you will not sleep a wink; the happiness awaiting you will take a thousand different forms in anticipation; after a morning of torment the hour strikes, and it seems as if each stroke were reverberating through your diaphragm. You make your way towards her street with a pounding heart and hardly have strength enough to drag yourself along. You catch sight of the woman you love, behind her blind; you go up, rallying your courage, . . . and you suffer the *fiasco through imagination*.

M. Rapture, an excessively artistic, highly-strung, and narrow-minded man, explained to me at Messina that not only every first attempt, but indeed every assignation, invariably brought him misfortune. Yet I am inclined to believe he was as much a man as the next; at any rate I know he has had two charming mistresses.

As for the man of wholly sanguine temperament (the true Frenchman, who looks on the bright side of everything; Colonel Mathis) an assignation for the following day at noon, far from torturing him with excess of feeling, casts a rosy light over everything leading to the lucky moment. If he had no assignation the sanguine type would be a little bored.

Look at the analysis of love made by Helvétius; I would wager that his feelings were of this nature, and he spoke for the majority of men. Such people have little propensity for *passionate love*; it would disturb their delightful tranquillity; I believe they would regard its transports as unhappiness; certainly they would be humiliated by its shyness.

The worst that can happen to the sanguine type is a kind of moral *fiasco*, when he has an assignation with Messalina and when at the very instant of entering her bed he is struck by the thought of how terrible is the judge before whom he is about to appear.

The man of shy melancholic temperament succeeds occasionally in emulating the sanguine, as Montaigne says, if he be drunk with the wine of Champagne, always provided it has not been purposely administered. He must console himself with the thought that the scintillating folk he envies so much and can never hope to rival know neither his sublime pleasures nor his failures, and that the fine arts, which thrive upon love's shyness, are closed books to them. The man who, like Duclos, aspires only to ordinary pleasure, often finds it, is never unhappy, and in consequence remains unmoved by the arts.

The athletic temperament only runs into this type of trouble from exhaustion or bodily weakness, in contrast with the nervous and melancholic temperaments, which seem expressly created to suffer from it.

These poor unfortunate melancholics often succeed in dulling their imaginations a little by tiring themselves with other women, and thus manage to cut a less distressing figure with the woman who is the object of their passion.

What conclusion can we draw from all this? That a wise woman should never surrender for the first time by pre-arrangement – it should be an unexpected good fortune.

Tonight at General Michaud's headquarters we were discussing *fiascos*, five handsome young fellows of twenty-five and myself. It appeared that with the exception of one popinjay, who was probably lying, we had all suffered a *fiasco* on our first occasion with our most notable mistresses. Admittedly, perhaps none of us had ever known what Delfante calls *passionate love*.

The idea that a *fiasco* is a very common misfortune should decrease the risk of its occurrence.

I knew a handsome lieutenant of Hussars, twenty-three years old, who, from excess of love, as I understand the matter, could do no more than kiss her and weep for joy throughout the first three nights he spent with a mistress whom he had adored for six months and who had treated him very harshly while she grieved over another lover killed in the war. Neither of them was ensnared.

The paymaster H. Mondor, well known to the whole army, suffered a *fiasco* for three nights in succession with the young and seductive Countess Koller.

But the king of *fiasco* is the handsome and rational Colonel Horse, who suffered an unbroken succession of *fiascos* for three months on end with the mischievous and enticing Nina Vigano, and was finally compelled to part from her without ever having possessed her.

Under this title, which I wish were more modest still, I have gathered a fairly generous selection from three or four hundred playing-cards scribbled over in pencil. Often what for want of a better name must be called the original manuscript consists of variously-sized pieces of paper written in pencil, which Lisio stuck together with wax to save himself the trouble of transcribing. He once told me that nothing he jotted down seemed an hour later to have been worth the effort of transcription. I mention this detail in the hope that it will serve to excuse the repetitions.

1

Everything can be acquired in solitude, except character.

2

In 1821; hatred, love, and avarice, the three most common passions; together with gambling, almost the only ones in Rome.

At first sight the Romans seem *wicked*; but in fact they are only mistrustful in the extreme, with an imagination that flares up on the slightest pretext.

If one of them is *wantonly* wicked it is because he is frightened and is trying to reassure himself by testing his gun.

3

If I were to say, as I believe, that kindliness is the distinguishing characteristic of Parisians, I am afraid I should offend them.

'I don't want to be kind!'

4

A sign of love has just struck me; it is when all the pleasures and all the pains attributable to all the other passions and all the other needs of a man cease abruptly to affect him.

5

Prudishness is a kind of avarice – the worst kind.

6

A dependable character is one which has a long and unshakable experience of life's disappointments and misfortunes. Such a man desires constantly or not at all.

7

Love as it exists in high society is a love of duelling or a love of gambling.

8

Nothing is more fatal to mannered love than gusts of passionate love in the partner.

Contessina L. Forli, 1819

9

A serious failing in women, the most shocking of all for a man worthy of the name. In matters of feeling, the public seldom rises above the level of meanness in ideas; yet women appoint the public as supreme judge of their lives. This applies even to the most distinguished women who are often quite unaware of it, and even believe and declare that the contrary is true.

Brescia, 1819

10

Prosaic is a new word which I used to think ridiculous, since there is nothing colder than our poetry; if there has been any warmth in France during the last fifty years it is certainly in our prose.

But the contessina Léonore used the word *prosaic*, and I love to write it.

The definition of it is in *Don Quixote* and in the 'Perfect contrast *between master and squire.*' The master, tall and pale; the squire, fat and ruddy. The former all heroism and courtliness; the latter all selfishness and servility; the first brimming with moving and romantic dreams; the second a model of good behaviour, a very symposium of prudent proverbs; the one for ever fortifying his spirit with some heroic and perilous contemplation; the other mulling over some careful course of action in which he does not fail to allow meticulously for the influence of every little shameful and selfish motive known to the human heart.

When the former ought to be disabused by the *non-success* of his dreams of yesterday, he is already fully occupied with today's castles in Spain.

It is better to have a prosaic husband and to take a romantic lover.

Marlborough had a *prosaic* mind; Henri IV, in love at fifty-five with a young princess well aware of his age, had a romantic heart.[1]

There are fewer prosaic minds among the nobility than among the middle class.

That is the disadvantage of trade; it makes one prosaic.

11

Nothing is so interesting as passion; everything about it is so unexpected, and its agent is also its victim. Nothing could be duller than mannered love, where everything is calculated, as in all the prosaic affairs of everyday life.

12

By the end of a visit one always finishes by treating one's suitor better than was intended.

L. 2nd November 1818

13

The influence of his class is always apparent in a parvenu, despite any genius he may have. Look at the way Rousseau fell in love with all the 'ladies' he met, or at his tears of joy because the Duke of Luxembourg, one of the dullest courtiers of the day, condescended to walk on the right instead of on the left, with a M. Coindet, a friend of Rousseau's.

L. 3rd May 1820

14

Ravenna, 23rd January 1820

Women here have no education except in material things; a mother has no scruples about showing despair or ecstatic joy, for love's sake, before her twelve- to fifteen-year-old daughters. Remember that in this happy clime many women are still very attractive at

1. Dulaure, *Histoire de Paris*. Silent scene in the queen's apartments the night Princesse de Condé fled; the ministers flattened speechless against the walls, the king striding up and down.

forty-five, and that most of them are married by the age of eighteen.

La Valchiusa, talking yesterday of Lampugnani: 'Ah, there was the man for me! He really knew how to love ... etc., etc.,' and carrying on this conversation for some time with a friend, in the presence of her daughter, a wide-awake young person of fourteen or fifteen, whom she also used to take along on her sentimental walks with this lover.

Now and then the girls pick up excellent maxims of behaviour. For instance, Madame Guarnacci, with her two daughters and two men whom she never set eyes on before or since, holding forth with profound maxims for half an hour, supported by examples they knew of (that of la Cercara in Hungary), concerning the precise moment when it is most suitable to punish by infidelity a lover who has misbehaved himself.

15

The sanguine type, the true Frenchman (Colonel Mathis), instead of torturing himself with excess of feeling, like Rousseau, when he has an assignation for the following evening at seven, sees everything in a rosy light until the lucky moment. Such people have but little propensity for passionate love; it would disturb their delightful tranquillity. I would go so far as to say they might regard its transports as unhappiness, and certainly they would be humiliated by its shyness.

16

Most men of the world, from vanity, from mistrust, from fear of disillusionment, refrain from falling in love with a woman until after intimacy.

17

The very sensitive need a woman to be easy of access if crystallization is to be encouraged.

18

A woman thinks to recognize the voice of the public in the first fool or false friend who claims to be a faithful interpreter of public opinion.

19

There is delicious pleasure in clasping in your arms a woman who has caused you much suffering, who has been your cruel enemy for a long time, and who is still ready to be so. Happiness of French officers in Spain, 1812.

20

To rejoice in one's heart and to love, one needs solitude, but to be a success one must get about in society.

21

All that the French have written about love has been well written, precise, and without exaggeration; but it has dealt only with superficial affections, said the good Cardinal Lante.

22

The whole *development of passion* in Goldoni's comedy of the *Innamorati* is excellent; it is the style and the thoughts which are so disgustingly and revoltingly mean; it is the opposite of a French comedy.

23

Youth in 1822. A serious inclination, an active disposition, mean a sacrifice of the present to the future; nothing is so elevating for the soul as the power and the habit of making such sacrifices. I see more likelihood of grand passions in 1832 than in 1772.

24

The bilious temperament, when it does not take too repulsive a form, is perhaps the most likely of all to strike and nourish imagination in women. When the bilious temperament does not occur in propitious circumstances like those of Lauzun in Saint-Simon's *Mémoires* (Vol. v, 380) it is difficult to grow accustomed to it. But once this character has been grasped by a woman it is bound to fascinate her: yes, even the wild and fanatical Balfour (*Old Mortality*). For women it is the exact opposite of the prosaic.

25

In love we are often in doubt of what we believe in most strongly (La R. 355). In every other passion, what we have once proved we no longer doubt.

26

Verse was invented as an aid to memory. Later it was preserved to increase pleasure by the spectacle of difficulty overcome. That it should still survive in dramatic art is a vestige of barbarism. Example – the cavalry orders written in verse by M. de Bonnay.

27

While that jealous suitor is regaling himself with boredom, avarice, hatred, and cold, poisonous passions, I spend a happy night dreaming of her – her who ill-treats me because she does not trust me.

—S.

28

Only a great mind dares express itself simply; this is why Rousseau filled *La Nouvelle Héloïse* with so much rhetoric, and this made it unreadable for anyone over thirty.

29

'Certainly the most serious reproach we can level against ourselves is that we should allow ideas of honour and justice, which occasionally well up in our hearts, to vanish like the slightest phantoms of a dream.'

Letter from Jena, March 1819

30

A respectable woman is at her country house and spends an hour in the hot-house with her gardener; people with whom she has been at variance accuse her of having taken the gardener as a lover.

What can she reply? Absolutely speaking, the thing is possible. She might say 'My character is my defence; examine my whole life,' but these things are equally beyond the perception of the wicked who refuse to see and of the fools who cannot see.

Salviati, Rome, 23 July 1819

31

I have seen a man discover that his rival was beloved, and the latter fail to perceive it because of his passion.

32

The more desperately a man is in love the greater the violence he must do his own feelings in daring to risk offending the woman he loves by taking her hand.

33

Ludicrous rhetoric but, unlike that of Rousseau, inspired by genuine passion: *Memoirs* of M. de Maubreuil, Sand's letter.

34

Naturalness

This evening I saw, or thought I saw, the triumph of naturalness in a young woman who I must admit seems to be a person of great character. It seems clear to me that she adores a cousin of hers, and she herself must certainly be aware of it. The cousin is in love with her too, but because she behaves towards him with great seriousness he thinks he does not please her and allows himself to be distracted by the advances of one Clara, a young widow who is a friend of Mélanie's. I believe he may marry her; Mélanie sees this and suffers all that a heart can suffer when it is proud and filled with a violent and irresistible passion. She need only change her manner a little, but she considers that to depart even for a moment from *naturalness* would be so contemptible as to demean her for the rest of her life.

35

Sappho saw in love only delirium of the senses or physical pleasure rendered sublime by crystallization. Anacreon regarded it as a recreation for the senses and the intellect. There was too little security in those ancient days to allow a man the leisure for indulging in a passionate love affair.

36

I only need to consider the previous fact to laugh a little at people who think Homer greater than Tasso. Passionate love did exist in Homer's day, and not very far from Greece.

37

Woman of sensibility, you who seek to know whether you are loved passionately by the man you adore, examine your lover's early youth. Every man of distinction was at the beginning of his life either absurdly fanatical or else dogged by misfortune. A man of cheerful, gentle disposition, easy to please, can never love with the passion your heart demands.

I call passion only what has stood the test of protracted misfortunes of a kind carefully avoided by novels, and which indeed novels *cannot* convey.

38

A stern resolve at once changes the direst misfortune into something bearable. On the evening after a lost battle a man is in headlong flight on a spent horse; he can clearly hear a group of horsemen galloping after him; suddenly he stops, dismounts, reloads his carbine and pistols, and resolves to defend himself. His vision of death is instantly changed into that of the cross of the Legion of Honour.

39

Basis of the English way of life. About 1730, when Voltaire and Fontenelle were already with us, a machine was invented in England to separate newly-threshed corn from the chaff; it was worked by a wheel which created enough draught to blow the chaff away; but in that *bible-ridden* country the peasants claimed that it was blasphemous to go against the will of Divine Providence and produce an artificial wind in this way, instead of praying fervently to Heaven for a wind to winnow the corn, and waiting for the moment ordained by the God of Israel. Compare this with the French peasantry.[1]

---

1. For the present state of English manners see *The Life of Mr Beattie* written by an intimate friend. There is an edifying description of Mr Beattie's profound humility as he received ten guineas from an old marchioness for slandering Hume. A trembling aristocracy relies for support on bishops with annual incomes of 200,000 livres, and repays *allegedly liberal* writers in hard cash or in esteem for insulting Chénier (*Edinburgh Review*, 1821).

Everything is pervaded by the most loathsome *cant*. Anything which is not a description of wild and energetic feelings is stifled by it; it is quite impossible to write a light-hearted page in English.

40

There is no doubt that it is madness for a man to lay himself open to passionate love. Sometimes, however, the cure acts too drastically. Young American girls in the United States are so imbued and fortified with rational ideas that love, the flower of life, has deserted their youth. In Boston a girl can quite safely be left alone with a handsome stranger, in the certainty that she will think of nothing but the income of her future husband.

41

In France men who have lost their wives are sad, while widows on the contrary are gay and happy. Women have a proverb about the felicity of widowhood. There is therefore no equality in the contract of marriage.

42

People who are happy in love have a look of profound concentration, which in a Frenchman means profound sadness.

Dresden, 1818

43

The more one pleases generally, the less one pleases profoundly.

44

The imitativeness of our early years makes us acquire the passions of our parents, even when these passions poison our lives. (Léonore's pride.)

45

The source of *feminine pride* most worthy of respect is the fear of demeaning oneself in a lover's eyes by some hasty step or by some action which he might consider unfeminine.

46

True love makes the thought of death frequent, easy, without terrors; it becomes merely a standard of comparison, the price one would pay for many things.

47

How often have I not exclaimed in a courageous moment: 'If someone were to shoot me through the head with a pistol I should thank him ere I died, if I had time!' Only by loving her less can one be courageous concerning one's beloved.

– S. *February* 1820

48

'I could never fall in love,' a young woman told me; 'Mirabeau and his letters to Sophie have quite put me off great souls.' Those fatal letters struck me with all the force of a personal experience. Look for what you never find in novels: that two years' constancy before intimacy proves you can rely on your lover's heart.

49

Ridicule frightens love away. Ridicule out of the question in Italy; what is good form in Venice is odd at Naples, hence nothing is odd. Consequently nothing which gives pleasure is culpable. It is this which disposes of foolish honour, and of one half of comedy.

50

Children get their way by tears, and when they cannot attract attention they hurt themselves purposely. Young women *pique* themselves with amour-propre.

51

It is often remarked, but for this reason easily forgotten, that sensitive people are daily becoming rarer, and cultured minds more commonplace.

52

Feminine Pride

Bologna, 18th April, two o'clock in the morning
I have just witnessed a striking example but, all things considered, it would take fifteen pages to give a fair account of it. I should prefer, if I had the courage, to record the consequences of what I observed

beyond any possibility of doubt. Here then is a conviction which I shall have to give up any thought of communicating. There are too many circumstantial details. This kind of pride is the opposite of French vanity. As far as I can remember, the only work where I have seen it described is the *Mémoires* of Madame Roland, in that part where she relates the little arguments she used to propound as a girl.

53

In France most women think nothing of a young man until they have turned him into a conceited fool. Only then can he flatter their vanity.

– Duclos

54

Modena, 1820

Zilietti told me at midnight, at the house of the charming Marchesina R—: 'I shan't dine with you tomorrow at San-Michele (an inn); yesterday I was joking and talking amusingly to Cl***, and it might make me conspicuou\`.'

Do not jump to the conclusion that Zilietti is foolish or shy. He is a prudent and wealthy citizen of this happy country.

55

What deserves admiration in America is the form of governmen and not the society. Elsewhere it is the government that does the harm. They have reversed the parts in Boston, and the government plays the hypocrite in order not to shock society.

56

The young women of Italy, when they fall in love, are entirely subject to natural feelings. At best they can rely for guidance only upon a few excellent maxims picked up by listening at doors.

As though fate had decided that everything here should combine to preserve *natural* behaviour, they do not read novels because there are none. In Geneva and France, on the contrary, girls fall in love at sixteen in order to make a novel out of life, and at each step, almost at each tear, they ask themselves: 'Am I not just like Julie d'Etanges?'

57

The husband of a young woman who is adored by a lover whom she ill-treats, and whom she will barely allow to kiss her hand, will at best enjoy only the coarsest physical pleasure where the lover would experience the most delicious and ecstatic happiness that exists on earth.

58

The laws of *imagination* are still so little understood that I venture the following observation, which may perhaps be quite wrong.

There seem to be two kinds of imagination:

1. Keen, impetuous, spontaneous imagination, leading instantly to action, chafing and languishing at a delay of even twenty-four hours; rather like Fabio's. It is characterized by impatience, and flares into anger against what it cannot obtain. It perceives external objects but these merely add fuel to its fire; it assimilates them and at once converts them to increase the passion.

2. Imagination which kindles only slowly, but which after a time no longer perceives external objects and succeeds in becoming exclusively concerned with, and dependent on, its own passion. This kind of imagination is quite compatible with slowness and even scarcity of ideas. It is conducive to constancy. It is to be found in most of those poor young German girls who die of love and consumption. This dismal spectacle, so frequent beyond the Rhine, is never seen in Italy.

59

Habits of imagination. A Frenchman is *genuinely* shocked by eight changes of scenery in one act of a tragedy. He finds it impossible to enjoy seeing *Macbeth*, and consoles himself by *damning* Shakespeare.

60

The provinces in France are forty years behind Paris in everything relating to women. A married woman in Corbeil told me that she had only allowed herself to read certain passages of Lauzun's *Mémoires*. Such stupidity stunned and bereft me of all reply; it's really not a book one can put down at will like that.

Failure to act naturally, great fault of provincial women. Their profusion of airs and graces. The leading lights in any town worse than the rest.

61

Goethe, or any other German genius, values money at its true worth. One must think of nothing but making money until one has an income of six thousand francs a year, and after that think of it no further. The fool, for his part, does not understand the advantage of feeling and thinking like Goethe; all his life he thinks and feels only in terms of money. It is by this process of double franchise that the prosaic in society seem to carry the day against those of noble heart.

62

In Europe desire is whetted by constraint; in America it is blunted by liberty.

63

The young have become possessed by a kind of mania for debate which distracts them from love. While they are considering whether Napoleon was useful to France, they let the age for loving slip by; even among those who are disposed to be young the affectations of cravat, spur, and martial aspect, the pre-occupation with self, all make them forget to glance at a girl walking demurely by, taking the weekly outing which is all her slender fortunes will permit.

64

I have withheld the chapter entitled *Prude*, and several others.

I am glad to have found the following passage in the memoirs of Horace Walpole:

The two Elizabeths. Let us compare the daughters of two ferocious men, and see which was sovereign of a civilized nation, which of a barbarous one. Both were Elizabeths. The daughter of Peter (of Russia) was absolute yet spared a competitor and a rival; and thought the person of an empress had sufficient allurements for as many of her subjects as she chose to honour with the communication. Elizabeth of England could neither forgive the claim of Mary Stuart nor her charms, but ungenerously emprisoned her (as George IV did Napoleon), when imploring protection and, without the sanction of either despotism or law, sacrificed many to her great and little jealousy. Yet this Elizabeth piqued herself on chastity; and while she practised every ridiculous art of coquetry to be admired at an unseemly age, kept off lovers whom she encouraged, and neither gratified her own desires nor their ambition. Who can help preferring the honest, open-hearted barbarian empress?

(Lord Oxford's *Memoirs*)

65

Excessive familiarity can destroy *crystallization*. A charming girl of sixteen was becoming too fond of a handsome young man of the same age, who used to make a practice of passing beneath her window every evening at nightfall.[1] Her mother invited him to spend a week with them in the country. It was a bold remedy, I admit, but the girl was of a romantic disposition, and the young man a trifle dull; within three days she despised him.

66

Bologna, 17th April 1817

Ave Maria (TWILIGHT), in Italy the hour for tenderness, for the pleasures of the soul and for melancholy: sensation enhanced by the sound of those lovely bells.

Hours for pleasures unrelated to the senses except through memories.

67

The first love affair of a young man entering society is generally one of ambition. It is seldom directed towards a gentle, lovable, innocent girl. How can one tremble, adore, and be aware of oneself in the presence of a divinity? An adolescent needs to love someone whose qualities raise him in his own estimation. It is in a man's declining years that he returns sadly to a love of the simple and the innocent, despairing of the sublime. Between the two comes true love, which thinks of nothing but itself.

68

Greatness of soul is never apparent, for it conceals itself; a little originality is usually all that shows. Greatness of soul is more frequent than one would suppose.

1. At the *Ave Maria*.

69

Oh, that moment when first you press the hand of the woman you love! The only comparable happiness is that exquisite enjoyment of power which ministers and monarchs affect to despise. This happiness also has its *crystallization* process, requiring a colder and more rational imagination. Think of a man whom, a quarter of an hour earlier, Napoleon has appointed to ministerial office.

70

Nature has given strength to the North and wit to the South, the celebrated Jean de Muller said to me at Cassel in 1808.

71

Nothing could be more fallacious than the saying 'no man is a hero to his valet,' or rather nothing could be more true in *monarchical* terms: the affected hero, like Hippolyte in *Phèdre*. Desaix, for example, would have been a hero even to his valet (admittedly I do not know whether he had one), and indeed more of a hero to his valet than to anyone else. But for good form and the necessary degree of comedy, Turenne and Fénelon might each have been Desaix.

72

Here is a piece of blasphemy: I, a Dutchman, make bold to say that the French take no real pleasure either in conversation or in the theatre; instead of recreation and perfect relaxation it is hard labour. Among the burdens which hastened the death of Madame de Staël, I have heard counted the strain of making conversation during her last winter.[1]

W.

73

The degree of tension necessary in the nerves of the ear to listen to each note, adequately explains the physical aspect of the enjoyment of music.

74

What degrades women of easy virtue is their own conviction, and that of others, that they are committing a great sin.

1. *Memoirs* of Marmontel, Montesquieu's conversation.

75

In the army, during a retreat, if you warn an Italian soldier of a danger which it is futile to risk, he will almost thank you, and carefully avoid it. If out of common humanity you point out the same danger to a French soldier he will think you are challenging him, his self-esteem will be *piqued*, and he will immediately expose himself to the danger in question. If he dared he would jeer at you.

Gyat, 1812

76

Any really useful idea, if it can be expressed only in very simple terms, will certainly be despised in France. *Mutual Instruction* would never have caught on had it been discovered by a Frenchman. It is exactly the opposite in Italy.

77

However little passion you may feel for a woman, provided your imagination has not run dry, if she be inept enough to say to you one evening, tenderly and bashfully: 'All right; come tomorrow at noon. I shall be alone,' you will be unable to sleep, and quite incapable of thought. After a morning of torment the hour strikes, and it is as if each stroke were reverberating through your diaphragm.

78

Between lovers the *sharing* of money increases love; the *giving* of money *destroys* love.

In one case present misfortune and, for the future, the grim prospect of the fear of want are dismissed; in the other case an element of *politics* is introduced, an awareness of being two which negates fellow-feeling.

79

(Messe des Tuileries, 1811)

The court functions at which women display their bare bosoms very much as officers do their uniforms – and, despite all their charms, with very little more effect – inevitably recall scenes from Aretino.

This is what people will do to curry a man's favour *for mercenary ends*; here is a whole society acting without morality and above all without passion. All this, added to the presence of women in low-cut dresses and bearing the stamp of viciousness, women who greet with a sardonic laugh everything but self-interest promptly paid with material pleasures, reminds one of scenes in the Bagnio, and drives far away any difficulty arising from virtue or the inner satisfaction of a mind at peace with itself.

I have noticed that a feeling of isolation in the midst of all this predisposes sensitive hearts to love.

80

If the soul is engaged in feeling false shame and in overcoming it, it cannot experience pleasure. Pleasure is a luxury; it requires for its enjoyment that security, which is a necessity, should not be imperilled.

81

A sign of love which self-interested women do not know how to simulate. Does reconciliation bring true joy? Or is there a weighing of the advantages to be gained from it?

82

The poor unfortunates who inhabit the monastery of La Trappe are wretched people who have not had quite enough courage to kill themselves. I except the leaders, who enjoy the pleasure of being leaders.

83

To have known Italian beauty is a misfortune; one becomes insensitive. Except in Italy one prefers the conversation of men.

84

Italian prudence tends towards self-preservation, which allows the imagination free play. (See an account of the death of the famous comic actor Pertica, 24th December 1821.) English prudence on the other hand, entirely concerned to amass and conserve enough money to cover expenses, demands a meticulous and unremitting precision, a habit which paralyses the imagination. But note that at the same time it lends the greatest strength to the idea of *duty*.

85

Immense respect for money, which is the besetting sin of the
English and the Italians, is less noticeable in France, and entirely
diminished to its just importance in Germany.

86

Frenchwomen, never having known the happiness of *genuine* passion, are not exacting about the happiness of their own households,
nor about *everyday* life.

Compiègne

87

'You may well talk of ambition as an antidote to boredom,' said
Kamensky; 'I used to gallop two leagues every evening to visit the
princess at Kolich, and all the time I was in the intimate society of a
despot whom I respected and in whose hands lay all my happiness
and the power to satisfy my every possible desire.'

Wilna, 1812

88

Perfection in their attention to minor manners and dress, great
kindness, no great intelligence, attentiveness to a hundred little
details every day, inability to be interested for more than three days
in any one event; a pretty contrast with puritan severity, biblical
cruelty, strict probity, shy and painful self-consciousness, universal
cant; and yet these are the two greatest peoples in the world!

89

Since among princesses there has been a Catherine the Second who
was an empress, why should there not have been among the bour-
geoises a female Samuel Bernard or Lagrange?

90

Alviza calls it an unforgivable lack of delicacy to dare write letters
in which you speak of love to a woman whom you adore, and who
swears, gazing at you tenderly the while, that she will never love you.

91

The greatest philosopher the French have ever had unfortunately did not live in some distant Alpine solitude, nor launch his book from there upon Paris without ever entering the city himself. When they saw Helvétius so simple and honest, affected and precious people like Suard, Marmontel and Diderot could never believe that here was a great philosopher. In all sincerity they doubted the profundity of his thought; in the first place it was simple, an unforgivable sin in France; in the second place the man – and not his book – was subject to one weakness: he attached excessive importance to what is known in France as glory, to being fashionable among his contemporaries such as Balzac, Voiture and Fontenelle.

Rousseau had too much sensibility and too little common-sense, Buffon was too hypocritical about his botanical garden, Voltaire too childish, for any of them to be capable of judging Helvétius's principle.

This philosopher made the little mistake of calling his principle *self-interest* instead of giving it the prettier name of *pleasure*;[1] but what can we think of the common-sense of a whole literary culture which allows itself to be misled by such a little slip of the pen?

A man of ordinary intelligence, Prince Eugene of Savoy for example, if he were in Regulus's shoes, would have stayed quietly in Rome, where he might even have derided the folly of the senate in Carthage; but Regulus went back. Prince Eugene would have been pursuing his own *interest* exactly as Regulus pursued his.

In nearly every situation in life a generous person will perceive a possible course of action of which the ordinary man has not the least inkling. The instant this course of action becomes clear to the generous person it is in *his interest* to take it.

If he did not perform the action once he had perceived it, he would despise himself and be unhappy. One's duties are in direct proportion to the scope of one's intelligence. The principle of Helvétius holds good even in the most frenzied ecstasies of love, even in the case of suicide. It is against his nature, it is impossible that man should not always, at any given moment, do what in that moment is possible and which gives him the most pleasure.

1. —Torva leœna lupum sequitur, lupus ipse capellam;
      Florentem cytisum sequitur lasciva capella.
    . . . . Trahit sua quemque voluptas.
                  Virgil, *Eclogue II.*

92

To have a strong character one must have experienced the effect produced by others upon oneself; therefore others are a necessity.

93

Love in Ancient Times

The love letters of Roman matrons have never been posthumously published. Petronius wrote a charming book, but has depicted only debauchery.

As regards *love* in Rome, apart from Dido[1] and the second Eclogue of Virgil, we have nothing more precise to go on than the writings of the three great poets Ovid, Tibullus, and Propertius.

Now the elegies of Parny or the letter from Héloïse to Abelard by Colardeau are very incomplete and vague descriptions by comparison with certain letters from *La Nouvelle Héloïse* or those of a Portuguese nun, Mlle de Lespinasse, Mirabeau's Sophie, Werther, etc.

Poetry, with its compulsory similes, its mythology in which the poet does not believe, its dignified Louis XIV style, and its whole paraphernalia of so-called poetic embellishment, is far less effective than prose in giving a clear and precise idea of the emotions of the heart; and in this sphere only clarity can move one.

Tibullus, Ovid, and Propertius had better taste than our poets; they showed love as it could have existed among the proud citizens of Rome; yet they lived under Augustus who, having closed the temple of Janus, sought to resorb the citizens into a state of loyal subjection to a monarchy.

The mistresses of these three great poets were unfaithful, venal coquettes from whom the poets sought only physical pleasure, and I am inclined to believe that they never had an inkling of the sublime feelings[2] which throbbed thirteen centuries later in the heart of tender Héloïse.

1. See the *look* in Dido's eyes, in the superb sketch by M. Guérin at the Luxembourg.

2. Since all the most beautiful things in the world have become a part of the beauty of your beloved, you feel ready to do all the most beautiful things in the world.

The following passage[1] is borrowed from a distinguished man of letters who knows the Latin poets far better than I:

'The brilliant genius of Ovid, the rich imagination of Propertius and the sensitive soul of Tibullus undoubtedly led them to write verse subtly different from each other's, but each loved a woman of almost the same type in the same way. They desired, they triumphed, they had fortunate rivals, they were jealous, they quarrelled and were reconciled, they were unfaithful in their turn, were forgiven and regained a contentment that was soon disturbed by the recurrence of the same happenings.

'Corinna is married. The first lesson Ovid teaches her is how she must cunningly deceive her husband; what signs they must employ in his presence and in public so that they may understand each other and yet be understood only be each other. Fulfilment follows soon after, then quarrels; then something unexpected from so gallant a man as Ovid, insults and blows; then apologies, tears and forgiveness. Sometimes he calls upon servants and underlings: his mistress's door-keeper, to let him in at night; an accursed old woman who corrupts her and teaches her to sell herself for gold; an old eunuch who guards her; a young slave-girl, to deliver writing-tablets requesting a meeting. The request is refused and he curses the tablets which have met with so little success. Later he is more fortunate, and exhorts Dawn not to interrupt his happiness.

'Soon he begins to accuse himself of frequent infidelities and of having a taste for all women. A moment later Corinna is also unfaithful; he cannot bear the thought of having taught her lessons from which she is now profiting in another's arms. Corinna in her turn is jealous; she behaves more like an angry woman than a tender one and accuses him of being in love with a young slave-girl. He swears that he is nothing of the sort, and writes to the slave-girl; and all that had angered Corinna turns out to be true after all. How can she have found out? What signs betrayed them? He insists that the slave-girl shall grant him a further meeting, and threatens, if she will not, to confess everything to Corinna. He jokes with a friend about his two loves and the hardships and pleasures they bring him. Shortly afterwards he is solely engrossed with Corinna. She is all his. He sings his triumph as though it were his first victory. After certain happenings which for several reasons are best left in Ovid's text, and others which

1. Guinguené, *Histoire Littéraire de l'Italie*, Vol. II, p. 490.

it would take too long to relate, he finds that Corinna's husband has become too acquiescent, and is no longer jealous. This displeases the lover who threatens to leave the man's wife unless he renews his jealousy. The husband obeys him to excess and has Corinna so closely watched that Ovid can no longer get near her. He complains of the surveillance he himself has provoked, but is sure he can outwit it; unfortunately he is not the only one to succeed in doing so. Corinna's infidelities begin again, more frequent than before, and her affairs become so public that Ovid begs her at least to grant him the favour of trying a little harder to deceive him, and of making it a little less obvious what she really is. This was the way of life of Ovid and his mistress, and such was the character of their loves.

'Cynthia is the first love of Propertius, and is to be the last. As soon as he is granted happiness he begins to be jealous. Cynthia is too fond of fine clothes; he begs her to eschew luxury and to love simplicity. He himself is given to more than one kind of debauchery. Cynthia is waiting for him but he does not arrive until morning, straight from the table and far gone in wine. He finds her asleep, and it is some time before she is awoken by all the noise he makes or even by the caresses he gives her. At last she opens her eyes and reproaches him as he deserves. A friend tries to estrange him from Cynthia; he waxes eloquent to this friend about her beauty and her talents. He is faced with the threat of losing her when she elopes with a soldier; she becomes a camp-follower and exposes herself to every indignity in the pursuit of her soldier. Propertius is not angry, but weeps and makes vows so that she shall be happy. He swears he will not leave the house from which she has departed; he will seek out strangers who have seen her, and ply them with questions about Cynthia. Her heart is touched by so great a love; she leaves the soldier and remains with the poet. Intoxicated with happiness he thanks Apollo and the Muses. This happiness is soon disturbed by new crises of jealousy, culminating in estrangement and parting. Absent from her he can think of nothing but Cynthia. Her past infidelities lead him to fear that she will commit new ones. Death holds no fears for him and his only anxiety is lest he lose Cynthia; if he could be sure she would be faithful to him he would gladly go to his grave.

'After further betrayals he thinks he is released from his love, but very soon resumes his shackles, painting the most ravishing portrait of his mistress, with her beauty, her elegant dress, her talent for singing, poetry, and dancing, each redoubling and vindicating his love. But Cynthia, as perverse as she is attractive, disgraces herself in the eyes of the whole city by such scandalous adventures that Propertius can no longer love her without shame. He blushes for it, but he cannot tear himself away from her. He will be her lover – her husband – never will he love anyone but Cynthia. They leave each other, and come together again. Cynthia is jealous, and he reassures her: he will never love another woman. It is indeed no single woman that he loves, but *all* women. He can never possess enough of them, and his need for pleasures is insatiable. He is only brought to himself when Cynthia again throws him over, and then his protests are as loud as if he had never been unfaithful himself. He wants to escape and seeks distraction in debauchery, having as usual drunk too much. He pretends that he is met by a host of Cupids who bring him back to Cynthia's feet. Their reconciliation is followed by renewed storms. While they are supping together Cynthia, as overheated with wine as he is himself, upsets the table and throws goblets at his head, which he finds charming. In the end further treacheries oblige him to break his bond; he must get away, and decides to make a journey to Greece; but when all his plans are complete he gives up the idea, only to find himself the victim of new injuries. Cynthia no longer confines herself to betraying him, but makes him a laughing-stock in the eyes of his rivals, until she is stricken with an illness and dies. She reproaches him for his infidelities and his capriciousness, for having abandoned her in her last hours, and swears that she herself, despite all appearances, was always faithful to him. Such are the adventures and behaviour of Propertius and his mistress, and such is the abridged account of their loves. So much for the woman whom a being of Propertius' calibre was reduced to loving.

'Ovid and Propertius were often unfaithful, but never inconstant. They were two confirmed libertines who often bestowed their favours at random, but who always returned to resume the same shackles. Corinna and Cynthia had to withstand the rivalry of all women, but not of any one woman in particular. The Muse of these two poets was faithful, even if their love was not, and no other name than that of Corinna or Cynthia appears in their verse. Tibullus, a more sensitive lover and poet, less lively and less wanton in his tastes, cannot boast the same constancy. One after another three beauties become the focus of his love and of his verse. The first and most famous is Delia, who is also the best loved. Tibullus has lost his fortune, but he still has the countryside and Delia; his only wishes are that he may possess her in the peace of the fields, that he may press her hand in his as he dies, and that she may follow his funeral procession in tears. Delia is placed in confinement by a jealous husband; he resolves to break into her prison despite the watchdogs and the triple locks, and in her arms to forget all his cares. He falls ill, and Delia alone preoccupies his thoughts. He urges her to remain chaste, *to despise gold*, to grant to him alone what he has obtained from her. But Delia does not take this advice. He had thought he could bear her unfaithfulness, but is overwhelmed and begs Delia and Venus to have mercy on him. In vain he seeks solace in wine; he can neither soften his regrets nor cure his love. He seeks out Delia's husband, who has been deceived like himself, and explains all the tricks she uses to attract and entertain her lovers. If the husband cannot keep her let him hand her over to Tibullus' care; the latter will know how to put the lovers off and keep safe from their snares the woman who has outraged them both. He grows calmer, and more reconciled to her; and remembers Delia's mother who used to champion their love; the recollection of this good woman re-opens his heart to tenderness and all Delia's ill-doings are forgotten. But she is soon guilty of further and graver transgressions. She has allowed herself to be corrupted by gold and presents; she gives herself to another, then to others. Tibullus finally breaks a shameful bondage and bids her farewell for ever.

'He falls under the spell of Nemesis and is none the happier; gold is her only love and she cares little for verses and the gifts of genius. Nemesis is a miserly woman who sells herself to the highest bidder; though he curses her avarice he loves her, and cannot live unless she will love him in return. He resolves to move her with touching pictures. She has lost her young sister, and he will go and weep over her grave, confiding his woes to the mute ashes. Her sister's shade will be displeased by the tears shed on Nemesis' account, and Nemesis should not regard that displeasure lightly, for the mournful ghost of her sister would visit her at night and disturb her sleep . . . But these sad memories wring tears from Nemesis, and he cannot bring himself to buy even happiness at such a price. His third mistress is Neaera. For a long time he basks in his love for her, and asks nothing more from the gods than that he may live and die with her, but she leaves him and goes away. He can think of no one else, and her name fills his prayers; he dreams that Apollo comes to tell him that Neaera has left him for ever, but he refuses to believe the dream, for he could never survive such a catastrophe; and yet the catastrophe has happened. Neaera is unfaithful, and he has once again been deserted. Such were the character of Tibullus and his fate, and such the triple and somewhat dismal story of his loves.

'It is chiefly Tibullus who is dominated by gentle melancholy, which lends even his pleasure that tinge of reverie and sadness wherein lies the charm. If any poet of antiquity can be said to have introduced morality into love, that poet was Tibullus; but those nuances of feeling which he expresses so well are *in himself*, and he is no more concerned than the other two to find or induce such nuances in his mistresses. Their graces and their beauty are what inflames him; their favours are what he covets or regrets; their faithlessness, venality, and wantonness are what tortures him. Of all these women immortalized in the verse of three great poets, Cynthia appears to be the most attractive. In addition to her other charms she has that of her talents; she cultivates singing and poetry; but for all these talents, which were fairly common among courtesans of a certain class, she is no more worthy; pleasure, gold, and wine are none the less her ruling passions; and Propertius, who only once or twice boasts of this taste she has for the arts, is none the less, in his passion for her, enslaved by quite another kind of power.'

These great poets were apparently among the most sensitive and fastidious souls of their time, and yet these were the women they loved and this was how they loved. All literary considerations must here be set aside. I am only looking to them for testimony about their times; two thousand years hence a novel by Ducray-Duminil will be testimony about our customs.

93a

One of my great regrets is not to have been able to see Venice in 1760;[1] a sequence of lucky accidents had apparently combined within that tiny area both the political institutions and the opinions most favourable to man's happiness. A gentle voluptuousness brought happiness within easy reach of all. There was no internal conflict and

1. Travels of President de Brosses in Italy; travels of Eustace, Sharp, Smollett.

no crime. Every brow was serene, no one was anxious to appear wealthier, and hypocrisy was pointless. I imagine that it must have been exactly the opposite of London in 1822.

94

If for a lack of personal security you substitute a healthy fear of lacking money, you will see that the United States of America, as regards the passion which is the subject of our present monograph, bears a strong resemblance to the ancient world.

In speaking of the more or less imperfect sketches of passionate love left to us by the ancients I see that I have omitted to mention the *Loves of Medea* in the *Golden Fleece*. Virgil copied them for his Dido. Compare this with love as it appears in a modern novel. *Le Doyen de Killerine*, for example.

95

The Roman feels the beauty of Nature and the arts with surprising strength, depth, and accuracy, but if he sets about trying rationally to discuss what he feels so forcefully the result is pitiful.

Perhaps it is because his feelings come from Nature, and his logic from the government.

One sees at once why the fine arts, outside Italy, are nothing but a bad joke; they are more rationally discussed, but the public cannot *feel*.

96

London, 20th November 1821

A very sensible man who has just arrived from Madras told me yesterday in two hours what I summarize below in twenty lines or so:

That *dreariness* which weighs inexplicably upon the character of the English is so deeply ingrained in their hearts that even in Madras, at the other end of the world, when an Englishman can obtain a few days' furlough he hastens to leave the rich and thriving city of Madras and to find relaxation in the little French town of Pondicherry which flourishes, without natural resources and almost without commerce, under the paternal administration of M. Dupuy. In Madras they drink Burgundy at thirty-six francs a bottle, while the poverty of the French in Pondicherry is such that even in the best circles the refreshments consist mostly of large glasses of water. But there is laughter there.

Nowadays there is more liberty in England than in Prussia. The climate is the same as that of Köenigsberg, Berlin, and Warsaw, none of which is noted for its cheerlessness. The working classes in these cities have less security and drink just as little wine as in England, and they are much less well-clothed.

Aristocratic circles in Venice and Vienna are not sad.

I can see only one difference in the gay countries; the Bible is little read and there is gallantry there. I apologize for lingering over the demonstration of something of which I am not sure. I am withholding twenty facts which bear out the foregoing.

97

In a fine castle near Paris I have just met a handsome, witty, wealthy young man of less than twenty; he chanced to be left almost alone there for a long time with an extremely beautiful girl of eighteen, talented, remarkably intelligent, and also very rich. Who would not have expected a passion to ensue? Nothing of the sort; both these pretty creatures were so eaten up with affectation that they were concerned only with themselves and with the effect they ought to produce upon each other.

98

I admit that from the moment of its great achievement this people has been led by a savage pride to commit all the errors and stupidities that opportunity offered. Here nevertheless is the reason why I cannot withdraw the words of praise I once uttered about this living counterpart of the Middle Ages.

The prettiest woman in Narbonne is a young Spanish girl, barely twenty, who lives in seclusion with her Spanish husband, an officer on half-pay. Some time ago the latter was obliged to slap the face of a certain coxcomb; the following day the coxcomb saw the young Spanish woman arrive at the place appointed for the duel; he burst out with a new torrent of affectation: 'But really, this is scandalous! How could you have admitted to your wife ... I suppose Madame has come to prevent us fighting?' '*I have come to bury you*,' replied the young Spanish woman.

Happy the husband who can tell his wife everything. The result does not belie the loftiness of the pronouncement. Such an action would have been regarded in England as most improper. Thus false propriety diminishes what little happiness this world affords.

99

That charming fellow Donézan said yesterday: 'In my young days, and indeed until quite late in my life (for I was fifty in '89), women used to powder their hair.

'I confess to you that a woman without powder is repugnant to me and always gives me the impression of being a chambermaid who has had no time to finish her toilette.'

This is the only argument against Shakespeare and in favour of the unities.

Since young people read nothing but La Harpe, a liking for great powdered wigs like those worn by the late Queen Marie-Antoinette may persist for a few years yet. I also know some people who despise Correggio and Michael Angelo, and certainly M. Donézan is an extremely intelligent man.

100

Cold, brave, calculating, mistrustful, argumentative, always in fear of being stimulated by someone who might secretly be laughing at them, a little jealous of those who had witnessed great things under Napoleon, such were the young people of this period, more to be respected than to be liked. Naturally they brought the government round to a debased left-of-centre position. The characteristics of these young people were to be found even among conscripts, whose only ambition was to reach the end of their service.

All systems of education, whether intentionally or fortuitously administered, fit men for a particular period in their lives. Education in the time of Louis XV singled out twenty-five as the ideal age in its pupils.[1]

The young people of this period will be at their best at forty, for they will have lost their mistrust and pretentiousness, and will have acquired gaiety and ease of manner.

---

1. M. de Francueil, when he wore too much powder. *Memoirs* of Mme d'Epinay.

101

Discussion between the man of good faith
and the man from the Academy

'In this discussion with the academician, the latter always extricated himself by quibbling over minor dates or other similar trivial errors; but he persisted in denying, or pretended not to understand, the consequence and natural quiddity of things; for example that Nero had been a cruel emperor, or that Charles II had forsworn himself. Now how can such things be proved, or in proving them how can one avoid interrupting the main argument, and losing the thread of it?

'I have ever observed this kind of argument taking place between such people, where one is but seeking truth and yet more truth, while the other seeks the favour of his master or party and the glory of eloquence. And I hold it a great deception and waste of time for the man of good faith to stop and talk with the aforesaid academicians.'

The Playful Works of Guy Allard de Voiron

102

Only a very small part of the art of being happy is an exact science, a kind of ladder, up one rung of which one is sure to climb every century; it is this part which depends upon the government (and this is only a theory; in my opinion the Venetians in 1707 were happier than are the people of Philadelphia today).

Moreover, the art of being happy is like poetry; despite the progress of all things towards perfection Homer, two thousand seven hundred years ago, had more talent than Lord Byron.

Reading Plutarch carefully I believe I can recognize that even without the invention of printing and iced punch they were happier in Sicily in the time of Dion than we know how to be today.

I would rather be a fifth-century Arab than a nineteenth-century Frenchman.

103

It is never that illusion which renews and dispels itself moment by moment which one goes to seek at the theatre, but the opportunity of proving to one's neighbour, or to oneself if one is so unlucky as to have no neighbour, that one's La Harpe has been properly conned and that one is a man of taste. This is a pleasure fit for old pedants, in which youth is indulging.

104

A woman belongs by right to a man who loves her and whom she loves *more than life*.

105

Crystallization cannot be induced by men who imitate others, and the most dangerous rivals are those who are the most unorthodox.

106

In a highly civilized society *passionate love* is just as natural as physical love among savages.

Métilde

107

If it were not for the nuances, there would be no happiness in possessing a woman one adored; in fact it would be impossible.

L. 7th October

108

Whence comes the intolerance of the Stoics? From the same source as that of the bigotedly devout. They are ill-tempered because they are in conflict with Nature, because they deny themselves and because they suffer. If they could be brought honestly to analyse the hatred they bear towards those who profess a less rigid ethic, they would acknowledge that it derives from the concealed jealousy of a happiness they envy and have forbidden themselves to enjoy, *without believing* in the rewards that would repay their sacrifices.

Diderot

109

Habitually ill-tempered women might well ask themselves if they are following the code of behaviour which they *sincerely believe* to be the road to happiness. Is there not perhaps within the heart of a prude a certain lack of courage accompanied by a degree of mean vengefulness? Look at the ill-humour of Madame Deshoulières in her latter days.

Note by M. Lemontey

110

Nothing could be more indulgent, because nothing is happier, than sincere virtue; but Mistress Hutchinson herself lacks indulgence.

111

Next to this happiness comes that of a woman who is young, pretty, and easy-going, and who is not given to self-reproach. In Messina when they spoke ill of the Contessina Vicenzella she replied: 'What do you expect; I'm young, free, rich, and perhaps not ugly. I wish as much to all the women in Messina.' This delightful woman, who never felt more than friendship towards me, was the one who introduced me to the sweet poetry in Sicilian dialect by the Abbé Meli; lovely poems, though still spoilt by mythology.

Delfante

112

The Parisian public has a capacity for concentration which lasts for three days; beyond that limit, whether you offer them the death of Napoleon or M. Béranger sentenced to two months' imprisonment, the result is the same; and to speak of it on the fourth day betrays a similar lack of tact in the speaker. Is every great capital like this, or has it to do with the kindly superficiality of the Parisian? Thanks to aristocratic pride and painful self-consciousness London is nothing but a vast congregation of hermits and not a capital at all. Vienna is nothing but an oligarchy of two hundred families surrounded by a hundred and fifty thousand artisans and servants in their employ, and is no more a capital than London. Naples and Paris are the only two capitals.

Extract from Birkbeck's Travels, p. 371

113

If there were a period when, going by the commonplace theories regarded as reasonable by commonplace men, prison might be bearable, that period would be a month or two before the release of a poor prisoner detained for a number of years. But *crystallization* ordains otherwise. The last month is more painful than the three previous years. M. d'Hotelans has known several prisoners serving long sentences in Melun gaol who *died* of impatience only a few months before they were due to be freed.

114

I cannot resist the pleasure of quoting a letter written in poor English by a young German girl. Thus it is proved that constant love does exist, and that not every man of genius is a Mirabeau. The great poet Klopstock is reputed in Hamburg to have been a likeable man; here is what his young wife wrote to an intimate friend:

After having seen him two hours, I was obliged to pass the evening in a company, which never had been so wearisome to me. I could not speak, I could not play; I thought I saw nothing but Klopstock; I saw him the next day, and the following and we were very seriously friends. But the fourth day he departed. It was a strong hour the hour of his departure! He wrote soon after and from that time our correspondence began to be a very diligent one. I sincerely believed my love to be friendship. I spoke with my friends of nothing but Klopstock, and showed his letters. They raillied at me and said I was in love. I raillied then again, and said that they must have a very friendshipless heart, if they had no idea of friendship to a man as well as to a woman. Thus it continued eight months, in which time my friends found as much love in Klopstock's letters as in me. I perceived it likewise, but I would not believe it. At the last Klopstock said plainly that he loved; and I startled as for a wrong thing; I answered that it was no love, but friendship, as it was what I felt for him; we had not seen one another enough to love (as if love must have more time than friendship). This was sincerely my meaning, and I had this meaning till Klopstock came again to Hamburg. This he did a year after we had seen one another the first time. We saw, we were friends, we loved; and a short time after, I could even tell Klopstock that I loved. But we were obliged to part again, and wait two years for our wedding. My mother would not let marry me a stranger. I could marry then without her consentement, as by the death of my father my fortune depended not on her; but this was a horrible idea for me; and thank heaven that I have prevailed by prayers! At this time knowing Klopstock, she loves him as her lifely son, and thanks God that she has not persisted. We married and I am the happiest wife in the world. In some few months it will be four years that I am so happy...

Correspondence of Richardson, Vol. III, p. 147

115

The only unions which are legitimate for ever are those ruled by a genuine passion.

Métilde

116

To be happy in a lax moral climate a woman must have a simplicity of character such as one finds in Germany and Italy, but never in France.

The Duchesse de C—

117

The Turks in their pride deprive their wives of everything which might provide matter for crystallization. For the last three months I have been living among a people whose titled folk, because of their pride, will soon have reached the same point.

The men give the name of *modesty* to the demands of a pride driven mad by aristocracy. How could one dare be found wanting in modesty? Also, as in Athens, intelligent men have a marked tendency to take refuge in the company of courtesans, that is to say women who through one outrageous mistake have found shelter from the affectations of *modesty*.

Life of Fox

118

Where love has been prevented by too early a victory, I have noticed that in sensitive people crystallization tries to set in afterwards. The woman says laughingly: 'No, I don't love you.'

119

The present system of education for women, that strange mixture of pious practices and lively songs (*di piacer mi balza il cor* from the *Gazza Ladra*), is the most effective way in the world to banish happiness. This education breeds the most illogical minds. Madame de R—, who feared death, has just died because she thought it was amusing to throw her medicine out of the window. These poor wretched women mistake inconsequence for gaiety, because gaiety is often apparently inconsequent. It is like the German who demonstrates his liveliness by throwing himself out of the window.

120

Vulgarity, by extinguishing imagination, has the immediate effect of boring me to death. The charming Countess K—, showing me her love-letters this evening, which I consider are coarse.

Forli, 17th March. Henri

Imagination had not been extinguished, but had merely lost its way, and from sheer distaste quickly gave up visualizing the coarseness of those dull lovers.

121

Metaphysical Reverie

Belgirate, 26th October 1816

Whenever a genuine passion encounters obstacles it probably produces more unhappiness than happiness; this idea may not hold good for a sensitive soul but is clearly true for the majority of men, and particularly for the cold philosophers who, in the sphere of passions, live almost entirely upon curiosity and self-esteem.

Yesterday evening, as we strolled along the terrace of the Isola Bella, on the east side, near the big pine, I related the foregoing to the Contessina Fulvia, who said to me: 'Unhappiness makes a much greater impression upon humanity than pleasure does.

'The most important quality of anything which claims to give us pleasure is that it should have a strong impact.

'Could one not conclude that, since life itself is entirely made up of sensations, the universal inclination of all living beings is towards awareness that their act of living depends on the strongest possible sensations? People from the North have little life; consider the slowness of their movements. The *dolce far niente* of the Italians is the pleasure of indulging in the emotions of the soul as one lies languidly upon a divan, a pleasure inconceivable to those who rush about all day on horseback or in a drosky like Englishmen or Russians. These people would die of boredom upon a divan. There is nothing in their souls for them to reflect upon.

'Love causes the strongest possible sensations; the proof of this is that in what physiologists would call moments of *inflammation* the heart forms those *associations of sensation* which seem so absurd to such philosophers as Helvétius and Buffon. The other day, as you know, Luizina fell into the lake; it was because she was watching a laurel leaf which had dropped into the water from a tree on the Isola Madre (Borromean Islands). The poor woman confessed to me that one day her lover, as he talked to her, was stripping the leaves from a laurel branch into the water, saying as he did so: "Your cruelties and the calumnies of your friend are denying me the enjoyment of life and the chance of glory."

'For some strange and quite incomprehensible reason, a soul which has known moments of anguish and intense unhappiness through the effects of some passion, ambition, gambling, love, jealousy, war, etc., *despises* the happiness of a peaceful life where everything seems made to order. A splendid castle in a picturesque situation, ample wealth, a good wife, three pretty children, numerous delightful friends: these are but a faint outline of all that our host General C— possesses, and yet you know he told us that he was tempted to go to Naples and take command of a guerilla band. A soul made for passion feels in the first place that this happy life *bores* him, and perhaps also that it only provides him with commonplace ideas. C— said to you: "I wish I had never known the fever of great passions, so that I might have profited by the apparent happiness about which I am paid such stupid compliments every day, and to which, as a crowning horror, I have to reply graciously." '

The philosopher in me rejoined: 'If you need a thousandth proof that we are not fashioned by a benign being, i t is that *pleasure* produces only about half as much impression upon our being as *pain* does . . .'[1]

The Contessina interrupted me: 'There are very few moral hardships in life which are not made more valuable by the *emotion* they excite; and if there is a fraction of generosity in the soul this pleasure is increased a hundredfold. A man condemned to death in 1815 and saved at the last moment (M. Lavalette for example), if he faced his torment bravely, must recall the occasion ten times a month; the coward who faces death sobbing and screaming (Morris the exciseman thrown into the lake; *Rob Roy* III, 120), if he too was saved at the last moment, can at best remember the occasion with pleasure only *because he was saved* and not because of any fund of generosity he discovered within himself, which rid the future of all its fears.'

Myself: 'Love, even unrequited love, provides a sensitive soul, for whom *what is imagined really exists*, with a fund of enjoyment of the same kind; sublime visions of happiness and beauty enwrap oneself and one's beloved. How often has Salviati not heard Léonore telling him, like Mademoiselle Mars in *Les Fausses Confidences*, with her

1. See the analysis of Bentham's *ascetic principle* in his *Traités de législation*, volume i.
One gives pleasure to a *benign* being by making oneself suffer.

bewitching smile, "Well, yes; I do love you!" Now these are illusions a prudent man never has.'

Fulvia (*raising her eyes to heaven*): 'Yes, for you and for me, love, even unrequited love, provided that our admiration of the beloved is infinite, is the greatest happiness of all.'

(Fulvia is twenty-three, and the most famous beauty in *****; her eyes were divine as she spoke, gazing up at the lovely midnight skies above the Borromean Islands; the very stars seemed to reply to her. I lowered my eyes, and could no longer find philosophical arguments to use against her). She continued: 'And all that the world calls happiness is not worth the trouble. I think only contempt can cure such a passion; not too great a contempt, for that would be torment; but for example, in the case of you men, to see the woman you adore loving a coarse and prosaic man, or giving you up for the sake of enjoying the trivial and dainty luxury she finds at the house of her friend.'

122

Will-power means the courage to run the risk of difficulty; to run such a risk means to tempt providence, to gamble. There are some soldiers who cannot exist without these gambles; this is what makes them quite unbearable in family life.

123

General Teulié told me this evening that he had discovered what made him so abominably taciturn and barren when there were affected women present in the drawing room. No sooner did he make a spirited exposition of his feelings in the presence of such creatures than he was smitten with bitter shame at having done so. (And if he did not speak from his heart, were it but of Punchinello, he had nothing to say. I noticed besides that he never knew the conventional or polite remark to make, and because of this he was always regarded as ridiculous and outlandish by affected women. Heaven had not created him to be elegant.)

124

At court irreligion is bad form because it is adjudged contrary to the interests of princes: it is also bad form in the presence of young girls, for it would prevent them from finding a husband. Doubtless, if God exists, he must find it pleasant to be honoured for motives such as these.

125

For a great painter or a great poet love is divine because it multiplies a hundredfold the scope and the pleasures of the art which gives his soul its daily bread. How many great artists there must be who never suspect the existence of their souls nor of their genius! Often they believe themselves untalented for the thing they adore, because they are at variance with the eunuchs of the seraglio, or with people like La Harpe; for such artists even unhappy love means happiness.

126

The picture of first love is the most universally moving one; why? Because it is nearly always the same in all classes, in all countries, and in all characters. Therefore this first love is not the most passionate.

127

Be reasonable! Be reasonable! That is the cry invariably hurled at a poor lover. In 1760, at the climax of the Seven Years War, Grimm wrote: '... There is no doubt that the King of Prussia could have prevented this war before it broke out, by ceding Silesia. This would have been a very wise action on his part. How many evils he would have prevented! What could the mere possession of a province have to do with the happiness of a king? And was not the Great Elector a most contented and respected prince without possessing Silesia? That is how a king might have acted in accordance with the soundest precepts of reason, and I have no idea why such a king would have become the object of the whole world's contempt, while Frederick, in sacrificing everything to the *necessity* of holding Silesia, covered himself with immortal glory.

'Cromwell's son undoubtedly did the wisest thing a man could do, in preferring security and peace to the difficulty and danger of governing a sombre, fiery, and proud people. This wise man has been despised both in his lifetime and by posterity, while his father has remained a great man in the judgment of the nations.

'*The Fair Penitent* is a sublime theme from Spanish drama[1] spoilt

1. See the Spanish and Danish ballads of the thirteenth century; they would appear dull or coarse to French taste.

in English and French by Otway and Colardeau. Calista has been seduced by a man she adores, the impetuous pride of whose character makes him detestable, though his talents, wit, and grace, in fact all his qualities, combine to make him attractive. Lothario might have been only too engaging had he known how to moderate his infamous vehemence; besides this, a bitter hatred has for generations divided his family from that of the woman he loves. These two families are the leaders of two factions that rend a town in Spain during the horrors of the Middle Ages. Sciolto, Calista's father, is the chief of the opposing faction, which at that time is the stronger; he knows that Lothario has had the insolence to wish to seduce his daughter. The weak Calista succumbs, tortured by shame and passion. Her father succeeds in having his enemy appointed to the command of a long and dangerous naval expedition, on which Lothario will probably lose his life. In Colardeau's tragedy he tells his daughter of this, at which her passion bursts forth:

> '*Oh, ye Gods!*
> *He is going! On your orders! Has it then come to this?*'

'Consider the danger in this situation; one word more and Sciolto will know the truth of his daughter's passion for Lothario. The dumbfounded father cries out:

> '*Do my ears fail me? Whither strays your heart?*'

'At this Calista, who has come to her senses, replies:

> '*Not his mere exile but his death I seek;*
> *O let him perish!*'

'With these words Calista nips her father's suspicions in the bud, but quite artlessly, for the feeling she is expressing is real. The continued existence, even at the other end of the world, of a man whom she loves and who has been capable of outraging her, must poison her life; only his death could bring her peace, if peace there were for the lovelorn . . . Soon afterwards Lothario is killed, and Calista has the good fortune to die.

' "A great deal of weeping and gnashing of teeth over very little" has been the comment of those cold people who affect the name of philosophers. A bold and violent man takes advantage of a woman's weakness for him, but this is no cause for mourning, or at least is insufficient reason for us to take an interest in the woes of Calista.

She has only to get over having slept with her lover, and will not be the first worthy woman to have resigned herself to that particular misfortune.'[1]

Richard Cromwell, the King of Prussia, and Calista, with the souls that Heaven had given them, could only find tranquillity and happiness by acting in the way they did. The behaviour of the latter two is eminently unreasonable, and yet they are the only ones to be respected.

Sagan. 1813

128

Constancy after happiness has been achieved can only be predicted in relation to that constancy which, despite cruel doubts, jealousy, and ridicule, existed before intimacy.

129

When a woman is in despair at the recent death of her lover on active service, and is obviously thinking of following him to the grave, one must first of all decide whether or not this would be a proper outcome. If the answer is negative, one must attack through that immemorial habit of humanity, her *instinct of self-preservation*. If the woman has an enemy, one can persuade her that this enemy has obtained a royal warrant for her summary imprisonment. If this threat does not increase her desire for death, she may begin to think of going into hiding to avoid incarceration. She should be in hiding for three weeks, fleeing from one refuge to another; she should be arrested, and escape three days later. Then under an assumed name she should be helped to find sanctuary in some very remote town as different as possible from the one where she was in despair. But who would wish to take up the cause of consoling so unhappy a being and one so unrewarding in friendship?

Warsaw. 1808

130

Academy scholars can see the customs of a people in its language: of all countries in the world Italy is the one where the word *love* is least used; it is always either *amicizia* or *avvicinar* (*amicizia* for love and *avvicinar* for courting crowned with success).

1. Grimm, vol. III, p. 107.

131

A dictionary of music has not yet been compiled nor even begun; it is only by chance that passages are found to express '*I am angry*' or '*I love you*' and their undertones. The composer only finds such passages when they are dictated to him by the presence of the particular passion in his heart, or by the recollection of it. Those young people who spend their ardent youth in study instead of in feeling can therefore never be artists – this whole mechanism is extremely simple.

132

The empire of women is much too extensive in France, and the empire of woman much too restricted.

133

The greatest flattery that the most frenzied imagination could invent, to describe the generation growing up amongst us to take possession of life, opinion, and power, turns out to be a truth clearer than daylight. The new generation has nothing to *continue* but everything to *create*. The great merit of Napoleon is that *he made a clean sweep*.

134

I should like to be able to say a few words about *consolation*. People make too little effort to be consoling.

The general principle is that one must be sure to develop a crystallization as far removed as possible from the cause of the suffering.

One must have the courage to engage in a little anatomy in order to discover an unknown principle.

If one cares to consult Chapter II of M. Villermé's work upon prisons (Paris, 1820), one will see that prisoners *si maritano fra di loro* (the phrase is prisoners' jargon). The women also *si maritano fra di loro*, and such unions are generally most faithful, which is not observed to be the case for men, and which is an effect of the principle of modesty.

'At Saint-Lazare,' M. Villermé writes on page 96, 'at Saint-Lazare in October 1818 a woman inflicted several knife-wounds upon herself because a newcomer was preferred to herself.

'It is normally the younger one who is the more attached to her partner.'

135

*Vivacità, leggerezza soggettissima a prendere puntiglio, occupazione di
ogni momento delle apparenze della propria esistenza agli occhi altrui: ecco i
tre gran caratteri di questa pianta che risveglia Europa nell 1808.*

The best among the Italians are those in whom a certain savagery
and taste for blood persist; those of Romagna and Calabria, and
among the more civilized the Brescians, Piedmontese, and Corsicans.

The middle-class Florentine is even more of a sheep than his
Parisian counterpart.

The espionage of Leopold has degraded him for ever. See M.
Courrier's letter about Furia the librarian and Puccini the chamber-
lain.

136

I find it laughable to see men of goodwill always unable to agree,
speaking ill of each other as a matter of course, and thinking worse.
To live is to feel life and to experience strong sensations. Since the
intensity of sensation differs according to the individual, what is too
painfully strong for one man is precisely what another requires to
arouse his interest. For example the sensation of coming unscathed
through cannon-fire, or the sensation of chasing those Parthians into
the depths of Russia; in the same way tragedy in Shakespeare and
tragedy in Racine, etc., etc.

Orcha, 13th August 1812

137

In the first place, pleasure does not produce half as much impression
as does pain, and in addition to this disadvantage of a lower emotional
yield the picture of happiness excites at most only half as much
sympathy as does the picture of misfortune. Hence poets can never be
too powerful in their portrayal of unhappiness; they must beware
only of one pitfall, themes which inspire disgust. Here again the
intensity of this sensation depends upon the monarchy or the republic.
The reign of a Louis XIV increases a hundredfold the number of
repulsive themes (Poems of Crabbe).

Through the very fact of the existence of a monarchy like that of
Louis XIV surrounded by his nobles, everything simple in the arts
becomes coarse. The noble personage before whom the simplicity is

displayed feels himself insulted, and this feeling is sincere and therefore to be respected.

Look what gentle Racine made of the heroic and time-honoured
friendship between Orestes and Pylades. Orestes addresses Pylades
in the second person singular, while Pylades replies to him as *my
lord*. And we are expected to find Racine our most moving author!
If an example such as this fails to convince, we had better change the
subject.

138

As soon as one sees a hope of revenge, hatred breaks out afresh.
Until my last few weeks in prison I had no thought of escaping or of
breaking the oath I had sworn to my friend. Two admissions made
tonight in my presence by a well-connected murderer who told us
his whole story.

Faenza, 1817

139

The whole of Europe put together could not produce a single one
of our good French books: *Les Lettres Persanes*, for instance.

140

I give the name of *pleasure* to anything which the soul would rather
perceive than not perceive.[1]

I give the name of *pain* to anything which the soul would rather not
perceive than perceive.

If I wish to go to sleep rather than feel what I am feeling, then it is
certainly *pain*. Therefore the desires of love are not pains, because the
lover will forgo the most pleasant company in order to dream at
his leisure.

The pleasures of the body are diminished by time while its pains
are augmented thereby.

As for the pleasures of the soul, they are augmented or diminished
by time according to the passions concerned; for example after six
months spent in studying astronomy one likes astronomy better; after
a year of avarice one prefers money.

The pains of the soul are diminished by time: 'How many genu-

1. Maupertuis.

inely heartbroken widows are consoled by the passage of time!' – Horace Walpole's Lady Waldegrave.

Suppose there is a man in a state of indifference, who experiences a pleasure.

Suppose there is another man in a state of acute pain, which ceases abruptly. Is the pleasure felt by the second of the same quality as that of the first man? M. Verri thinks it is, and I do not.

Not all pleasures are the result of the cessation of pain.

For a long time a man has had an income of six thousand francs a year; he wins five hundred thousand francs in a lottery. This man has lost the habit of desiring those things which only great wealth can afford. (I might say in passing that one of the inconvenient things about Paris is the ease with which this habit can be lost.)

The quill-sharpener has now been invented; I bought one this morning, and it is a great pleasure to me, for I grow impatient at sharpening my pens; but certainly I was not unhappy yesterday for not knowing about this machine. Do you suppose Petrarch was unhappy because he never drank coffee?

It is useless to define happiness, for everyone knows what it is: for example one's first partridge brought down on the wing at twelve; the first battle from which one emerges safe and sound at seventeen.

Pleasure which is merely the cessation of a pain is soon over, and after a few years even the memory of it is no longer agreeable. A friend of mine was wounded in the side by a shell at the battle of the Moskova; some days later he was threatened with gangrene, and within a few hours M. Béclar, M. Larrey, and several renowned surgeons were together in consultation, and the result was that my friend was informed that he did not have gangrene. In that instant I saw his happiness, which was great, and yet not unmixed. Secretly in his own mind he did not feel quite free of it, and went over the work the surgeons had done, deliberating whether he could entirely rely on them. The possibility of gangrene still hovered before his eyes. Today, eight years afterwards, when this consultation is mentioned to him he experiences a feeling of pain, at the unexpected vision of one of the misfortunes of life.

The pleasure caused by the cessation of pain consists in:

1. winning a victory over all one's successive misgivings;
2. reviewing all the advantages one was about to lose.

The pleasure caused by the acquisition of five hundred thousand francs consists in anticipating all the new and extraordinary pleasures in which one is going to indulge.

There is one singular exception: we must determine whether this man is too much or too little in the habit of desiring a great fortune. If he is too little in this habit, if he is small-minded, the feeling of encumbrance will last two or three days.

If he is often in the habit of desiring a great fortune he will have used up the enjoyment of it in imagination beforehand.

This misfortune does not occur in passionate love.

A burning soul does not imagine the ultimate favour, but the nearest one. For example, with a mistress who treats you severely you dream of holding her hand. Imagination does not naturally reach beyond the first step, and if it is forced it will very soon retreat for fear of profaning what it adores.

When pleasure has entirely run its course it is clear that one sinks back into indifference, but an indifference which is not the same as before. This second state differs from the first in that it appears we are no longer able to take such delight in enjoying the pleasure we have just experienced.

The organs employed in feeling it are tired, and the imagination is no longer so capable of presenting images attractive to desires which are now satisfied.

But if in the midst of pleasure we are wrenched away from it, suffering will result.

141

The disposition to physical love and even to physical pleasure is not at all the same for the two sexes. Unlike men, nearly all women are at least susceptible to one kind of love. From the very first novel a woman opens surreptitiously at fifteen she awaits in secret the advent of passionate love. She sees a grand passion as proof of her merit. This anticipation is intensified at about the age of twenty, when she has outgrown her early blunders; whereas men no sooner reach the age of thirty than they believe love is impossible or absurd.

142

From the age of six we become accustomed to seek happiness along the same paths as our parents. The unhappiness of the charming

Contessina Nella derives from the pride of her mother, and she perpetuates it with the same mad pride.

Venice, 1819

143

On the Romantic Style

I am told in a letter from Paris that they have just seen a thousand or so pictures (Exhibition of 1822) representing scenes from the Holy Scriptures, painted by painters who have little belief in them, admired and judged by people who don't believe in them, and then bought by people who don't believe in them either.

And yet we seek a reason for the decadence of art.

With no belief in what he is expressing, the artist is always afraid lest he appear exaggerated and absurd. How can he attain the *grandiose* when nothing lifts him towards it?

Lettera di Roma, Giugno, 1822

144

In my opinion one of the greatest poets in these latter days is Robert Burns, a Scottish peasant who died of poverty. As an excise agent he had a wage of seventy louis for himself, his wife, and four children. It must be agreed, for example, that the tyrant Napoleon was more generous to his enemy Chénier. Burns had none of the prudishness of the English. His was a latin genius bereft of chivalry and honour. Space does not permit me to relate the story of his love for Mary Campbell, which culminated in mournful catastrophe. But I notice that Edinburgh is in the same latitude as Moscow, which may to some extent upset my system of climates.

'One of Burns' remarks, when he first came to Edinburgh, was that between the men of rustic life and the polite world he observed little difference, that in the former, though unpolished by fashion and unenlightened by science, he had found much observation and much intelligence; but a refined and accomplished woman was a being almost new to him, and of which he had formed but a very inadequate idea.'

London, 1st November 1821, Vol. V, p. 69

145

Love is the only passion which rewards itself in a coin of its own manufacture.

146

The compliments paid to little girls of three constitute the best possible form of education for teaching them the most pernicious vanity. To be pretty is chief among the virtues, and the greatest advantage there is. To have a pretty dress is to be pretty.

These stupid compliments are only current among the bourgeoisie; fortunately among those who own carriages they are considered bad form, as being too facile.

147

Loretto, 11th September 1811

I have just seen a very fine battalion of the men of this region; they are all that remain of four thousand men who went to Vienna in 1809. I walked through the ranks with their colonel, and at my request several soldiers told me their stories. Here is the virtue of the medieval republics, more or less debased by the Spaniards,[1] the priesthood,[2] and two centuries of cowardly and cruel governments who have each in their turn spoilt this land.

Brilliant chivalric *honour*, sublime and irrational, is an exotic plant imported only within fairly recent years.

There is no sign of it in 1740. See de Brosses. The officers of Montenotte and Rivoli too often had occasion to display genuine virtue to their neighbours for them to seek to *imitate* an honour little known within the cottage homes of the soldiers of 1796, and one which would have seemed very strange to them.

In 1796 there was neither a Legion of Honour nor enthusiasm for any one man, but a great deal of simplicity and virtue in the manner

1. About 1580 the Spaniards, outside their own country, were nothing but the active agents of despotism, or players of guitars beneath the windows of beautiful Italian women. At that time the Spaniards used to visit Italy as nowadays one visits Paris; and their only pride was to ensure the triumph of the king *their master*. They have lost Italy, and in losing it have degraded it. In 1626 the great poet Calderon was an officer in Milan.

2. See the *Life of Saint Charles Borromeo*, who transformed Milan and degraded it. He induced people to desert the fencing-schools and take up the rosary. Merveilles murders Castiglione, 1533.

of Desaix. Hence *honour* was imported into Italy by people too rational and too virtuous to be really brilliant. One feels it is a far cry from the soldiers of '96 winning twenty battles in a year, and often without shoes or uniform, to the brilliant regiments at Fontenoy, doffing their hats and saying politely to the English: 'Will you fire first, gentlemen?'

148

I am prepared to believe that the goodness of a way of life must be judged through its representatives. For instance Richard Cœur-de-Lion on his throne appeared to be a paragon of heroism and valorous chivalry, though he was really a ridiculous king.

149

Public opinion in 1822. A man of thirty seduces a girl of fifteen, and it is the girl who is dishonoured.

150

Ten years later I met Countess Ottavia again; she wept copiously at seeing me again; I reminded her of Oginski. 'I can no longer love,' she told me; I answered her in the words of the poet: 'How changed, how saddened, yet how elevated was her character!'

151

Just as the English way of life came into existence between 1688 and 1730, that of France will be created between 1815 and 1880. Nothing will be so beautiful, just, or happy as the moral atmosphere of France in about 1900. At present it is none of these. What is infamous in the Rue de Belle-Chasse is heroic in the Rue du Mont-Blanc, and in the midst of all the exaggerations, people genuinely worthy of contempt escape by moving into the next street. We had one recourse, the freedom of the press, which in the end tells all and sundry the truth about themselves, and if this truth happens to coincide with public opinion it endures. This safeguard is now being wrested from us, which will somewhat delay the advent of morality.

152

The Abbé Rousseau was a poor young man (1784) reduced to chasing about all over the city from morning to night giving history and geography lessons. In love with one of his pupils, like Abelard with Héloïse, like Saint-Preux with Julie; less happy, certainly, but probably very near to being so; with as much passion as the latter, but more honest, more fastidious, and above all more courageous, he appears to have sacrificed himself to the object of his passion. Here is what he wrote before he blew out his brains, after having dined at a restaurant near the Palais-Royal where he betrayed no sign of anxiety or insanity; the text of the note is taken from the investigation report drawn up on the spot by the police inspector and his officers, and is sufficiently remarkable to merit preservation.

'The inexpressible contrast which exists between the nobility of my feelings and the meanness of my birth, my love for an adorable girl,[1] as violent as it is insuperable, the fear of being the agent of her dishonour, the necessity of choosing between crime and death, all these have made me resolve to abandon life. I was born to be virtuous, I was about to be criminal; I preferred to die.'

Grimm, Third Part, Vol. II, p. 495

This is a suicide worthy of admiration, and one which would be simply absurd in the moral climate of 1880.

153

In the fine arts, however hard they try, the French will never transcend the *pretty*.

Comedy requiring a *spirited* audience and actors with *brio*, the delightful jokes of Palomba played by Casaccia at Naples, impossible in Paris; prettiness and ever more prettiness, though sometimes, it is true, announced as sublime.

The reader will note that I am not in the habit of speculating about national honour.

154

'We like a beautiful picture very much,' say the French, and they are quite right; but we make it an essential condition of beauty that it should have been executed by a painter who stands on one leg whenever he is working. Verse in dramatic art.

---

1. It appears that the lady in question was a Mademoiselle Gromaire, daughter of M. Gromaire, a copying-clerk at the Vatican.

155

Far less *envy* in America than in France, and far less wit.

156

Tyranny in the manner of Philip II has so degraded men's minds since 1530 that it has cast its shadow over the garden of the world, so that the poor Italian authors have not yet had the courage to *invent* their own national novel. Nevertheless, in view of the rule that everything must be *natural*, nothing could be simpler; they must have the courage to copy quite openly what stares them in the face in society. Look at Cardinal Conzalvi in 1822, gravely thumbing over the libretto of a comic opera for three hours, and saying anxiously to the composer: 'But you will often repeat this word *cozzar, cozzar*.'

157

Héloïse speaks to you of love, and some ass speaks to you of his love; don't you sense that these two things have nothing but the word in common? They are like a love of concerts and a love of music. Love of the delights of vanity offered you by your harp in the midst of dazzling society, or love of a tender, solitary, unassuming reverie.

158

When one has just seen the woman one loves, the sight of every other woman damages the vision and physically hurts the eyes; I can see why.

159

Answer to an objection.

Perfectly natural behaviour and intimacy can exist only in passionate love, for in every other kind one is aware that a rival may be favoured.

160

In a man who has taken poison to release himself from life the moral being is dead; stunned by what it has done and what it must experience it pays no further attention to anything; some rare exceptions.

161

An old sea-captain, the author's uncle, to whom I dedicate the present manuscript, thinks that nothing could be more ridiculous than to devote six hundred pages to anything as frivolous as love. This frivolous thing is nevertheless the only weapon with which one can assail strength of soul.

What stopped M. de Maubreuil from sacrificing Napoleon in the forest of Fontainebleau in 1814? The contemptuous glance of a pretty woman entering the Chinese Baths.[1] What a difference it would have made to the destiny of the world if Napoleon and his son had been killed in 1814!

162

I quote the following lines from a letter I received from Znaïm written in French, and would add that in the whole province there is not a single man fit to understand the intelligent woman who wrote it to me.

'. . . chance plays a great part in love. When I have not read English for a year, I am delighted by the first novel I happen to pick up. The habit of loving a prosaic soul, that is to say one which is slow and shy towards anything delicate and which only feels passion for the coarser pursuits of life – love of gold, pride in fine horses, physical desires, etc. – may easily lead a person to regard as offensive the actions of a burning and impetuous genius with an impatient imagination, one who feels nothing but love and forgets all else, and who is continuously engaging in impetuous action in situations where the other lacked initiative and never acted of his own accord. The surprise such a genius arouses may offend what we called feminine pride (last year at Zithau); is this a French concept? To the second, the reaction is one of *surprise*, a feeling unknown in relation to the first (and as the first died unexpectedly in the army he has remained a synonym for perfection); a feeling moreover which a soul full of dignity, and lacking that ease of manner which stems from the experience of several love affairs, can easily confuse with what is offensive.'

1. *Memoirs* of Maubreuil, p. 88, London edition.

163

Geoffroy Rudel of Blaye was a very great nobleman, prince of Blaye, and he became enamoured of the Countess of Tripoli, though he had not seen her, by reason of the great good and the great courtesy he heard tell of her from the pilgrims coming from Antioch; he made many beautiful songs for her with good melodies and weak words; and wishing to see her he crossed himself and embarked on the sea to go to her. And it happened that on the ship he was stricken with a grievous sickness, so that those who were with him believed him dead, but went so far as to take him to an inn at Tripoli, as a dead man. The Countess being told of this, she came to his bedside and took him in her arms. He knew that she was the Countess and recovered his sight and his hearing, and praised God, and thanked Him for having spared his life until he had seen her. And thus he died in the arms of the Countess, who had him honourably buried in the House of the Temple at Tripoli. And that same day she took the veil of a nun, because of her grief for him and for his death.[1]

164

Here is a curious proof of the madness called crystallization, taken from the *Memoirs* of Mistress Hutchinson:

'. . . He told to Mr Hutchinson a very true story of a gentleman who not long before had come for some time to lodge in Richmond, and found all the people he came in company with, bewailing the death of a gentlewoman that had lived there. Hearing her so much deplored he made enquiry after her, and grew so in love with the description, that no other discourse could at first please him, nor could he at last endure any other; he grew desperately melancholy, and would go to a mount where the print of her foot was cut, and lie there pining and kissing of it all the day long, till at length death in some months space concluded his languishment. This story was very true.'

Vol. I, p. 83

165

Lisio Visconti was nothing if not a great reader of books. Besides what he had been able to observe as he went about the world this essay is also based upon the memoirs of fifteen or twenty famous

1. Translated from a thirteenth-century Provençal manuscript.

people. In case one of its readers should perchance consider these trifles worthy of a moment's attention, here are the books from which Lisio drew his reflections and conclusions:

Life of Benvenuto Cellini, by himself.

The *Short Stories* of Cervantes and Scarron.

Manon Lescaut and *Le Doyen de Killerine* by the Abbé Prevôt.

The *Latin Letters of Héloïse to Abélard*.

Tom Jones.

Letters of a Portuguese Nun.

Two or three novels by Auguste La Fontaine.

History of Tuscany by Pignotti.

Werther.

Brantôme.

Memoirs of Carlo Gozzi (Venice, 1760); only the 80 pages dealing with the story of his loves.

Memoirs of Lauzun, Saint-Simon, d'Epinay, de Staal, Marmontel, Bezanval, Roland, Duclos, Horace Walpole, Evelyn, Hutchinson.

Letters of Mademoiselle Lespinasse.

166

One of the greatest figures of the time, one of the most outstanding men in Church and State, told us at the home of Mme de M— this evening (January 1822) about the very real dangers he had run during the Terror.

'I had the misfortune to be one of the best-known members of the Constituent Assembly; I stayed in Paris, trying with indifferent success to hide myself, as long as there was some hope that the cause of right would triumph. At length, as the tide of danger was rising and the foreigners did nothing energetic to help us, I made up my mind to leave, but it had to be done without a passport. Since everybody seemed to be making for Coblenz I thought I should try to make my exit through Calais. But my portrait had been so widely circulated eighteen months earlier that I was recognized at the last staging-post, though they let me pass. I reached an inn at Calais where, as you may imagine, I scarcely slept a wink, and this was extremely lucky because at about four in the morning I heard my name spoken distinctly. As I rose and dressed in haste I could see, despite the darkness, national guards with their muskets, coming into the courtyard of the inn through the main gate which had been opened for them. Fortunately it was pouring with rain and a very dark and windy winter morning. The darkness and the noise of the wind enabled me to escape through the back yard and the stables, and there I was in the street at seven in the morning, with no resources whatever.

'I assumed that my pursuers would follow me from the inn, and with no very clear idea what I was doing I made my way to the port and on the jetty. I admit that I had to some extent lost my head, and could see nothing but the prospect of the guillotine.

'There was a packet putting out from the port in a heavy sea, and already twenty fathoms from the jetty. All at once I heard shouts from the direction of the sea, as if I were being hailed. I saw a small boat coming up. "Come along, Sir. You're expected." Mechanically I stepped aboard the boat, in which was a man who whispered to me: "When I saw you walk on to the jetty looking so frantic I thought you might well be an unfortunate outlaw. I said you were a friend I was expecting; you must pretend to be seasick and hide yourself below in a dark corner of the cabin."'

'Oh, what a magnificent gesture!' cried the lady of the house breathlessly, moved to tears by the long and well-told recital of the Abbé's dangers. 'How you must have thanked this generous stranger! What was his name?'

'I do not know his name,' replied the Abbé in some confusion; and there was a moment of dead silence in the drawing-room.

167

Father and Son

A dialogue of 1787

The father, (Minister for War):

'I congratulate you, my boy; it's a very pleasant thing for you to have been invited to M. le duc d'Orléans. It's an honour for a man of your age. Make sure you are at the Palais-Royal at six o'clock precisely.'

The son:

'I believe, sir, that you are to dine there as well?'

The father:

'M. le duc d'Orléans, who has always been most good to our family, has been kind enough to invite me as well, as he is requesting your presence for the first time.'

The son, a well-born young man of most distinguished intelligence, was at the Palais-Royal without fail at six o'clock. Dinner was served at seven. The son found himself sitting opposite his father. Each guest had a naked girl sitting beside him. Twenty footmen in full livery were serving.[1]

168

London, August 1817

Never in my life have I been so struck and overawed by the presence of beauty as I was this evening at a concert given by Mme Pasta.

She was surrounded as she sang by three rows of young women so lovely, so pure and celestial in their beauty, that I felt myself lower my eyes respectfully instead of raising them to admire and enjoy. I have never felt the like in any country, not even in my beloved Italy.

169

If there is one thing utterly out of the question in the arts in France it is verve. For a man to be enthusiastic would be too ridiculous; *he would look too happy.* But see a Venetian reciting Buratti's satires.

170

In Valencia in Spain there lived two friends, very respectable women belonging to distinguished families. One of them was courted by a French officer who loved her passionately, even to the point of forgoing his medal after a battle because he stayed with her in his billet instead of going to headquarters to curry favour with the general in command.

In the end she came to love him. After seven months of coldness as heartbreaking at the end as it was in the beginning, she said to him one evening: 'Dear Joseph, I am yours.' There remained an obstacle in the shape of a husband, an extremely intelligent but excessively jealous man. In my capacity of friend I had to read through with the husband the whole of Rulhière's History of Poland, which he did not understand very well. Three months went by without our having been able to deceive him. Telegraph messages were sent on feast days to indicate which church they would attend for mass.

One day I noticed that my friend was more depressed than usual;

1. FROM DECEMBER 27, 1819 TILL JUNE 3, 1820, MILAN.

here is what was going to happen. Dona Inezilla's friend was dangerously ill, and she asked her husband's permission to go and spend the night with the invalid. This was agreed immediately on condition that the husband should choose the day. One evening he took Dona Inezilla round to her friend's house, and apparently on the spur of the moment said playfully that he would sleep very well on a sofa in a little drawing-room which gave into the bedroom, and of which the door was left open. For eleven days the French officer spent two hours every evening hidden under the invalid's bed. I dare not add the sequel.

I do not think vanity would permit a Frenchwoman to exhibit this degree of friendship.

APPENDIX

THERE were courts of love in France between the year 1150 and the year 1200. So much has been proved. The existence of these courts of love probably dates back to a very much earlier period.

The ladies assembled in the courts of love gave judgment both upon questions of law – for instance: Can love exist between people who are married? – and also upon individual cases brought before them by lovers.[1]

As far as I can imagine, the moral aspect of this judicature must have been similar to what the court of the Marshals of France, established by Louis XIV for the *point of honour*, might have been had its institution been endorsed by public opinion.

André, chaplain to the King of France, who wrote about the year 1170, mentions the *courts of love* of:

The ladies of Gascony,
Ermengarde, Viscountess of Narbonne (1144–94),
Queen Eleanor,
The Countess of Flanders,
The Countess of Champagne (1174).

André gives an account of nine judgments pronounced by the Countess of Champagne, and mentions two pronounced by the Countess of Flanders.

Jean de Nostradamus says in his *Vie des poètes provençaux* (page 15):

Tensons were arguments about love which took place between poet knights and ladies, discussing among themselves some fine and subtle point of love; and when they could not reach agreement they would send the cases to the illustrious ladies-president who held open and plenary court of love ât *Signe* and *Pierrefeu*, or at *Romanin*, where before others they delivered judgments upon them which were called '*Lous Arrests d'Amours*'.

Here are the names of some of the ladies who presided over the courts of love at Pierrefeu and Signe:

Stephanette, lady of Baulx, daughter of the Comte de Provence,
Adalasie, Viscountess of Avignon,
Alalète, lady of Ongle,
Hermissende, lady of Posquières,

1. André the Chaplain, Nostradamus, Raynouard, Crescimbeni, Aretino.

Bertrane, lady of Urgon,
Mabille, lady of Yères,
The Countess of Dye,
Rostangue, lady of Pierrefeu,
Bertrane, lady of Signe,
Jausserande of Claustral.

Nostradamus, p. 27

It is probable that the same court of love assembled sometimes at the castle of Pierrefeu and sometimes at that of Signe. The two villages lie very close to each other, almost exactly half-way between Toulon and Brignoles.

In the *Vie de Bertrand d'Alamanon* Nostradamus says:

'This troubadour was enamoured of Phanette or Estephanette de Romanin, lady of that place, of the house of Gantelmes, who in her time held open and plenary court of love in her castle at Romanin, near the town of Saint-Rémy in Provence. She was the aunt of Laurette of Avignon of the house of Sado, immortalized by the poet Petrarch.'

In the article on Laurette we read that Laurette de Sade, immortalized by Petrarch, lived at Avignon about the year 1341; that she was taught by Phanette de Gantelmes her aunt, lady of Romanin; that 'both were quick at making ballads in every kind of Provençal rhythm, according to what has been written of them by the monk of the Golden Isles, whose works bear ample witness to their doctrine . . . It is true (says the monk) that Phanette or Estephanette, being very excellent in poesy, had a fury or divine inspiration, the which fury was thought to be truly a gift of God; they had as companions several . . . illustrious and generous ladies[1] of Provence who flourished

---

1.   'Jehanne, lady of Baulx,
           Huguette de Forcarquier, lady of Trects,
           Briande d'Agoult, Countess of the Lune,
           Mabille de Villeneufve, lady of Vence,
           Béatrix d'Agoult, lady of Sault,
           Ysoarde de Roquefueilh, lady of Ansoys,
           Anne, Viscountess of Tallard,
           Blanche de Flassans, surnamed Blankaffour,
           Doulce de Monstiers, lady of Clumane,
           Antonette de Cadenet, lady of Lambesc,
           Magdalène de Sallon, lady of the same place,
           Rixende de Puyverd, lady of Trans.'
                          Nostradamus, p. 217

then in Avignon when the Roman court was there, devoted themselves to the study of literature, held open court of love and defined the questions of love which were proposed and sent to them . . .

'Guillen and Pierre Balz and Loys des Lascaris, counts of Vintimille, Tende, and La Brigue, and figures of great renown, being come to Avignon about this time to visit Pope Innocent VI, went to listen to the definitions and judgments of love pronounced by these ladies; amazed and enraptured by their beauty and learning, they found themselves in love.'

Often at the end of their *tensons* the troubadours would name the ladies who were to give judgment on the questions they were debating between them.

A judgment of the court of the ladies of Gascony reads:

'The court of the ladies assembled in Gascony has established, by consent of *the whole court*, this constitution in perpetuity, etc., etc.'

The Countess of Champagne, in a judgment in 1174, says:

'This judgment, which we have upheld with extreme prudence, is based upon the opinion of a very great number of ladies . . .'

In another judgment we find:

'The knight, by reason of the deception practised upon him, disclosed this whole affair to the Countess of Champagne, and humbly begged that the offence be submitted to the judgment of the Countess of Champagne and of the other ladies.

'The Countess, having summoned sixty ladies to her, gave this judgment,' etc., etc.

André the Chaplain, from whom this information is drawn, states that a court composed of a large number of ladies and knights had published the code of love.

André has preserved for us the petition addressed to the Countess of Champagne, when she decided the following question in the negative: *Can true love exist between the married?*

But what was the penalty for failing to obey the judgments of the courts of love?

We see the court of Gascony ordering that one of its judgments should be observed as constitutional in perpetuity, and that ladies disobeying it should incur the enmity of every honest woman.

To what extent did public opinion sanction the judgments of the courts of love?

Was it as shameful to evade them as it is nowadays to shirk an affair of honour?

I can find nothing either in André or in Nostradamus which might enable me to resolve that question.

Two troubadours, Simon Doria and Lanfranc Cigalla, once argued the question: 'Which is the more worthy to be loved; he who gives liberally or he who gives against his will in order to be regarded as liberal?'

This question was submitted to the ladies of the court of love of Pierrefeu and Signe, but the two troubadours were dissatisfied with the judgment given, and appealed to the supreme court of love of the ladies of Romanin.[1]

The phraseology of judgments corresponds with that of the courts of law of the period.

Whatever opinion the reader may hold of the degree of importance assumed by the courts of love in the minds of the people of the day, I beg him to consider what are nowadays, in 1822, the subjects of conversation among the wealthiest and most respected ladies of Toulon and Marseilles.

Were they not gayer, wittier, and happier in 1174 than they are in 1822?

Nearly all the judgments of the courts of love take some cognizance of the rules of the code of love.

This code of love will be found in its entirety in the work of André the Chaplain.

There are thirty-one articles, as follows:

Code of Love for the Twelfth Century

I

The plea of marriage is not a legitimate defence against love.

2

Who knows not how to conceal knows not how to love.

3

No one can surrender to two loves.

1. Nostradamus, p. 131.

4

Love can always increase or diminish.

5

There is no savour in what one lover takes by force from the other lover.

6

The male normally loves only when he has reached full puberty.

7

A lover shall, on the death of the other lover, remain unattached for two years.

8

No one, except for more than sufficient reason, shall be deprived of his right in love.

9

No one can love unless urged by the persuasion of love (by the hope of being loved).

10

Love is normally driven out of the house by avarice.

11

It is improper to love a woman whom one would be ashamed to desire in marriage.

12

True love desires caresses only from the beloved.

13

Love disclosed seldom endures.

14

Success too easily won soon strips love of its charm; obstacles enhance its value.

15

Every lover grows pale at the sight of the beloved.

16

One trembles at the unexpected sight of the beloved.

17

New love drives out the old.

18

Only merit is worthy to be loved.

19

Waning love dies quickly and seldom revives.

20

A lover is always timorous.

21

True jealousy always aggravates the condition called love.

22

Suspicion and the jealousy which derives from it aggravate the condition called love.

23

Those besieged by thoughts of love sleep less and eat less.

24

The lover's every action ends with the thought of the beloved.

25

True love finds nothing good but what it knows will please its beloved.

26

Love can refuse love nothing.

27

A lover cannot be sated by the enjoyment of the beloved.

28

A slight presumption leads a lover to suspect the worst of the other lover.

29

Too excessive a habit of pleasure prevents the birth of love.

30

A person in love is unremittingly and uninterruptedly occupied with the image of the beloved.

31

Nothing forbids a woman to be loved by two men, or a man by two women.[1]

Here is the purview of a judgment given by a court of love:

QUESTION: 'Can true love exist between married persons?'

JUDGMENT of the Countess of Champagne: 'We say and affirm, by the tenor of these presents, that love may not extend its rights over two married persons. For lovers grant each other all things mutually and freely without constraint of any motive of necessity, whereas the married are in duty bound reciprocally to submit to the will of the other, and to refuse each other nothing . . .

I. 1. Causa conjugii ab amore non est excusatio recta.
    2. Qui non celat amare non potest.
    3. Nemo duplici potest amore ligari.
    4. Semper amorem minui vel crescere constat.
    5. Non est sapidum quod amans ab invito sumit amante.
    6. Masculus non solet nisi in plena pubertate amare.
    7. Biennalis viduitas pro amante defuncto superstiti prœscribitur amanti.
    8. Nemo, sine rationis excessu, suo debet amore privari.
    9. Amare nemo potest, nisi qui amoris suasione compellitur.
   10. Amor semper ab avaritiœ consuevit domiciliis exulare.
   11. Non decet amare quarum pudor est nuptias affectare.
   12. Verus amans alterius nisi suœ coamantis ex affectu non cupit amplexus.
   13. Amor raro consuevit durare vulgatus.
   14. Facilis perceptio contemptibilem reddit amorem, difficilis eum parùm facit haberi.
   15. Omnis consuevit amans in coamantis aspectu pallescere.
   16. Il repentinâ coamantis visione, cor tremescit amantis.
   17. Novus amor veterem compellit abire.
   18. Probitas sola quemcumque dignum facit amore.
   19. Si amore minuatur, cito deficit et raro convalescit.
   20. Amorosus semper est timorosus.
   21. Ex verâ zelotypiâ affectus semper crescit amandi.
   22. De coamante suspicione perceptâ zelus interea et affectus crescit amandi.
   23. Minus dormit et edit quem amoris cogitatio vexat.
   24. Quilibet amantis actus in coamantis cogitatione finitur.
   25. Verus amans nihil beatum credit, nisi quod cogit amanti placere.
   26. Amor nihil posset amori denegare.
   27. Amans coamantis solatiis satiari non potest.
   28. Modica prœsumptio cogit amantem de coamante suspicari sinistra.
   29. Non solet amare quem nimia voluptatis abundantia vexat.
   30. Verus amans assiduâ, sine intermissione, coamantis imagine detinetur.
   31. Unam feminam nihil prohibet a duobus amari, et a duabus mulieribus unum.   —Fol. 103

'Let this judgment, which we have given with extreme prudence and according to the opinion of a great number of other ladies, be constantly and inviolably true for you. Thus judged in the year 1174, on the third day of the Kalends of May, VIIth Indiction.'[1]

Note on André the Chaplain

André appears to have written in 1176 or thereabouts.

In the *Bibliothèque du roi* (No. 8758) there is a manuscript of André's work which once belonged to Baluze. The first title is: 'Hic incipiunt capitula libri de Arte amatoriâ et reprobatione amoris.'

This title is followed by the index of chapters.

Then appears this second title:

'Incipit liber de Arte amandi et de reprobatione amoris, editus et compillatus a magistro Andreâ, Francorum aulae regiae capellano, ad Galterium amicum suum, cupientem in amoris exercitu militare: in quo quidem libro, cujusque gradus et ordinis mulier ab homine cujusque conditionis et status ad amorem sapientissimè invitatur; et ultimo in fine ipsius libri de amoris reprobatione subjungitur.'

Crescimbeni, in the article on Percivalle Doria in his *Vite de' poeti provenzali*, mentions a manuscript in the library of Nicolo Bargiacchi at Florence, and quotes various passages; this manuscript is a translation of the treatise of André the Chaplain. The *della Crusca* academy admits it among the works which furnished examples for its dictionary.

There were various editions of the Latin original. Frid. Otto Menckenius, in his *Miscellanea Lipsiensia nova*, Lipsiae, 1751, vol. VIII, section I, pp. 545 et seq., makes reference to a very early edition with neither date nor place of publication, which he considers dates back to the beginnings of printing: 'Tractatus amoris et de amoris remedio Andreae capellani papae Innocentii quarti.'

1. 'Utrum inter conjugatos amor possit habere locum?

'Dicimus enim et stabilito tenore firmamus amorem non posse inter duos jugales suas extendere vires, nam amantes sibi invicem gratis omnia largiuntur, nullius necessitatis ratione cogente; jugales vero mutuis tenentur ex debito voluntatibus obedire et in nullo seipsos sibi ad invicem denegare. . . .

'Hoc igitur nostrum judicum, cum nimiâ moderatione prolatum, et aliarum quamplurium dominakrum consilio roboratum, pro indubitabili vobis sit ac veritate constanti.

'Ab anno M.C.LXXIV, tertio calend, maii, indictione VII.'   Fol. 56.

This judgment is in accordance with the first rule of the code of love: 'Causa conjugii non est ab amore excusatio recta.'

Another edition in 1610 bears the following title:

'*Erotica seu amatoria* Andreae capellani regii, vetustissimi scriptoris ad venerandum suum amicum Guualterium scripta, nunquam antehac edita, sed saepius a multis desiderata; nunc tandem fide diversorum mss. codicum in publicum emissa a Dethmaro Mulhero, Dorpmundae, typis Westhovianis, anno Vna Castè et Verè amanda.'

Yet a third edition reads: 'Tremoniae, typis Westhovianis, anno 1614.'

André methodically divides the subject he proposes to treat, as follows:

1. Quid sit amor et undè dicatur.

2. Quis sit effectus amoris.

3. Inter quos possit esse amor.

4. Qualiter amor acquiratur, retineatur, augmentetur, minuatur, finiatur.

5. De notitia mutui amoris, et quid unus amantium agere debeat altero fidem fallente.[1]

Several paragraphs are devoted to each of these questions.

André makes the lover and the lady speak alternately. The lady raises objections and the lover tries to convince her with more or less subtle reasoning. The author puts the following passage in the mouth of the lover:

... Sed si fortè horum sermonum te perturbet obscuritas, eorum tibi sentenciam indicabo.

Ab antiquo igitur quatuor sunt in amore gradus distincti:

Primus, in spei datione consistit.

Secundus, in osculi exhibitione.

Tertius, in amplexus fruitione.

Quartus, in totius concessione personae finitur.[2]

1. What love is and whence it takes its name.
   What the effect of love is.
   Between whom love can exist.
   How love is acquired, retained, increases, diminishes, ends.
   By what signs one recognizes one is loved in return, and what one lover must do when the other breaks faith.

2. But if by chance the obscurity of this discourse puzzle you, I shall provide you with a summary of it.

From time immemorial there have been four different degrees of love:

    The first consists in the giving of hope.

    The second in the offering of a kiss.

    The third in the enjoyment of the most intimate embraces.

    The fourth in the granting of the whole person.

The Salzburg Bough

AT the salt mines of Hallein near Salzburg the miners throw a leafless wintry bough into one of the abandoned workings. Two or three months later, through the effect of the waters saturated with salt which soak the bough and then let it dry as they recede, the miners find it covered with a shining deposit of crystals. The tiniest twigs no bigger than a tom-tit's claw are encrusted with an infinity of little crystals, scintillating and dazzling. The original little bough is no longer recognizable; it has become a child's plaything very pretty to see. When the sun is shining and the air is perfectly dry the miners of Hallein seize the opportunity of offering these diamond-studded boughs to travellers preparing to go down the mine. This descent is a peculiar operation. You sit astride great pine trunks which lead downwards one after the other in a sloping line. The trunks are extremely thick, and having performed the office of horse for a century or two they have become completely smooth. In front of the saddle on which you sit and which slips along the pine trunks placed end to end a miner takes up his position and, sitting on his leather apron, slides in front of you to stop you from going down too fast.

Before they undertake this swift journey the miners request the ladies to don an immense pair of grey serge trousers over their dresses, which gives them a most comical appearance. I visited the mines in the summer of 18— in company with Madame Gherardi. Originally we had only intended to escape the intolerable heat we were suffering in Bologna, and to go and enjoy the cool of Mont Saint-Gothard. In three nights we had crossed the pestilential marshes of Mantua and lovely Lake Garda, and reached Riva, Bolzano, and Innsbruck.

Mme Gherardi thought these mountains so beautiful that what began as an outing ended as a real journey. Following the valley of the Inn and then that of the Salza we came down to Salzburg. The delightful coolness of this northern slope of the Alps, compared with the stifling air and the dust we had just left behind in the plain of Lombardy, gave us new pleasure every morning and encouraged us to press forward. At Golling we bought peasant coats. Often we found it difficult to obtain lodging or even food, for our caravan was

quite large; but these difficulties and misfortunes were so many
pleasures.

From Golling we came to Hallein, unaware even of the existence
of the pretty salt mines I have mentioned. We found a great crowd
of sight-seers there with whom we mingled in our peasant coats, the
ladies with the enormous peasant hoods they had bought. We went
to the mine without the slightest intention of going down into the
subterranean galleries; the thought of riding three quarters of a
league mounted on a piece of wood seemed strange, and we were
afraid we might suffocate down that ugly black hole. Madame
Gherardi looked at it for a moment, then declared that as far as she was
concerned she was going down, and that we might do as we pleased.

While we were getting ready, which took some time, for before
being swallowed up in so deep a cavity we had to find dinner, I
amused myself by watching what was happening to the thoughts of a
handsome fair-haired young officer of the Bavarian light horse. We
had just made the acquaintance of this likeable young man, who
spoke French and was most useful in making us understood by the
German peasants of Hallein. The young officer, although handsome,
was no conceited fool; on the contrary he appeared to be a man of
intelligence, as Madame Gherardi found out. I could see the officer
visibly falling in love with the charming Italian woman, who was
wildly ecstatic at the prospect of going down a mine and at the
thought that we should soon be five hundred feet below ground.
Madame Gherardi, entirely taken up with the beauty of the mines and
their great galleries, and with difficulties overcome, was a thousand
miles from any thought of pleasing and even further from thoughts
of being attracted to anyone. Soon I was surprised at the strange confidences uttered unawares by the Bavarian officer. He was so engrossed in the celestial features, animated by an angelic spirit, which
were sharing his table in a little mountain inn barely illuminated by
green glass windows, that I noticed he often spoke without knowing
what he was saying or to whom he was saying it. I signalled to
Madame Gherardi who, but for me, would have missed the spectacle,
one by which a young woman is perhaps never unmoved. What
struck me was the undertone of madness which grew moment by
moment in the discourse of the officer; each moment he saw in this
woman perfections more and more invisible to my eyes. Each moment what he said bore *less resemblance* to the woman he was beginning

to love. I thought to myself: 'La Ghita is certainly no more than a pretext for all the raptures of this poor German.' For example he began to praise Madame Gherardi's hand, which had been curiously marked by smallpox in her childhood and had remained very pocked and rather brown.

'How shall I explain what I can see?' I wondered. 'Where shall I find a comparison to illustrate my thought?'

Just at that moment Madame Gherardi was toying with the pretty branch covered with sparkling diamonds which the miners had given her. The sun was shining (it was the third of August) and the little salt prisms glittered like the finest diamonds in a brightly-lit ballroom. The Bavarian officer, who had chanced to obtain a branch of even stranger brilliance, suggested that Madame Gherardi should exchange with him. She consented, and on receiving her branch he pressed it to his heart with so comical a gesture that all the Italians began to laugh. In his agitation the officer paid Madame Gherardi the most exaggerated and heartfelt compliments. As I had taken him under my wing I attempted to justify the folly of his praises. I told Ghita: 'The effect produced on this young man by the nobility of your Italian features and those eyes of which he has never seen the like is precisely similar to the effect of crystallization upon that little branch of hornbeam you hold in your hand and which you think so pretty. Stripped of its leaves by the winter it was certainly anything but dazzling until the crystallization of the salt covered its black twigs with such a multitude of shining diamonds that only here and there can one still see the twigs as they really are.'

'And what are you trying to deduce from that?' interjected Madame Gherardi.

'That this branch is a faithful representation of la Ghita as viewed by the imagination of this young officer.'

'Implying, my dear sir, that you perceive just the same difference between what I really am and the way this charming young man sees me, as between a little dried-up stick of hornbeam and the pretty spray of diamonds the miners gave me.'

'Madame, the young officer is discovering qualities in you that we who have long been your friends have never seen. For example, we could never perceive an air of tender and compassionate kindness in you. Since this young man is a German the most important quality in a woman, for him, is *kindness*, so he immediately reads into your features an expression of kindness. If he were English he would see in you the aristocratic and LADY-LIKE mien of a duchess; but if he were myself he would see you just as you are, because for a long time it has been my misfortune to be able to imagine nothing more attractive.'

'Ah, now I understand,' said Ghita, 'from the moment you begin to be interested in a woman, you no longer see her *as she really is*, but as it suits you to see her. You're comparing the flattering illusions created by this nascent interest with the pretty diamonds which hide this leafless branch of hornbeam – and which are only perceived, mark you, by the eyes of this young man falling in love.'

'And that's why,' I pursued, 'a lover's conversation sounds so absurd to sensible people who know nothing of the phenomenon called crystallization.'

'Oh, you call it *crystallization*,' laughed Ghita. 'Well then, will you crystallize for me?'

The metaphor, unusual perhaps, captured Madame Gherardi's imagination, and when we had reached the great hall of the mine, lit by a hundred little lamps that seemed ten thousand by virtue of the salt crystals which reflected them on every side, she said to the young Bavarian: 'Now this is really pretty; I crystallize for this vault; I feel I overrate its beauty. And what about you; are you crystallizing?'

'Yes, Madame,' replied the young officer naively, delighted to have a feeling in common with the beautiful Italian, but none the wiser as to what she meant. This simple reply made us laugh until we wept, because it confirmed the jealousy of the fool with whom Ghita was in love, and who was beginning to be seriously jealous of the Bavarian officer. He began to abominate the word *crystallization*.

When we emerged from the mine of Hallein I informed my new friend the young officer, whose involuntary confidences interested me far more than the details of salt-mining, that Madame Gherardi's name was *Ghita*, and that it was customary in Italy to call her *la Ghita* in her presence. The poor boy, trembling at his own daring, addressed her as *la Ghita*, and Madame Gherardi, amused by the shyly passionate expression of the young man and the angry scowl of a certain other person, invited the officer to lunch with us the following day, before we left for Italy. No sooner had he departed than the certain person exploded: 'And now, my dear friend, will you kindly explain why you propose to inflict upon us the company of that washed-out, tow-headed fellow with the dazed eyes?'

'Because, Sir, having travelled with me day in and day out for ten days you all see me just as I am, while those sensitive and (as you call them) *dazed* eyes see me as perfect. Isn't that so, Filippo,' she added looking at me, 'those eyes clothe me with a shining *crystallization*; to them I am perfection itself; and best of all, whatever I do, whatever stupidity I happen to utter, I shall not cease to be perfect in the eyes of my handsome German; that's most convenient. Now you, Annibalino' (the lover we all thought a bit of a fool was called Colonel Annibal), 'I'll wager that at this very moment you don't find me exactly perfect, do you? You think I'm wrong to admit this young man into my circle. Do you know what's the matter with you, my friend? You've stopped *crystallizing* for me.'

The word *crystallization* became current among us, and so struck the imagination of the beautiful Ghita that she used it for everything.

When we returned to Bologna she scarcely ever heard an anecdote about love related to her in her box without turning to me and saying: 'That feature confirms (or destroys) such and such of our theories.' Repeated acts of madness, in which a lover sees all the perfections together in the woman with whom he is falling in love, were always referred to between us as *crystallization*. The word recalled our most enjoyable journey. Never in my life have I felt so keenly the touching and solitary beauty of the shores of Lake Garda; we spent wonderful evenings afloat there, despite the stifling heat. We knew unforgettable moments; it was one of the brightest periods of our youth.

One evening someone came and told us that Princess Lanfranchi and the beautiful Florenza were contending for the heart of the young painter Oldofredi. The poor princess was, it appeared, really in love with him, while the young Milanese artist seemed to be solely interested in the charms of Florenza. We debated whether Oldofredi was in love. But I beg the reader to believe that I am not attempting to justify this kind of conversation, in which we were so impertinent as not to conform to French conventions. I do not know why, but that evening it became a point of personal pride to determine whether or not the Milanese painter was in love with the beautiful Florenza.

We became immersed in the discussion of a great number of minor facts. When we had grown tired of concentrating upon almost imperceptible nuances which were, in the end, not very conclusive, Madame Gherardi began to tell us the romantic story which, according to her, was unfolding in the heart of Oldofredi. Unhappily from the very beginning of her story she made use of the word *crystalliz-ation*; Colonel Annibal, with whom the handsome face of the Bavarian officer still rankled, pretended not to understand, and asked us for the hundredth time exactly what we meant by this word *crystalliz-ation*. 'It's what I don't feel for you,' flashed Madame Gherardi. After which she abandoned him in his corner with his ill humour and turned to us saying: 'When I see a man being sad I believe he is falling in love.' We all protested at once: 'What! in love, *that ex-quisite feeling which begins so wonderfully* . . .' 'And which sometimes ends so badly in ill temper and quarrels,' said Madame Gherardi laugh-ing and looking towards Annibal. 'I understand why you protest. You coarse males see only one thing in the birth of love; either one loves or one does not love. In just the same way common people imagine that all nightingales sing the same song, but we who take pleasure in listening to them, realize that there are in fact ten varying nuances from one nightingale to another.' 'It seems to me nevertheless, Madame,' said someone, 'that one either loves or does not love.' 'Nothing of the sort, Sir; that is like saying that a man who leaves Bologna on his way to Rome has already arrived at the gates of Rome when from the crest of the Apennines he can still see our tower of Garisenda. It's a long way from one town to the other, and the traveller may be a quarter, or a half, or three quarters of the way there without on that account having reached Rome, although he has certainly left Bologna.' 'In that fine comparison,' I said, 'Bologna apparently represents *indifference* and Rome *perfect love*.' 'When we are at Bologna,' continued Madame Gherardi, 'we are entirely indifferent; we are not concerned to admire in any particular way the woman with whom we shall perhaps one day be madly in love; even less is our imagination inclined to overrate her worth. In a word, as we used to say at Hallein, *crystallization* has not yet begun.'

At these words Annibal rose in a fury and left the box, saying he would return when we chose to speak Italian. Immediately the con-versation was resumed in French, and everyone laughed, including Madame Gherardi. 'Well,' she said, 'love has now departed,' and we all laughed again. 'One leaves Bologna, climbs the Apennines, and takes the road to Rome . . .' 'But, Madame,' said someone, 'all this is a long way from the painter Oldofredi.' Madame Gherardi made a little gesture of impatience which probably banished all thought of Annibal and his abrupt exit. 'Would you like to know,' she asked us, 'what happens when one leaves Bologna? In the first place I think the departure has nothing to do with one's will; it is an instinctive movement. I don't say it's not accompanied by a great deal of pleasure. One admires, and then tells oneself: "How pleasant to be loved by this charming woman!" Then hope emerges, and after hope (often lightly conceived, for the least trace of hot-bloodedness removes all doubts), after hope, I say, one delights in overrating the beauty and the merit of the woman whose love one hopes to win.'

While Madame Gherardi was speaking I took a playing-card and wrote on the back of it; Rome on the right, Bologna on the left, and between Bologna and Rome the four stages Madame Gherardi had just described.

BALOGNE.   ROME.

1. Admiration.

2. One reaches this second stage on the road when one says: 'How pleasant to be loved by this charming woman!'

3. The appearance of hope marks the third stage.

4. One arrives at the fourth stage when one delights in overrating the beauty and merit of the woman one loves. This is what we the initiated call by the word *crystallization*, which puts Carthage to flight. It really is rather difficult to understand.

Madame Gherardi continued: 'Throughout these four movements of the soul, or states of being, which Filippo has just drawn, I can't see the least reason why our traveller should be sad. The fact is that the pleasure is keen, and claims all the attention of which the soul is capable. One is serious but one is not sad, and there's a great difference.' 'We gather,' said one of the company, 'that you are not referring to those poor unfortunates for whom all nightingales sing the same song.' 'The difference between being serious and being sad (*esser serio* and *esser mesto*),' resumed Madame Gherardi, 'is decisive when it comes to resolving a problem such as this one: Does

Oldofredi love the beautiful Florenza? I think Oldofredi *is* in love, because following his strong interest in la Florenza I have seen him not only serious but also sad. He is sad because what has happened to him is this. After having overrated the happiness he might derive from the character implied by that Raphaelesque face, the lovely shoulders and arms, in short the form worthy of Canova of the beautiful Marchesina Florenza, he probably sought to obtain confirmation of the hopes he had dared to conceive. Very probably too, la Florenza, afraid of loving a stranger who might leave Bologna at any moment, and above all extremely annoyed that he should have been able to entertain hopes so soon, will have dashed them pitilessly.'

We had the good fortune to see Madame Gherardi every day; our circle was on terms of perfect intimacy and we understood one another's slightest hints; I have often noticed laughter at jokes where never a word had been spoken in the telling: a mere glance had given the whole story. At this point the French reader will perceive that a pretty Italian woman surrenders wildly to every crazy notion which comes into her head. At Rome, Bologna, or Venice a pretty woman is an absolute queen; nothing could be more absolute than the despotism she exercises over her circle. A pretty woman in Paris is always afraid of public opinion, and of public opinion's executioner: *ridicule*. In her heart she goes in constant fear of becoming a laughing-stock, as an absolute king goes in fear of a charter. The secret thought of this comes to disturb her in the full enjoyment of her pleasures, and suddenly makes her look serious. To an Italian woman the limited authority which a Parisian woman can wield in her own drawing-room would seem quite absurd. The former is literally all-powerful over the men who surround her, and whose happiness, at any rate for the evening, invariably depends upon one of her caprices; I mean the happiness of ordinary friendship. If you fail to please the woman who holds court in her theatre box you see boredom reflected in her eyes, and you might as well vanish for the rest of that day.

One day I was riding along the road to the *Cascata del Reno* with Madame Gherardi when we met Oldofredi alone, very excited and with a look of extreme preoccupation, though not at all gloomy. Madame Gherardi called him over and spoke to him, the better to observe him. 'If I am not mistaken,' I said to her, 'poor Oldofredi is completely overwhelmed by his passion for la Florenza; pray tell your humble servant what stage of the disease called love you think he has reached.' 'I see him,' replied Madame Gherardi, 'walking alone, repeating to himself over and over again: "Yes, she loves me." Then he busies himself to find new charms in her and new reasons for loving her to distraction.' 'I don't think he's quite as happy as you suppose. He must be a prey to cruel doubts; he can't be so sure that la Florenza loves him, for he does not know as we do how little wealth, rank, and social graces count with her in affairs of this kind.[1] Oldofredi is pleasant enough, certainly, but he's only a poor stranger.' 'Never mind,' said Madame Gherardi, 'I'll wager we found him just now at a moment when he was carried away by reasons for hope.' 'But he looked too deeply disturbed,' I said; 'he must be experiencing moments of frightful unhappiness, and asking himself: "But does she love me?"' 'I admit,' resumed Madame Gherardi, almost forgetting that she was talking to me, 'that when one gives oneself a satisfactory answer to that question there are moments of sublime happiness unlike anything else in this world. They are probably the best thing in life.

'When the tired soul, as if crushed by such violent feelings, at last comes to its senses through sheer weariness, what remains on the surface after such a spate of opposing emotions is this certainty: "With *him* I shall find a happiness that *only he* in all the world can give me."'

Little by little I edged my horse further from Madame Gherardi's. We covered the three miles that separated us from Bologna in complete silence, practising the virtue known as discretion.

1. France and Italy are in complete contrast with each other in every detail. For example, beyond the Alps wealth, high birth, and perfect education are conducive to the growth of love, yet discourage it in France.

Ernestine
or
The Birth of Love

PREFATORY NOTE

A WOMAN of great intelligence and some experience was maintaining one day that love is not born so suddenly as is commonly
supposed. 'It seems to me,' she said, 'that I can distinguish seven quite
distinct phases in the birth of love'; and to prove her point she related
the following story. We were in the country, it was pouring with
rain, and we were only too happy to listen to her.

IN the unattached heart of a girl who is living in a secluded château
in the depths of the country the least touch of surprise arouses profound interest. A young huntsman, for example, whom she sees
unexpectedly in the woods near the château.

It was just such a simple event which led to the misfortunes of
Ernestine de S— The castle where she lived alone with her old
uncle, the Comte de S—, had been built in the Middle Ages upon
one of those huge masses of rock which jut out into the valley of the
Drac and narrow its course; it overlooked one of the finest beauty
spots in the Dauphiné. The young huntsman of whom chance had
given her a glimpse had, Ernestine considered, an air of nobility. His
image came into her mind several times, for what on earth could one
think about in this ancient manor-house? She lived there in magnificence of a sort, with a large domestic staff at her beck and call,
but both master and servants had been old for twenty years, all things
were done according to the same routine, and conversation was confined to finding fault with everything and lamenting over trifles. One
spring evening as daylight faded Ernestine sat at her window looking
out at the little lake and the wood beyond it; the quiet beauty of the
scene perhaps contributed to her mood of profound reverie. All at
once she again caught sight of the young huntsman she had seen a
few days earlier; again he was in the little wood beyond the lake; he
held a bunch of flowers in his hand, and stopped as if to look at her.
She saw him kiss the flowers and place them with a kind of tender
respect in the crook of a great oak by the lake shore.

What a surge of thoughts this single gesture awoke, thoughts keenly interesting by comparison with the humdrum sensations which had hitherto filled Ernestine's life! That life now entered a new phase; dare she go and look at the bouquet? 'Heavens, what imprudence!' she told herself with a start; 'and suppose that just as I reach the great oak the young huntsman happened to come out of the bushes nearby! How shameful! Whatever would he think of me?' This handsome tree was nevertheless the habitual goal of her solitary walks, and she would often go and sit on its gigantic roots which rose above the lawn like so many natural seats surrounding the trunk and sheltered by its spreading shade.

That night Ernestine could hardly sleep a wink, and at five the following morning, at the very first glimmer of dawn, she climbed to the topmost part of the castle. Her eyes sought for the great oak beyond the lake, and no sooner did she catch sight of it than she stood motionless and breathless. The turbulent happiness of the passions was replacing the aimless and almost mechanical contentment of early youth.

Ten days went by. Ernestine was counting the days now! She only saw the young huntsman once; he was by the beloved tree upon which as before, he placed a bouquet. The old Comte de S— noticed that she spent all her time tending an aviary she had installed in the attics of the castle; the fact was that sitting beside a little shuttered window she could survey the whole extent of the wood beyond the lake. She was quite sure that her unknown could not see her, and in this way she could think of him without constraint. One idea occurred to her and tormented her. If he believed that no attention was being paid to his bouquets he would conclude that his tribute, which was, after all, only a gesture of politeness, was despised, and as a man of honour he would return no more. Four more days elapsed, but how slowly! On the fifth, as she chanced to pass near the great oak, the girl could not resist the temptation to glance into the little hollow in which she had seen the flowers placed. She was with her governess and had nothing to fear. Ernestine expected to see only withered flowers but to her inexpressible joy she saw a bouquet of the rarest and prettiest blooms, fresh and sparkling; not a petal of the most delicate flowers was withered. No sooner had she glimpsed all this out of the corner of her eye than she began to run as lightly as a gazelle round that part of the wood within a hundred paces of the tree, without losing sight of her governess. She saw no one; sure of being unobserved she returned to the great oak and dared to look delightedly at the charming bouquet. Heavens! there was a tiny piece of paper nestling in the knot of the bouquet. 'Ernestine! What's the matter?' said the governess in alarm at the little shriek which accompanied this discovery. 'Nothing, dearest, it was just a partridge rising at my feet.' A fortnight earlier Ernestine would never have thought of lying. She drew closer and closer to the charming bouquet, bent her head and, her cheeks burning like fire, without daring to touch it, she read the little note:

'It is now a month since I began to bring a bouquet every morning. Will this one know the happiness of being noticed?'

Everything about this delicious note was ravishing; the Italian hand in which the words were written was most elegantly formed. In the four years since she had left Paris and the most fashionable convent in the Faubourg Saint-Germain, Ernestine had not seen anything so pretty. All at once she blushed fiercely, ran to her governess and insisted that they return to the castle. Instead of going up the valley and round the lake as usual Ernestine took a short cut along the path over the little bridge, which led directly back to the castle. She was deep in thought and promised herself never to go that way again; for she had at last recognized that this was a kind of billet-doux which someone had dared to write to her. 'It wasn't sealed though,' she murmured to herself. From that moment her life was beset by a dreadful anxiety. Was she then never to be able to see her beloved tree again, even from a distance? This was countered by her sense of duty. 'If I cross to the far shore of the lake,' she told herself, 'I shall never be able to keep the promises I have made to myself.' When at eight o'clock she heard the porter shut the gate of the little bridge the sound, which cut off all hope, seemed to relieve her of an enormous burden that was oppressing her; now she could no longer fail in her duty even if she were weak enough to succumb.

The next day nothing could banish her mood of sombre reverie; she was pale and downcast; her uncle noticed it and had the horses put to the old berlin. They drove round the neighbourhood and as far as the avenue of Mme Dayssin's château, three leagues away. As they were returning the Comte de S— called a halt in the little wood beyond the lake; the berlin drew up on the grass, for he wanted to look at the huge oak to which he always referred as *Charlemagne's contemporary.* 'The great emperor may have seen it,' he said, 'as he crossed our mountains on his way to defeat King Didier in Lombardy'; and the burden of almost eighty years seemed to be lightened for the old man by this thought of so long a life. Ernestine was paying no attention to her uncle's remarks; her cheeks were burning. So she was once again to be near the old oak! She promised herself not to look into the little hiding-place. Instinctively, without realizing what she was doing, she glanced into it, saw the bouquet and turned pale. It was made up of roses streaked with black. 'I am very unhappy, and must depart for ever. The one I love will not deign to notice my tribute.' Thus ran the little note attached to the bouquet. Ernestine had read it before she had time to forbid herself to see it. She felt so weak that she had to lean against the tree for support; soon she burst into tears. That evening she told herself: 'He'll go away for ever and I shall never see him again!'

The following day, in the full noonday light of the August sun, as she was walking with her uncle under the plane trees which stretched along the lake, looking across to the other side she saw the young man go up to the great oak, seize his bouquet, throw it into the lake and disappear from view. Ernestine had the feeling that his gesture was partly one of vexation, and she soon had no doubt of it at all. She was surprised that she could have doubted it for a moment; clearly, seeing himself despised he was about to go, and she would never see him again.

It was an anxious day in the castle, which relied solely upon her to provide a little gaiety. Her uncle declared that she was decidedly unwell; a deathly pallor and a certain pinched look had transformed the ingenuous face which once had radiated the tranquillity of early youth. When the time for the evening walk drew near Ernestine did not demur when her uncle led her in the direction of the lawn beyond the lake. As she passed by, her sad eyes filled with hardly-restrained tears, she glanced into the little hiding-place three feet above the ground, sure that there would be nothing there; had she not seen the bouquet thrown into the lake? But heavens! There was another one there. 'Take pity on my agony, and deign to take the white rose.' As she re-read these astonishing words her hand, all unawares, plucked the white rose from the middle of the bouquet. 'He must be very unhappy, then,' she thought. At that moment her uncle called her and she went after him, but she was happy. She held her white rose wrapped in her little cambric handkerchief of which the material was so fine that for the rest of the walk she could see the colour of the rose through the delicate fabric. She held the handkerchief in such a way as not to crush the beloved rose.

No sooner was she indoors than she ran up the steep staircase leading to her little tower at the corner of the castle. Only then did she dare to gaze freely upon the adorable rose and to feast her sight through the sweet tears that welled from her eyes.

What did these tears mean? Ernestine did not know. If she had been able to guess at the feeling which was their source she would have had the courage to sacrifice the rose she had just placed so carefully in its crystal vase on her little mahogany table. But if the reader grieves at all for the time when he was twenty he will divine that such tears have nothing to do with suffering, but are the inseparable companions of the unexpected sight of extreme happiness; they signify: 'How sweet it is to be loved!' It was at a moment when the shock of the first happiness in her life had led her judgment astray that Ernestine made the mistake of taking that flower. But as yet she was ready neither to see the indiscretion nor to reproach herself for it.

We who have fewer illusions can recognize the third stage of the birth of love: the appearance of hope. Ernestine did not realize that her heart was saying, as it contemplated the rose: 'It is certain now that he loves me.'

But can it really be true that Ernestine was on the point of being in love? Is this not in flat contravention of all the rules of simple common sense? Why, she had only seen him three times, this man for whom she was now weeping ardent tears! And furthermore she had only seen him across the lake, from a distance of at least five hundred yards. Worse still, if she were to meet him without his gun and hunting-jacket she might perhaps not even recognize him. She did not know his name, nor what he was, and yet all her days were spent regaling herself with passionate feelings which I cannot here describe at length since I have insufficient space in which to write a novel. These feelings were simply variations on the idea: 'What happiness to be loved by him!' Or else she would deliberate that other and far more important question: 'Dare I hope he loves me truly? Is he not just amusing himself by saying he loves me?' Even though she lived in a castle built by Lesdiguières, and belonged to the family of one of the noblest companions of the famous High Constable, Ernestine did not raise within herself the further objection: 'Perhaps he is the son of a local peasant.' Why? Because she lived in complete solitude.

Ernestine was certainly far from recognizing the nature of the feelings which held sway in her heart. Had she been able to foresee whither they were leading her she would have had a chance of escaping their dominion. A young German, English, or Italian girl would have recognized love; however, our wise educational system having chosen to deny the existence of love to young girls, Ernestine was only vaguely alarmed by what was taking place in her heart; on profound reflection she could see nothing there but simple friendship. If she had taken that one rose it was because she feared lest in doing otherwise she might have hurt her new friend and driven him away. 'And besides,' she told herself, after much thought, 'one must not be found wanting in politeness.'

Ernestine's heart was riven by the most violent feelings. For four days, which seemed like four centuries to the young recluse, she was held back by an indefinable apprehensiveness and did not leave the castle. On the fifth day her uncle, increasingly anxious about her health, insisted that she accompany him to the little wood; she found herself beside the fatal tree, and read on the little scrap of paper hidden in the bouquet:

'If you deign to take the variegated camellia I shall be at your village church on Sunday.'

At the church Ernestine saw a man dressed with severe simplicity, who might have been about thirty-five. She noticed that he did not even wear a cross. He was reading and holding his prayer-book in such a way as never to take his eyes off her for a moment. Which meant that Ernestine throughout the service was quite incapable of thought about anything. She dropped her prayer-book as she left the old family pew, and nearly fell as she was picking it up. She blushed crimson at her clumsiness. 'He must have thought me so awkward,' she at once told herself, 'that he will be ashamed of his interest in me.' And indeed from the moment this little accident occurred she lost sight of the stranger. In vain once she was in her carriage did she stop to distribute a few coins to the little village boys; nowhere among the groups of peasants who gossiped beside the church could she see the person at whom she had never dared to look during the mass. Ernestine, who until now had been sincerity itself, pretended to have lost her handkerchief. A servant went back into the church and searched for some time in the family pew for the handkerchief he could not hope to find. But the delay resulting from her little strategem was useless, and she did not see the huntsman again. 'It's quite plain,' she thought; 'Mlle de C— once told me I was not pretty and that I had something imperious and repellent in my looks, and now to crown it all I have to be clumsy; he must certainly despise me.'

She was possessed by these dismal thoughts all through the two or three calls that her uncle paid before returning to the castle.

No sooner were they back at the castle, at about four o'clock, than she ran along the plane-tree walk beside the lake. As it was Sunday the gate to the causeway was closed, but fortunately she caught sight of a gardener whom she called and begged him to take out the boat and ferry her to the other side of the lake. She landed a hundred paces from the great oak. The boat kept close inshore, always near enough to reassure her. The low and almost horizontal branches of the huge oak spread nearly to the water's edge. With a determined step and a kind of sombre cold-blooded resolve she approached the tree, as though she were marching to the scaffold. She was certain she would find nothing in the hiding-place; and indeed all it contained was one wilted flower which had been part of the previous day's bouquet. 'If he had been pleased with me,' she thought, 'he would not have omitted to thank me with a bouquet.'

She had herself rowed back to the castle and ran to her room; once she was in her little tower and safe from interruption she burst into tears. 'Mlle de C— was right,' she told herself; 'to find me pretty, people must see me from five hundred yards away. And since in this district full of liberals my uncle never sees anyone but peasants and parish priests, my manners must have acquired a certain uncouthness, perhaps even coarseness. I probably look imperious and repellent.' She crossed to her mirror to examine this expression, and saw a pair of dark blue eyes swimming with tears. 'Just now, at any rate,' she thought, 'no one could say I have an imperious look which would always prevent me from being attractive.'

The bell rang for dinner, and she was hard put to it to dry her tears. At last she arrived in the drawing-room where she found M. Villars, an old botanist who came every year to spend a week with M. de S— to the great regret of the latter's maid, styled as a governess, who during the visit lost her place at the table of M. le Comte. All went well until the champagne was served; when the icepail was passed to Ernestine the ice had entirely melted. She summoned a servant and said to him: 'Change this water and put in some ice at once.' 'That imperious little manner suits you very well, my dear,' laughed her kindly great-uncle. At the word *imperious* Ernestine's eyes became so flooded with tears that she could not hide them, and was obliged to leave the drawing-room; as the door shut she could be heard choking with sobs. The old men were dumbfounded.

Two days later she passed by the great oak; she looked into the hiding-place, as though she wished to revisit the scene of her former happiness. Imagine her rapture at finding there two bouquets! She snatched them up, together with the little notes, and placed them in her handkerchief, then ran towards the castle quite heedless whether the stranger, hidden in the wood, might have been watching her movements, an idea which until that day had been ever-present in her mind. Out of breath and quite unable to run further, she had to stop half-way across the causeway. As soon as she had got her breath back a little she ran on again as fast as she could. At last she reached her little room, took the bouquets from her handkerchief and, without reading her little notes, began to kiss the flowers ecstatically; she blushed when she realized what she was doing. 'Oh, I'll never look imperious again,' she kept telling herself; 'I'll turn over a new leaf.'

At last, when she had lavished all her tenderness upon the pretty bouquets made of the rarest flowers, she read the notes. (A man would have read them first.) The first, which bore Sunday's date, read: 'Five o'clock. I forbade myself the pleasure of seeing you after the service; I could not be alone; I feared lest my eyes should betray the burning love I feel for you.' She re-read these words three times: '*the burning love I feel for you*'; then she went to her mirror to see whether she looked imperious, and continued: '*the burning love I feel for you*. If your heart is free, deign to take away this note, which might compromise us.'

The second note, which was Monday's, had been written or rather scrawled in pencil, but Ernestine was beyond the stage where the pretty Italian hand of her stranger was one of his charms for her; she was concerned with matters too serious to allow her to notice such details.

'I came. I have been fortunate enough to meet someone who spoke of you in my presence. I learned that you crossed the lake yesterday.

I see that you did not deign to take the note I left for you. This settles my fate. You are in love, but not with me. It was madness at my age to form an attachment for a girl of your tender years. Farewell for ever. I shall not add the burden of importunity to that of having too long engaged you with a passion which you perhaps regard as ridiculous.' *'A passion,'* sighed Ernestine, raising her eyes to heaven. It was a sweet moment. This young girl, remarkable for her beauty, and in the full bloom of youth, cried out in rapture: 'He condescends to love me; oh, God in Heaven, how happy I am!' She dropped on her knees before a charming Madonna by Carlo Dolci which one of her ancestors had brought back from Italy: 'Ah yes, I shall be good and virtuous,' she cried, her eyes bright with tears. 'Oh God, only show me my faults, I pray, so that I may correct them; everything is now within my power.'

She stood up and read the notes twenty times over. The second in particular made her ecstatically happy. She soon realized a truth which had long been latent in her heart: that she could never have become attached to a man of less than forty. (The stranger spoke of his age.) She recalled that at church, with his slight baldness, he had seemed to be about thirty-four or thirty-five. But she could not be sure of this; she had hardly dared to look at him, and had been so flustered! Throughout the night Ernestine never closed her eyes. Never in her life had she visualized happiness like this. She got up and wrote in English in her prayer-book: *'Never be imperious. This I vow, September 30th, 18—.'*

During that night she became more and more convinced of the fact that it would be impossible to love a man of less than forty. Lying there dreaming of the fine qualities of her stranger it occurred to her that besides the advantage of being forty years old he probably possessed that of being poor. Nothing could equal her joy at this discovery. 'He'll never look stupid and inane like our friends Messieurs So-and-so when they come, at the feast of Saint-Hubert, to do my uncle the honour of killing his deer, and at mealtimes tell us about the exploits of their youth without being asked.

'Oh great Heavens, may he indeed be poor! In that case nothing is wanting to complete my happiness!' She got up a second time, lit her nightlight, and looked out a statement of her fortune which one of her cousins had once written down for her in a book. She found that she would have an annual income of seventeen thousand francs when she married, and eventually forty or fifty thousand. As she was pondering this figure four o'clock struck, and she gave a start. 'Perhaps it's light enough for me to see my beloved tree.' She opened her shutters, and could indeed see the great oak and its dark mass of foliage, but it was thanks to the moonlight and not to the first rays of dawn, still far off.

When she came to dress in the morning she said to herself: 'The friend of a man of forty must not be dressed like a child,' And for an hour she ransacked her wardrobe for a dress, a hat and a belt which made such an original ensemble that when she appeared in the dining-room her uncle, her governess and the old botanist could not repress a burst of laughter. 'Come here,' said the old Comte de S—, former Knight of Saint-Louis, wounded at Quiberon, 'come here, my Ernestine; you're dressed this morning as though you wanted to disguise yourself as a woman of forty.' At these words she blushed and her features assumed an expression of the keenest happiness. 'Heaven preserve me,' said her uncle at the end of the meal, turning to the old botanist, 'it's a wager, that's what it is; and isn't it true, sir, that Mademoiselle Ernestine is behaving exactly like a woman of thirty this morning? In particular she's using a little patronizing tone in talking to the servants, which delights me by its absurdity; I've put it to the test two or three times to make quite sure of it.' This remark redoubled Ernestine's happiness, if one may use the expression in speaking of a felicity already absolute.

It was with difficulty that she excused herself after lunch. Her uncle and his friend the botanist persisted in teasing her about her little air of old age. She went back to her room and looked at the oak. For the first time in twenty hours a cloud dimmed her felicity, though she did not understand this sudden change. What diminished the rapture in which she had been living since that moment the evening before when, in the depths of despair, she had found the bouquets in the tree, was the question: 'How must I behave towards my friend to make him respect me? A man of so much intelligence, who has moreover the advantage of being forty, must be very particular. His respect for me will quite disappear if I make a false move.'

As Ernestine was indulging in this soliloquy, seated in the place most proper for the serious meditations of a young woman: before her mirror, she noticed with horrified surprise that at her belt hung a golden hook from which depended by little chains a thimble, scissors, and their little case – a charming bauble which even the previous day she had been for ever admiring, and which her uncle had given her for her birthday less than a fortnight before. What caused her to look at the trinket with horror and to take it off hurriedly was that she remembered her maid telling her it had cost eight hundred and fifty francs, and had been bought of the most famous jeweller in Paris, Laurençot. 'What would my friend who has the honour to be poor think of me if he were to see me with such an absurdly expensive jewel? What could be more ridiculous than to show off in this way the token of a good housewife; because that's what they mean, these scissors, thimble, and case; something one always has about one; and the good housewife never stops to think that every year this jewel also costs the interest upon its price.' She began to calculate in earnest and found that the trinket cost almost fifty francs a year.

This fine excursion into domestic economy, which Ernestine owed to the excellent education received from a conspirator hidden for several years in her uncle's castle, this excursion, I say, only served to defer the difficulty. When she had hidden the absurdly expensive jewel in her chest of drawers she was still faced with the awkward question: what ought she to do to retain the respect of such an intelligent man?

Ernestine's meditations (which the reader will perhaps have recognized as simply the fifth stage of the birth of love) would lead us far afield. The girl had a fair and penetrating mind, as keen as the air of her mountains. Her uncle, who had once been intelligent and was still so about the two or three subjects which continued to interest him, had noticed that she could immediately perceive all the consequences of an idea. The kind old man, on his happier days (and the governess had noticed that this joke was an infallible sign of such days), was in the habit of chaffing Ernestine about what he called her *military glance*. It was perhaps this quality which later enabled her to play so brilliant a part when she entered society and acquired the confidence to talk. But at the time we are considering, Ernestine became utterly muddled in her arguments despite her intelligence. Twenty times she was on the point of resolving not to take her walk in the direction of the tree: 'A single blunder,' she told herself, 'by betraying the childishness of a little girl, could ruin my friend's opinion of me.' But despite extremely subtle arguments to which she bent all her powers of thought, she had not yet mastered the difficult art of controlling her passions by her intellect. The love by which the poor girl was possessed unawares falsified all her arguments and led her all too soon, for her happiness' sake, to turn her steps towards the fatal tree. After much hesitation she found herself there with her maid at about one o'clock. She drew a little apart from the woman and went up to the tree, radiant with joy, poor child! She seemed rather to glide than to walk across the lawn. The old botanist, who had joined them for the walk, said as much to the chambermaid as Ernestine ran from them.

All Ernestine's happiness suddenly vanished in the twinkling of an eye. It was not that she found no flowers in the hollow of the tree; there was a charming and quite fresh bouquet there, which at first gave her keen pleasure. So it was not long since her friend had stood in precisely the spot where she was standing now. She examined the turf for traces of his footprints; what was even more delightful was that instead of a simple note there was a letter, a long letter. Her eyes flew to the signature; she had to know his Christian name. As she read it, the letter fell from her hands, and so did the flowers. She was seized with a dreadful shudder. The name she had read at the foot of the letter was that of Philippe Astézan. Now M. Astézan was known at the castle of the Comte de S— to be the lover of Madame Dayssin, an extremely wealthy and elegant Parisian who came and scandalized the neighbourhood every year by daring to spend four months alone in her château with a man who was not her husband. Worst of all she was a widow, young and pretty, and might very well marry M. Astézan. All these sad facts, which were true as here stated, took on a far more lurid complexion when discussed by the gloomy folk, great enemies one and all of the errors of youth, who occasionally came to stay at the old manor house belonging to Ernestine's great-uncle. Never was so pure and keen a happiness (it was the first in her life) replaced in a few seconds by such an aching and hopeless misery. 'He has played a cruel trick on me,' thought Ernestine, 'he's tried to enliven his hunting expeditions by turning a little girl's head, perhaps so that he can amuse Madame Dayssin by telling her about it. And I was thinking I might marry him! Oh, what childishness! What humiliation!' And with that she sank to the ground in a faint beside the fatal tree at which she had so often gazed during the past three months. At least that was where the chambermaid and the old botanist found her motionless half an hour later. To make matters even worse, when she had been revived Ernestine saw Astézan's letter on the ground beside her, lying open in such a way that the signature could be read. Like lightning she jumped up and put her foot upon the letter.

She explained away her accident and was able to pick up the fatal letter unobserved. She was given no chance to read it, for her governess made her sit down and would not leave her. The botanist called a man working in a field nearby and sent him to the castle to fetch the carriage. To avoid replying to questions about her accident Ernestine made a pretence of being unable to speak; a splitting headache gave her an excuse to hold a handkerchief over her eyes. The carriage arrived. Left to herself once she was settled in the carriage, she was torn by unspeakable suffering all the way back to the castle. The worst of it was that she felt obliged to despise herself. Through her handkerchief she could feel the fatal letter burning her hand. Night fell as they made their way back to the castle and she was able to open her eyes unobserved. The sight of the stars, so brilliant on a fine night in the South of France, cheered her a little. Even though she was suffering the effects of turbulent passions her young simplicity was far from being aware of what was happening. After two hours of the most atrocious moral agony Ernestine owed her first respite to a courageous decision. 'I shall not read this letter of which I have seen only the signature; I shall burn it,' she said to herself as she reached the castle. Thus she was able at least to respect herself for being courageous, since love's faction, although apparently worsted, had not omitted to insinuate modestly that this letter might perhaps satisfactorily explain the relations between M. Astézan and Madame Dayssin.

As soon as she entered the drawing-room Ernestine threw the letter into the fire. The following morning at eight she once again applied herself to her piano, which for two months she had greatly neglected. She returned to the collection of *Mémoires sur l'Histoire de France* published by Petitot, and resumed her copying of long extracts from the *Mémoires* of the bloodthirsty Montluc. She was clever enough to persuade the old botanist to renew his offer of giving her a course in natural history. At the end of a fortnight the good fellow, who was as simple as his plants, could not refrain from commenting upon the astonishing diligence of his pupil; he was amazed by it. As for Ernestine, it was all one to her; every idea only led back to despair.

Her uncle was seriously alarmed; Ernestine was growing visibly thinner. She chanced to have a slight cold, and the good old man who, unlike most people of his age, did not centre upon himself all the interest he was able to summon up in the affairs of life, took it into his head that she was consumptive. Ernestine believed it too, and it was to this idea that she owed the only tolerable moments she experienced at this period; the hope that she would soon die helped her to bear life without impatience.

Through a long month she knew no other feeling than that of a suffering the more intense in that it flowed from her self-contempt; having no experience of life she was unable to comfort herself with the thought that no one in the world could have suspected what had taken place in her heart, or that the cruel man who had so much engaged her attention would probably never guess the hundredth part of what she had felt for him. Though beset by unhappiness she was not lacking in courage, and without hesitation threw two letters into the fire unread when she recognized the deadly Italian hand in which they were addressed.

She had promised herself never to look at the lawn beyond the lake, and would never raise her eyes before the windows which looked out in that direction. One day almost six weeks after she had read Philippe Astézan's name, her natural history tutor, the good M. Villars, decided to give her a lesson upon aquatic plants; he went out with her in a boat and had it rowed to that part of the lake which stretched up the valley. As Ernestine was stepping aboard the boat an oblique and almost involuntary glance reassured her that there was no one near the great oak; she barely noticed a part of the bark of the tree, of a slightly lighter grey than the rest. Two hours later as she was returning past the great oak after the lesson, she shivered as she realized that what she had taken to be a blemish in the bark of the tree was in fact the colour of Philippe Astézan's hunting-jacket, and that he had been sitting there for two hours on the roots of the oak, as motionless as if he were dead. Ernestine herself, as she made the mental comparison, used the words: *as if he were dead*, and they startled her. 'If he were dead there would no longer be any harm in my thinking about him so much.' For a few minutes this supposition provided an excuse for surrendering to a love made all-powerful by the sight of the beloved.

This chance discovery worried her a good deal. The following

evening a neighbouring parish priest who had called at the castle
asked the Comte de S— for the loan of *le Moniteur*. While the old
manservant was fetching the month's collection of the papers, the
Comte asked: 'But, Curé, you seem to have lost your interest in the
news this year; it's the first time you've asked me for *le Moniteur*!'
'M. le Comte,' replied the priest, 'my neighbour Madame Dayssin
has been lending it to me while she was down here, but she left a
fortnight ago.'

This random remark produced such an upheaval in Ernestine that
she thought she would faint; she felt her heart leap at the priest's
words, which was most humiliating. 'So this is how I succeed in
forgetting him!' she thought.

That evening she smiled for the first time in many days. 'At all
events,' she thought, 'he has stayed in the country a hundred and
fifty leagues from Paris, and has let Madame Dayssin return alone.'
She recalled his immobility on the roots of the oak tree, and grieved
that her thoughts should dwell upon this memory. Her only happiness
in the last month had consisted in persuading herself that she was
suffering from consumption; the following day she caught herself
thinking that it was getting very chilly in the evenings now that the
snow had begun to cover the mountain-tops, and that it would be
wise to wear warmer clothes. A common person would not have
omitted to take the same precaution; Ernestine thought of it only
after the priest's remark.

The feast of Saint-Hubert was drawing near, and with it the occasion of the only full-scale dinner party held in the castle during the
year. Ernestine's piano was brought down to the drawing-room.
When she opened it the following day she found on the keyboard a
scrap of paper bearing a line of writing:

'Do not cry out when you see me.'

It was so short that she read it before recognizing the hand of the
writer; the writing had been disguised. Since chance, or perhaps the
mountain air of the Dauphiné, had endowed Ernestine with strength
of mind, she would most certainly have shut herself in her room and
stayed there until after the party, had it not been for the priest's words
about Madame Dayssin's departure.

Two days later the great annual Saint-Hubert dinner took place.
Ernestine, very elegantly dressed, and seated opposite her uncle, did
the honours of the table, which was surrounded by a more or less

complete assembly of the local priests and mayors, as well as five or six provincial fops who talked of themselves and of their feats in war, in the chase, and even in love, and above all of the length of their pedigrees. They never had the misfortune to make less impression upon the heiress to the castle. Her extreme pallor combined with the beauty of her features to give Ernestine an expression little short of disdainful, and the fops who tried to make conversation felt quite nervous when they spoke to her. She herself was far from demeaning her thoughts to their level.

The whole of the first part of the dinner passed without her noticing anything unusual, and she was just beginning to breathe again when towards the end of the meal she looked up and met the eyes of a peasant already past middle age who seemed to be the valet of one of the mayors from the Drac valley. She again felt that strange movement in her breast which had earlier been caused by the priest's words; yet she could be sure of nothing. This peasant did not look at all like Philippe. She plucked up courage and took a second look at him; her doubts vanished; it was he. He had disguised himself to look extremely ugly.

It is time to say a little about Philippe Astézan, for here he was behaving like a man in love, and we may perhaps find something in his story to verify our theory of the seven stages of love. Shortly after he arrived at the Château de Lafrey with Madame Dayssin five months earlier, one of the priests whom she used to entertain in order to curry favour with the church made a very pretty remark. Philippe, surprised to hear wit from the lips of such a man, enquired who had made the remark in the first instance. 'The niece of the Comte de S——,' replied the priest, 'she's a girl who will one day be very rich, but she's been given a terrible education. Not a year goes by but she receives a whole boxful of books from Paris. I fear she will come to a sad end and may not even succeed in marrying. Who would want to be responsible for such a woman?' And so forth.

Philippe asked a few more questions, and the priest felt bound to deplore Ernestine's rare beauty, which would certainly be her downfall; he described the tedium of life at the castle of the Comte so vividly that Madame Dayssin protested: 'Oh, enough, please, M. le Curé, you're quite spoiling your beautiful mountains for me.' 'One cannot cease to love a countryside where one does so much good,' replied the priest, 'and the money that Madame has given to help us buy the third bell for our church will ensure . . .' Philippe was no longer listening; he was thinking of Ernestine and of what must be taking place in the heart of a girl in the seclusion of a castle which seemed tedious even to a country priest. 'I must give her some amusement,' he thought; 'I will pay court to her in a romantic way, and this will give her something new to think about, poor girl.' The following day he went hunting in the direction of the Comte's castle, noticed the situation of the wood with the lake lying between it and the castle, and hit upon the idea of doing homage to Ernestine with a bouquet; we already know what he did with flowers and little notes. When he was out hunting in the neighbourhood of the great oak he would place them there himself and on other days would send his servant. Philippe was doing all this quite philanthropically, and did not even think of meeting Ernestine; it would have been too difficult and too tedious to call formally upon her uncle. When Philippe saw Ernestine at church his first thought was that he was much too old to attract a girl of eighteen or twenty. He was touched by her beauty and above all by a kind of noble simplicity which characterized her face. 'It's a naive face,' he thought to himself, and a moment later found her charming. When he saw her drop her prayer-book as she left the family pew, and her delightful awkwardness as she tried to pick it up, he thought of loving her, for he began to hope. He stayed in the church after she had gone, meditating upon a subject not particularly pleasant for a man beginning to fall in love; he was thirty-five, and his hair had begun to recede in such a way that he might soon have a fine forehead in the manner of Dr Gall, but it undoubtedly added another three or four years to his age. 'If my years haven't ruined everything at first sight,' he thought, 'she will have to be made to doubt my heart and so forget my age.'

He moved to a little gothic window which gave on to the square, and saw Ernestine getting into her carriage; he thought her figure and her foot were charming; she distributed alms, and it seemed to him that her eyes were seeking someone. 'Why,' he wondered, 'should her eyes be looking into the distance when she is handing out coins quite near her carriage? Can I have aroused her interest?'

He saw Ernestine giving instructions to a footman, and as he watched he drank in her beauty. He saw her blush, for he was very close to her, the carriage being no more than ten paces from the little gothic window; he saw the servant enter the church and look for

something in the family pew. While the servant was away he became
certain that Ernestine's eyes were directed above the heads of the
crowd which surrounded her, and were therefore seeking someone;
but that someone need not necessarily be Philippe Astézan, whom she
perhaps believed to be fifty, or even sixty, who could tell? At her age
and with her fortune would she not have a suitor among the neighbouring squirelings? 'Though I saw none present at Mass.'

As soon as the Comte's carriage had gone Astézan mounted his
horse, took a detour through the woods to avoid meeting her and
quickly made his way to the strip of lawn. To his inexpressible pleasure he was able to reach the great oak before Ernestine had an opportunity of seeing the bouquet and note which he had had placed
there that morning; he removed the bouquet, plunged deep into the
wood, tied his horse to a tree, and walked up and down in agitation.
Acting on impulse he hid in the thickest part of a little wooded knoll
a hundred yards from the lake. From this concealed retreat, thanks to
a clearing in the trees, he could observe both the great oak and the
lake.

Imagine his rapture when shortly afterwards he saw Ernestine's
little boat gliding over those clear waters softly ruffled by the midday breeze! It was a decisive moment; the picture of the lake and of
Ernestine, whom he had just seen looking so lovely at church, en-
graved itself indelibly on his heart. From that moment Ernestine
possessed something which in his eyes distinguished her from all
other women and only hope was wanting to make him love her to
distraction. He saw her go eagerly to the tree, and observed her disappointment at finding no bouquet there. The moment was so
exquisitely sharp that when Ernestine ran away Philippe thought he
must have been mistaken in thinking he saw grief in her expression
when she failed to find flowers in the hollow of the tree. The whole
fate of his love depended on this circumstance. He told himself she
had looked sad as she left the boat, even before she reached the tree.
'But,' argued his hopefulness, 'she did not look sad at church; she
was on the contrary radiant with freshness, beauty, and youth, and a
little stirred; her eyes shone with vitality.'

When Philippe Astézan could no longer see Ernestine, who had
disembarked under the plane-tree walk on the other side of the lake,
he left his hiding-place, a very different man from the one who had
entered it. As he galloped back to Madame Dayssin's château he was

possessed by two thoughts: 'Did she look sad when she found no flowers in the tree? Isn't that sadness merely the result of disappointed vanity?' Eventually this more likely supposition triumphed, and restored him to the rational outlook of a man of thirty-five. He was very thoughtful. He found a whole crowd of visitors at Madame Dayssin's, and during the evening she twitted him upon his gravity and his conceit. He could no longer pass a mirror, she said, without stopping to gaze at himself. 'I detest this habit of fashionable young people,' said Madame Dayssin. 'You never used to cultivate it; now please stop it at once, or I shall get my own back by having all the mirrors removed.' Philippe was in difficulties; he did not know how best to explain away an absence he was planning. Besides it was perfectly true that he had been gazing into mirrors to see whether he looked old.

The next day he again took up his position on the knoll whence he had an excellent view of the lake; he was armed with a good spy-glass, and only left his hiding place at nightfall.

The following day he took a book with him, but would have been hard put to it to say what was contained in the pages he read. On the other hand, if he had not had a book he would have wished for one. At last, to his great joy, at about three o'clock he saw Ernestine walking slowly towards the line of plane trees at the edge of the lake, and taking the path to the causeway. She was wearing a big Italian straw hat, and looked downcast as she approached the fatal tree. With the help of his spy-glass he made quite certain of the downcast look. He saw her take the two bouquets he had put there in the morning, wrap them in her handkerchief and run away out of sight as quick as lightning. This simple gesture completed the conquest of his heart; it was so quick, so swift that he had no time to see whether she was still looking sad or whether her eyes were shining with joy. What was he to make of this curious action? Was she going to show the two bouquets to her governess? In that case Ernestine was no more than a child, and he was even more of a child than she, to have spent so much time and interest on a little girl. 'Fortunately,' he thought, 'she does not know my name; I alone know my folly, and have forgiven myself many such.'

Coldly Philippe left his retreat and went thoughtfully to fetch his horse which he had left with a peasant half a league away. 'It must be admitted that I am still a great idiot!' he said to himself as he dismounted in the courtyard of Madame Dayssin's château. By the time he entered the drawing-room his face was a frozen, bewildered mask. He was no longer in love.

The next day, as he put on his cravat, Philippe thought he looked very old. On the one hand he had little inclination to go and hide in a thicket three leagues away in order to watch a tree, and yet he had no desire to go anywhere else. 'The whole thing's ridiculous,' he thought. Yes, but ridiculous in whose eyes? Besides, one must be faithful to one's destiny. He began to write a very careful letter in which, like another Lindor, he declared his name and his status. It may be remembered that this carefully executed letter was unlucky enough to be burnt without being read by anyone. Only the words to which our hero had devoted least thought, the signature *Philippe Astézan*, were given the privilege of perusal. In spite of some excellent reasoning our reasonable man was none the less hidden in his customary refuge at the moment when his name produced so much effect; he saw Ernestine faint as she opened his letter, and was extremely surprised.

The day afterwards he had to admit to himself that he was in love: his behaviour was proof of it. Every day he would return to the little wood where he had experienced such keen sensations. As Madame Dayssin was soon to go back to Paris, Philippe arranged for a letter to be written to him, and announced that he was leaving the Dauphiné to spend a fortnight with a sick uncle in Burgundy. He left by the stage-coach, and managed things so well, returning by another route, that only one day elapsed without his visiting the little wood. He took lodgings two leagues from the castle of the Comte de S—, in the lonely region of Crossey which lay in the opposite direction from Madame Dayssin's château. From there he came every day to the shore of the little lake. He came for thirty-three days in succession without seeing Ernestine there; she no longer appeared at church, for mass was being said at the castle; he went up to the castle in disguise, and twice had the good fortune to catch a glimpse of her. Nothing, he felt, could compare with her expression, at once noble and naive. 'Never,' he thought, 'should I know satiety with such a woman as she.' What touched him most were her extreme pallor and her air of suffering. I should write ten volumes like Richardson if I were to undertake a description of all the ways in which this man, for all his good sense and experience, sought to explain Ernestine's swoon and her sadness. At last he resolved to have it out with her, and for this purpose to enter the castle. Shyness – fancy being shy at thirty-five! – shyness had long prevented him from doing so earlier. He made his preparations with all possible intelligence, and yet without the intervention of chance, which caused an unconcerned outsider to break the news of Madame Dayssin's departure, all Philippe's cunning would have been wasted, or at any rate he would have been able to see Ernestine's love only in her anger. He would probably have explained this anger as surprise at being loved by a man of his age. Philippe would have thought himself despised, and to forget this painful feeling would have had recourse to gambling or the foyers of the Opéra; he would have become harder and more self-centred, thinking that his youth was entirely gone.

A man who was *half a gentleman*, as they say in those parts, the mayor of one of the mountain villages, who had been chamois-hunting with Philippe, consented to smuggle him in, disguised as his servant, to the great dinner at the Comte's castle where he was recognized by Ernestine.

Ernestine, feeling that she was blushing crimson, was struck by a dreadful thought: 'He's going to think I love him madly without knowing him; he'll despise me for being a child, and leave for Paris to join his Madame Dayssin, and I shall never see him again.' This agonizing thought gave her the courage to rise from table and go to her room. She had been there for two minutes when she heard the outer door of her apartments open. She thought it was her governess, and got up, seeking an excuse to send her away. As she went towards the door of her room it opened, and Philippe was at her feet.

'In God's name forgive this intrusion,' he implored her; 'I have been in despair for two months. Will you have me for a husband?'

It was a wonderful moment for Ernestine. 'He's asking me to marry him,' she thought; 'I needn't fear Madame Dayssin any more.' She was searching for a haughty answer, and despite incredible efforts might perhaps not have found one. Two months of despair were forgotten; she was at the zenith of happiness. Fortunately at this moment the door of the outer room was heard to open. Ernestine said: 'You are dishonouring me.' 'Admit nothing!' exclaimed Philippe in a low voice, and slipped adroitly down between the wall and Ernestine's pretty pink and white bed. It was the governess, much alarmed for the well-being of her charge, and the state in which she found her did nothing to allay her qualms. She would not be got rid of for a long time, and while she was in the room Ernestine had time to accustom herself to her good fortune and regain her self-control. Once the governess had gone she dealt superbly with Philippe upon his reappearance.

Ernestine was so beautiful in her lover's eyes, and her expression so stern, that the first words of her reply gave Philippe the idea that all he had hitherto assumed was nothing but illusion, and that his love was in fact not returned. His expression changed instantaneously to one of complete despair. Ernestine was shaken to the depths of her being by his air of hopelessness but nevertheless had the strength to dismiss him. All she could remember of this extraordinary encounter was that when he had begged to be allowed to ask for her hand she had replied that his business affairs as well as his affections no doubt required his presence in Paris. He had cried out that the only business which concerned him was to be worthy of Ernestine's heart, that he swore before her never to leave the Dauphiné while she was in it, nor ever to return to the château where he had dwelt before he knew her.

Ernestine's happiness knew no bounds. The following day she returned to the foot of the great oak, but safely escorted by her governess and the old botanist. She duly found a bouquet there and, more important, a letter. Within a week Astézan had almost persuaded her to reply to his letters, and then she learned that Madame Dayssin had returned to the Dauphiné from Paris. Acute anxiety filled Ernestine's heart to the exclusion of all other feelings. The gossips of the neighbouring village, who at this juncture were unwittingly deciding the course of her life, and whom she lost no opportunity of encouraging to chatter, told her at last that Madame Dayssin, angry and jealous, had come to fetch her lover Philippe Astézan who was said to have stayed in the neighbourhood with the intention of becoming a Carthusian monk. To accustom himself to the austerities of the order he had withdrawn to the solitude of Crossey. They added that Madame Dayssin was in despair.

Ernestine learned a few days later that Madame Dayssin had not succeeded in seeing Philippe and that she had left for Paris, white with fury. While Ernestine was trying to confirm this sweet certainty Philippe was in despair; he was passionately in love and believed that his love was not returned. Several times he waylaid her, and was received in such a way as to make him think he had offended the pride of his young mistress by his forwardness. Twice he left for Paris, and twice turned back after twenty leagues or so, to return to his hut among the rocks of Crossey. Having flattered himself with hopes which he now came to regard as too lightly conceived, he tried to renounce his love, and found that all the other pleasures of life were now meaningless to him.

Ernestine was happier for she both loved and was loved. Love held full sway in her soul which we have seen pass through the seven successive and distinct phases which separate indifference from passion, phases in whose stead the vulgar can perceive but one change, and cannot explain its nature.

As for Philippe Astézan, we leave him, as a punishment for having abandoned an old friend on the threshold of what one might call old age for women, a prey to one of the most agonizing states into which a human being can sink. He was loved by Ernestine but could not obtain her hand. She was married the following year to an old lieutenant-general who was exceedingly wealthy and a knight of several orders.

An Example of Love among the Wealthy Class in France

I HAVE received a large number of letters prompted by *Love*. Here is one of the most interesting.

Saint-Dizier, . . June 1825

My dear philosopher,

I am not quite sure whether you are entitled to class as *vanity-love* that little speculation in vanity by the young Frenchwoman whom you met last summer taking the waters at Aix-en-Savoie, and whose story I promised to tell you; because in the entire comedy, which was in any case very dull, there did not appear the slightest shadow of love; that is to say passionate reverie which exaggerates the happiness of intimacy.

Please do not conclude from this that I did not understand your book; I am only protesting against an ill-chosen term.

In all the different species of the *genus love* there ought to be some common characteristic: the characteristic proper to the genus is the desire for perfect intimacy. Now in *vanity-love* this characteristic is not present.

When one is accustomed to the faultless precision of the language of the physical sciences one is easily shocked by the imperfection of the language of the metaphysical sciences.

Madame Félicie Féline is a young Frenchwoman of twenty-five with a superb estate and a delightful château in Burgundy. She herself is, as you know, quite plain, though she has a good enough figure (nervous-lymphatic temperament). She is far from being a fool, but she is certainly not intelligent; she has never had a strong or trenchant idea in her life. As she was brought up by an intelligent mother among people of great distinction she has had a great deal of *practice* at being intelligent; she repeats the words of others perfectly and with a surprising air of originality. As she repeats them she even registers the slight look of surprise which accompanies invention. In this way she passes for a charming and highly intelligent woman among people who see her seldom or fools who see her often.

She has exactly the same kind of talent for music as she has for conversation. At seventeen she could play the piano perfectly; well enough to give lessons at eight francs a time (not that she gives any, for her fortune is more than comfortable). When she has been to a new opera by Rossini she can pick out at least half of it at her piano the following day. Being very musical she plays the most difficult scores at sight, and with great expression. While she has this particular knack she nevertheless does not *understand* difficult *things*, either in her reading or in her music. I am sure Madame Gherardi would have grasped Berzelius's theory of chemical proportions in two months. Madame Féline on the other hand is incapable of understanding one of the early chapters of Say or the theory of continuous fractions.

She took lessons in harmony from a tutor highly renowned in Germany, and never understood a word.

For having had a few lessons from Redouté she outshines her master's talent in some respects. Her roses are even more delicate than those of the artist. For several years I have been watching her play with her colours, and she has never looked at any pictures but those in the exhibition; never, at the time she was learning to paint flowers, and when we still possessed the masterpieces of Italian painting, did she have the curiosity to go and see them. She understands neither the perspective of a landscape nor light-and-shade effects (*chiaroscuro*).

This inability of the intellect to grasp difficult things is characteristic of Frenchwomen; as soon as anything becomes arduous it palls and is dropped forthwith.

This is why your book *Love* will never be a success among women. They will read the anecdotes and skip the conclusions, and they will deride all they skip. It is exceedingly polite of me to put all this in the future tense.

Madame Féline made a marriage of convenience when she was eighteen. She found herself wedded to an honest young man of thirty, a little lymphatic and sanguine, entirely anti-bilious and nervous, kind, gentle, equable, and very stupid. I know of no other man more completely devoid of intellect. Her husband had nevertheless been very successful in his studies at the École Polytechnique where I had known him, and his *merit* had been well and truly puffed in the circles in which Félicie grew up, in order to blind her to his stupidity, which is all-embracing – except for his first-class skill at managing his mines and foundries.

The husband did all he could to make her welcome, which in this case means that he did a very great deal; but he was up against an icy creature quite impervious to everything. That kind of tender gratitude which husbands usually inspire even in the most indifferent girls did not last a week in her case.

However, once she began to live with him she soon realized that she had been saddled with the company of a fool, and, more frightful still, a fool who sometimes appeared ridiculous in society. She felt that this more than outweighed the pleasure of having married an extremely wealthy man and of receiving frequent compliments on her husband's merit.

So she took a dislike to him.

The husband, who was not so well-born as she, thought she was putting on airs. He at once withdrew in his turn. He was however an extremely busy and accommodating fellow, and as there was nothing more convenient for him than his wife between the checking of a foreman's report and the testing of a machine he would occasionally attempt a little love-making with her. This duly changed his wife's dislike into downright aversion, especially when he was clumsy, coarse, and ill-bred enough to make his advances before a third party, such as myself.

I think I should have been inclined to box his ears if he had said and done these things to another woman in my presence. But I knew Félicie to be so arid, so completely devoid of any genuine sensibility, I was so often impatient of her vanity, that I confined myself to feeling a little sorry for her when I saw her suffering for that vanity because of her husband, and I used to retire from the scene.

The couple carried on in this way for several years (Félicie has never had a child). During that time the husband, who kept good company while he was in Paris (and he only spent six weeks each summer at his Burgundy ironworks), acquired Parisian tone and improved a great deal; although he was still stupid he almost entirely ceased to be ridiculous, and went from strength to strength in his business affairs, as you may have concluded from the large purchases he has since made and from the last report by the judges of the exhibition of national industrial products.

As a result of his wife's frequent rebuffs M. Féline five or six times imagined in all good faith that he was a little in love with her. She used to lead him a fine dance. Her little game at this time consisted in saying pleasant things to him in public and then finding excuses to keep him at a distance when they were alone. She thus aroused his desire further, and when she condescended to allow . . . he would pay all her furnisher's bills, those of Leroy and of Corcelet, and would think her expenditure quite moderate when it was in fact absurd.

For the first two or three years, until she was twenty or twenty-one, Félicie's pleasure-seeking was confined to the satisfaction of the following vanities:

'To own more beautiful clothes than any of the young women of her acquaintance.

'To give better dinner-parties.

'To receive more compliments than others when she played the piano.

'To be considered more intelligent than others.'

At twenty-one ensued *vanity in her feelings*.

She had been brought up by an atheist mother among a society of atheist philosophers. Only once had she ever been to church, to get married – and then she had not wanted to do so. After her marriage she read all kinds of books. Rousseau and Madame de Staël came into her hands: this marked an epoch and proves how dangerous those books are.

First of all she read *Emile*, and at once believed she was justified in despising intellectually all the young women of her acquaintance. Note that she had not understood a word of the metaphysic of the 'vicaire savoyard'.

But Rousseau's sentences are extremely elaborate, subtle, and very difficult to memorize. She confined herself to an occasional religious sally hazarded *to create an effect*, in an irreligious circle where such matters were of no more interest than the king of Siam.

She read *Corinne*, in fact it is this book that she has read most of all. The sentences are written for effect and are easily memorized, and she stuffed a good number of them into her head. In the evening she would pick out the young and fairly stupid men in her drawing-room, to whom without a word of warning she would then prettily repeat her lesson of the morning.

Some of them fell into the trap, thought her a woman capable of passion, and paid her attentions.

However, she had brought to this point only the commonest and most inane of her guests, and she was never entirely sure that the others were not making mild fun of her. Her husband, who was continually away from home on business and a good enough fellow to boot (*what concern is it of mine?*), either did not see or else took not the slightest notice of these intellectual coquetries.

Félicie read *La Nouvelle Héloïse*, and at once discovered a whole fund of sensibilities in her soul; she confided this secret to her mother and to an old uncle who had played the part of a father to her; both of them laughed at her as though she were a child. None the less she persisted in her belief that one could not live without a lover, a lover in the style of Saint-Preux.

In her circle there was a young Swede, a strange enough fellow indeed. After he left the University at the early age of eighteen he distinguished himself several times in the 1812 campaign, and reached a high rank in his country's militia; later he travelled to America and spent six months living among the Indians. He is neither stupid nor witty, but he has a strong character, and in some ways he touches the sublime in virtue and greatness. Besides this he is more lymphatic than anyone I have ever known; he has quite a handsome face, and a simple though prodigiously earnest manner. Hence there is a great show of respect and consideration towards him.

'This,' said Félicie to herself, 'is the man I must pretend to have for a lover. As he is the coldest of them all, his passion will do me the greatest honour.'

Weilberg, the Swede, was very much a friend of the family, and in the summer, five years ago, a journey was arranged which included the husband and himself.

As he was a man of extremely strict principles, and more especially as he was not the least in love with Félicie, he saw her as she really was, very unattractive. Besides, he had not been told before they left what part he was expected to play. The husband, bored by all this pother and also anxious to turn to good use a journey undertaken to please his wife, left her to her own devices whenever they reached a stopping-place; he made a round of the factories, works, and mines, and said to Weilberg: 'Gustave, look after my wife for me.'

Weilberg's French was atrocious; he had never read Rousseau or Mme de Staël, which suited Félicie's book admirably.

So the little lady made a fine show of being ill in order to dismiss her husband through sheer boredom and to excite the pity of the kind young man with whom she was constantly left alone. To melt his heart she spoke of the love she bore her husband and of her sorrow at observing his lack of response.

Weilberg was not amused by this theme and listened to it purely out of politeness. She thought she had made greater headway, and spoke of the bond of sympathy which existed between them. Gustave took up his hat and went out for a walk.

When he came back she was angry with him and claimed that he had insulted her by interpreting a mere friendly remark as the beginning of a declaration of love.

When they travelled at night she would rest her head on Gustave's shoulder and he would endure it for the sake of politeness.

For two months they travelled in this fashion, simply eating up money, and growing more and more bored.

On their return Félicie went off on an entirely new tack. If she had been able to circulate a formal announcement she would have notified all her friends and acquaintances that she loved M. Weilberg the Swede with a violent passion, and that M. Weilberg was her lover.

Balls and fine clothes were a thing of the past; she neglected her former friends and offended her former acquaintances. In short she sacrificed everything she enjoyed to foster the belief that she was deeply in love with this M. Weilberg, this kind of Indian savage who had been a colonel in the Swedish militia at eighteen, and that the man was madly in love with her.

She began by telling her mother the day they returned home. Her mother, according to Félicie, was guilty of having married her to a man she did not love, so she should now assist, with all the means at her disposal, Félicie's love for the man she had chosen and whom she adored; she must therefore persuade the husband to install Weilberg somehow in their house. If she did not have him at home all the time she threatened to go and seek him in his apartments.

The mother, like a fool, believed all this and so well managed things with her son-in-law that Weilberg had no option but to go and live in their home. Charles would not take no for an answer, and the mother too showed Gustave so much courtesy and was so insistent that the poor young man, not knowing what was expected of him, and exceedingly anxious to do the right thing among people who had received him with perfect civility, dared not refuse a thing.

Women can weep at will, as you know.

One day when I was alone with Félicie she began weeping, squeezed my hand and said: 'Oh, my dear Goncelin, with your clear-sighted friendship you must have guessed the secret of my heart! You used to be very friendly with Gustave, but since we came back you've changed; you seem to hate him.' (In fact I seemed nothing of the sort. I knew exactly what was up.) 'Ah, my friend, I was not happy before . . . It's only since . . . If only you knew how dreadful Charles was on the journey! If you knew Gustave better! . . . If only you knew how touchingly attentive, how tender! . . . Could I have resisted? . . . If only you knew what an ardent soul, what frightening passions burn in this man who appears so cool and impassive! No, my dear, you would not despise me then! . . . Alas, I am well aware that something is lacking in me . . . This happiness is not pure . . . I know only too well what I owed to *Charles*. But oh! my friend, that continual contrast between the indifference and contempt of the one and the attentions and love of the other . . . and that enforced familiarity that comes from travelling together . . . So many dangers! . . . Could I have resisted so great a love? or for that matter could I have resisted his violence?' etc., etc., etc.

So here was poor Weilberg, the soul of honesty, accused of having violated his friend's wife, and it must be believed since she was the one to say so; she boasted of it to two people I know and doubtless also to others whom I do not.

The foregoing declaration is pretty much what she told me: her words have remained clear in my memory. Only a few days afterwards I met one of the women in whom she had similarly confided. I begged her to try and remember the actual words and she repeated precisely the same rendering that I myself had heard, which made me laugh.

Her confession complete, Félicie held out her hand to me and said that she counted on my discretion, that I should behave to Weilberg exactly as before and pretend to notice nothing. 'The wild virtue of that sublime man frightened her.' Whenever he left her she was always afraid lest she might never see him again; she feared that he might unexpectedly resolve to leave for Sweden at once. For my part I promised to keep our conversation absolutely secret.

Meanwhile all the friends of the family found it outrageous that poor Weilberg, hitherto so upright, should have *seduced* a young woman in whose house he was virtually a guest, and whose husband had helped him in a thousand ways. I apprised him of the idiotic role he was being made to play. He embraced me and thanked me for telling him, and swore he would never set foot in their house again. It was he who told me then what had happened on the journey.

For several days Félicie had to do without Weilberg, who had previously dined with her regularly, and she simulated despair. She said it was all her husband's doing, and that he had driven such a virtuous man away. (She had told me and two other people that this virtuous man had violated her on the moss at the foot of a pine in the Black Forest, in the approved fashion for that sort of thing.) She also politely suggested that her mother, after having aided and abetted her, had then made off with her daughter's virtuous lover. (Note that the mother was then a poor old woman of sixty, who hadn't had a thought in her head for twenty years.) From a first-rate cutler Félicie ordered a dagger with a Damascus blade, and had it delivered one day right in the middle of dinner; I saw her pay forty francs for it and put it neatly away in her writing-desk next to the sealing-wax, in full view of us all. A dozen or so apothecaries' errand boys each brought a little bottle of tincture of opium which all together amounted to quite a considerable quantity. She put them away in her dressing-table.

The following day she informed her mother that unless Gustave was persuaded to return she would poison herself with the opium and stab herself to death with the dagger which she had ordered for that very purpose.

The mother, who had no illusions about Weilberg's love, and who feared a scandal, went to see him. She told him her daughter was mad, that she was pretending to be very much in love with him and saying that he was in love with her, and that she had sworn to kill herself if he did not return. 'Go back to her,' begged the mother, 'humiliate her thoroughly; then she'll loathe you and you need never return any more.'

Weilberg was a good fellow; he took pity on the old woman who had come to him with this appeal, and agreed to become a party to the tedious play-acting for the sake of avoiding the scandal the mother so much feared.

So he went back. The young woman made no comment beyond amiably reproaching him for his five days' absence. When they were alone together she knew better than to speak to him of love, ever since that day during the journey when he had taken his hat and walked out as soon as she began a declaration. Weilberg was fond of music, and she spent her time playing the piano; since she played remarkably well he was willing enough to stay and listen to her. In public it was quite a different matter; she spoke to him of nothing but love, but it must be admitted that she did it most artfully. Fortunately his knowledge of French was poor, and she managed to convey to all those present that he was her lover, without his being any the wiser.

All the friends of the household were privy to the secret of the game, but as yet the mere acquaintances were not. The question of M. Weilberg's outrageous behaviour was again raised among them, and once again he went away and refused to return.

Félicie took to her bed and told her mother she proposed to starve to death. She would take nothing but tea, and though she got up for dinner she ate precisely nothing.

After six days of this diet she was seriously indisposed, and doctors were sent for. She declared that she had poisoned herself, that she wanted nobody's attentions, and that everything was useless. Her mother and two friends were present together with the doctors; she said she was dying for love of M. Weilberg, whose affections had been alienated from her. In addition she begged that her poor husband should be spared the grief of learning the truth, since fortunately he knew nothing of all this, etc., etc.

She did however agree to take some medicine, and was given an emetic, whereupon she who had lived on nothing but tea for six days brought back some three to four pounds of chocolate; her illness and poisoning were nothing more than appalling indigestion. I had predicted as much.

Not knowing what story to tell her mother next, to induce her to take new steps which might lure Weilberg back to the house, she threatened to tell Charles everything. The husband would have taken his wife's word for it and would undoubtedly have had no more to do with her. With this new scandal looming the mother returned to the charge and once again persuaded Gustave to go back. He and I used to see a good deal of each other at that time; we were doing some work together; he had taken a fancy to me and I was pretty well his favourite Frenchman. We used to spend part of our days together; he was giving me lessons in Swedish, and I was teaching him descriptive geometry and differential calculus, for he had developed a passion for mathematics which often obliged me to refer to our books and brush up my already fading memories of the École Polytechnique. Then I would take up my violin, and being far more tolerant than you are he would willingly sit and listen to me for hours.

Félicie lavished her attentions upon me, to procure my constant presence at her house; she knew it was one way of attracting Weilberg to go there. One morning when we were all three breakfasting there together she fancied she would undertake to *prove her love* for Gustave in my presence, and affected a liberty of behaviour with him such as normally exists only between people who are living on terms of the most complete intimacy. At first Gustave did not understand, but she dotted her *i*'s and crossed her *t*'s to such an extent that he had to realize it; he looked at me, laughed, and swallowed his mouthful without making a move. Félicie suggested he should make some slight adjustment to her dress. 'Good God,' he snapped brutally, 'you've got a maid to dress you, haven't you?' And she whispered in my ear: 'You see how discreet he is; I was certain that he wouldn't even put a pin in my fichu.'

However she was not so pleased as she would have had me believe about her alleged lover's discretion and restraint. It was, I recall, Easter Sunday. When we had finished breakfast but for our cups of tea, she said to her servant: 'Paul, tell my maid I have no need of her, and that she had better take the chance to go to mass.'

We sat there sipping tea. The servant did not reappear, and she drew very close to the fire. 'I'm terribly cold,' she said holding out her hand to Weilberg. 'Don't you think I'm feverish?' 'Egad, I know nothing about these things, but here's Goncelin who plays the doctor to his peasants in the country; he ought to know all about fever; he'll tell you.' I felt her pulse. 'No fever there at all,' I said. 'It's strange,' she replied, 'I'm in such a state; I feel as if I were going to faint. There, I *am* going to faint; I'm suffocating; unfasten my stays, M. Gustave, unfasten my stays. Please, Goncelin, go to my husband's room and fetch . . .' 'What?' 'Some balsam, to burn it; there's some in his medal-cabinet.' 'I know where it is,' said Weilberg, 'I'll go. Goncelin will help you; I'll be back in a moment.' And he returned five minutes later.

I amused myself by unlacing her. Apart from her face she was not bad: young, with a good figure and soft white skin. I had uncovered her bosom; she would have let herself be stripped naked. I made tolerably good use of the uncovered part, and said: 'Your heart's beating quite gently; don't worry, there's absolutely nothing wrong.' She was registering mild faintness. At last Weilberg returned after deliberately dawdling outside for some time; he put the balsam on the mantelpiece and placidly resumed eating biscuits and swallowing cups of tea. Félicie, seeing all this, although she was pretending not to, could stand it no longer. In addition I had told Gustave that neither her pulse nor her respiration were in any way abnormal, and he had rejoined: 'In that case it's very odd that she should faint!' Félicie, at the end of her tether, gradually came to herself; she re-arranged her dress and begged us to leave her.

In view of the great importance she attached to appearing genuinely unconscious before Gustave I believe that had I attempted to satisfy a whim (which did not tempt me) she would have allowed it, only saying later how unworthy it had been of me and how unhappy it had made her. And, mind you, since up to that time she had been physically honest, and was besides quite insensitive to that particular pleasure, she would most certainly have suffered had she been thus violated.

Having always talked to me of him as if he were the most passionate lover, Félicie was so cruelly humiliated by Weilberg's manifestation of indifference towards her in my presence that it made her really ill. Weilberg did not want to return to her house after such a ridiculous farce; however, as she was confined to bed for some time and as he had previously been a constant visitor to her home, he put in an appearance in order that his absence should not cause comment. His visits gradually became less and less frequent, but it was only eight months later that he entirely ceased from calling on her. Throughout those eight months she continued to represent him to all and sundry as her lover, even when he was scarcely ever seen at her house.

Félicie is very fond of music. As she had no box at the *Opéra Bouffes* she very seldom had the chance of going there. One day some friends lent us their box, and she arranged that Weilberg and I should escort her; her husband was to join us there later. You must understand that by this time, in her heart of hearts, she loathed Weilberg; she had insisted on his coming so that he should sit with her at the front of the box. Gustave said he felt too hot, and walked out of the theatre, leaving her alone with me. He was for ever giving her the lie in this way, and upon my word, from that day forth she changed her tune, and having spent a year talking of Weilberg's passion and his love she now began to hint at his inconstancy and the grief he was causing her.

At the same time it came to my ears that I was supposed to be her lover. I went to see her and told her so, and added that I had no wish to pass for her lover without at least reaping the benefits of the position. I took her on my lap and gave her short shrift. As I knew for certain that she was most averse to being violated and that she felt this was imminent, I told her I intended to merit the reputation she had built for me, and so forth ... It was during the day; someone might have entered her room at any moment; she was deucedly frightened, and implored me to leave her alone; she said she had never loved anyone but Weilberg and that she would never love anyone else. At last she struggled free of me, and rang the bell. A servant came in and she told him to make up the fire, pull the curtains, and bring her some tea. I left. Since then we have more or less parted company. She lets it be known everywhere that I am a kind of villain of the Iago type; that I have long entertained a disgusting passion for her, and that it is I who have estranged her lover Weilberg from her. She has even gone so far as to bring out certain familiar and friendly letters which I wrote to her six years ago when I was in Rome with you, and to proclaim them as declarations of my passion.

Félicie's vanity is at present employed in other directions. In speaking of Weilberg she repeats dismal quotations from the third volume of *Corinne*; she is making a show of mourning a grand passion; she no longer goes out, nor does she dress elaborately at home; but she gives excellent dinner parties which are attended by aged imbeciles who are supposed to have been clever in their day, and by poor devils who have nothing to eat at home. She speaks admiringly of Lord Byron, Canaris, Bolívar, and M. de la Fayette. In her little circle she is pitied as being a very unhappy young woman, and praised for her great sensitivity and intelligence; and she is tolerably contented with her lot. In all, it is one of those bourgeois households which you so much detest.

Was I not right to tell you that this tedious tale would be of no use to you? By its very nature it is dull. In *vanity-love* there is nothing but talk, and talk is tedious when it is narrated; the merest particle of action is worth more.

Moreover I do not think that this is *vanity-love* as you understand it. Félicie has a trait which, even if not exclusively hers, is rare: she finds it disagreeable to fulfil the obligations of womanhood, and it mattered very little to her whether she made the man she proclaimed as her lover believe that she really loved him.

– Goncelin

MORE ABOUT PENGUINS, PELICANS AND PUFFINS

For further information about books available from Penguins please write to Dept EP, Penguin Books Ltd, Harmondsworth, Middlesex UB7 0DA.

In the U.S.A.: For a complete list of books available from Penguins in the United States write to Dept DG, Penguin Books, 299 Murray Hill Parkway, East Rutherford, New Jersey 07073.

In Canada: For a complete list of books available from Penguins in Canada write to Penguin Books Canada Ltd, 2801 John Street, Markham, Ontario L3R 1B4.

In Australia: For a complete list of books available from Penguins in Australia write to the Marketing Department, Penguin Books Australia Ltd, P.O. Box 257, Ringwood, Victoria 3134.

In New Zealand: For a complete list of books available from Penguins in New Zealand write to the Marketing Department, Penguin Books (N.Z.) Ltd, P.O. Box 4019, Auckland 10.

In India: For a complete list of books available from Penguins in India write to Penguin Overseas Ltd, 706 Eros Apartments, 56 Nehru Place, New Delhi 110019.

BALZAC IN THE PENGUIN CLASSICS

—

SELECTED SHORT STORIES
Translated by Sylvia Raphael

In addition to the longer novels Balzac wrote some fifty stories during his working life. The twelve included here provide examples of many varied aspects of his art: tragic, melodramatic, sentimental, pathetic and comic. With the ability to tell a gripping tale Balzac combined a lively imagination, a minute observation and a keen sense of the irony of the human condition.

URSULE MIROUËT
Translated by Donald Adamson

In 1842, eight years before his death, Balzac described *Ursule Mirouët* as the masterpiece of all the studies of human society that he had written; he regarded the book as 'a remarkable *tour de force*'.
An essentially simple tale about the struggle and triumph of innocence reviled, *Ursule Mirouët* is characterized by that wealth of penetrating observation so readily associated with Balzac's work. The twin themes of redemption and rebirth are illuminated by a consistently passionate rejection of both philosophic and practical materialism in favour of love. In this case love is added by supernatural intervention, which itself effectively illustrates Balzac's lifelong fascination with the occult.

COUSIN BETTE
Translated by Marion Ayton Crawford

Cousin Bette (1847) was one of the last and greatest of Balzac's novels. It is the story of the Hulot family: risen to eminence under Napoleon I, their aristocratic values leave them bewildered and vulnerable in the money-ridden bourgeois Paris of the 1840s. It is also the story of Bette herself, the poor relation whose patient malice finally leads to their destruction.

ZOLA IN THE PENGUIN CLASSICS

—

LA BÊTE HUMAINE

Translated by Leonard Tancock

'Love and death, possessing and killing, are the dark foundations of the human soul.'
La Bête Humaine is a taut thriller of violent passions and sexual jealousy. But the book is also a fascinating study of the criminal mind and a bitter attack on the French judicial system.

GERMINAL

Translated by Leonard Tancock

Germinal was written by Zola (1840–1902) to draw attention to the misery prevailing among the poor in France during the Second Empire. The novel depicts the grim struggle between capital and labour in a coalfield in northern France. Yet through the blackness of this picture, humanity is constantly apparent, and the final impression is one of compassion and hope for the future, not only of organized labour, but also of man.

THE DEBACLE

Translated by Leonard Tancock

The Debacle is the climax of Zola's great Rougon-Macquart series. Its subject is the Franco-Prussian War of 1870, the defeat at Sedan, and the Paris Commune, the traumatic humiliation which brought about the collapse of the corrupt and vulgar Second Empire, transformed France, and left scars which have remained unhealed to this day. Zola's account of these tragic events is remarkably factual; his descriptions of armaments, of strategy and tactics, and of the behaviour of the participants, both great and small, are based on intensive research. But *The Debacle* is much more than a documentary. It is at once one of the greatest war novels ever written and a grimly prophetic vision of the realities of our time.

STENDHAL IN THE PENGUIN CLASSICS

—

THE CHARTERHOUSE OF PARMA

Translated by Margaret R. B. Shaw

Stendhal's second great novel, *La Chartreuse de Parme*, was published in 1839. He adapted the theme from a sixteenth-century Italian manuscript and set it in the period of Waterloo. Amid the intrigues of the small court of Parma the hero, Fabrizio, with his secret love for Clelia, emerges as an 'outsider' whose destiny is shaped by events in which his character plays relatively little part. Fabrizio's final withdrawal into a monastery emphasizes his lack of contact with real life and his similarity to the ingrown hero of the twentieth century.

THE LIFE OF HENRY BRULARD

Translated by Jean Stewart and B. C. J. G. Knight

In 1835, Stendhal, then middle-aged, began an introspective account of his childhood and youth in an attempt to discover the truth about himself. Unfinished and unrevised, it is nonetheless one of the most remarkable and entrancing of autobiographies, with all the spontaneity and vividness of a work written at the moment when memory was unlocking itself.

SCARLET AND BLACK

Translated by Margaret R. B. Shaw

To Stendhal (1783–1842) the novel was a mirror of life reflecting 'the blue of the skies and the mire of the road below'. *Scarlet and Black*, his greatest novel, reflects without distortion the France of the decades after Waterloo – its haves and have-nots, its Royalists and Liberals, its Jesuits and Jansenists. Against this crowded backcloth moves the figure of Julien Sorel, a clever, ambitious, up-from-nothing hero whose tragic weakness is to lose his head in a crisis. Margaret Shaw's translation keeps intact the plain, colloquial style of a writer who, in an age of Romantics, set the pattern for later realists such as Flaubert and Zola.